S0-FBX-639

CAN INFLATION BE CONTROLLED?

CAN INFLATION BE CONTROLLED ?

By HAROLD G. MOULTON
President-Emeritus, The Brookings Institution

ANDERSON KRAMER ASSOCIATES
Washington, D.C. 1958

MANUFACTURED IN THE UNITED STATES OF AMERICA
BY GEORGE BANTA COMPANY, INC.,
MENASHA, WISCONSIN

LIBRARY OF CONGRESS CARD NO. 58-13970

To my son and daughter
John R. and Barbara Moulton

Acknowledgments

The author is deeply indebted to the Maurice and Laura Falk Foundation for generous financial assistance in carrying out this research project. However, the Foundation assumes no responsibility for the conclusions reached.

As this book has been written since my retirement, the Brookings Institution has had no connection with the project. I am indebted to Mr. Harlan Youell for invaluable assistance in assembling statistical and other data; to Mr. Max Sasuly for critical appraisal of statistical issues; to Mrs. Louise Bebb Williams for preparing the charts; and to Mrs. Eleanor McMeekin for secretarial assistance.

Harold G. Moulton
October, 1958

Contents

CHAPTER IV

CHAPTER V

CHAPTER VI

CHAPTER VII

CHAPTER VIII

CHAPTER IX

APPENDIX A

APPENDIX B

CAN INFLATION BE CONTROLLED?

Introductory

The economic problem with which this book is concerned is strikingly indicated in the diagram on the accompanying page, which reveals the wide variations in the general level of commodity prices in modern times. The phenomenon of rapid changes in the price level is one of the oldest subjects of discussion and controversy in the realm of economics. This is, of course, attributable to the fact that rising prices (inflation) produce grave inequities in the distribution of income, enriching some groups while impoverishing others, and that falling prices (deflation) are commonly attended by general economic depression and widespread unemployment.

Many and varied explanations of rising prices have been advanced. In early times they were commonly ascribed to the extravagance of rulers, the activities of speculators, or the extortions of middlemen and monopolists. But they have also long been conceived to be in some way related to monetary conditions or policies. It is said that when Alexander, in the fourth century B.C., used the bullion which had been accumulating for two centuries in the Achaemenian treasuries in paying his mercenary legions, the "sudden increase in the volume of currency worked havoc among the peasants and artisans. Prices soared, and the financial revolution reduced to pauperism an element in the body social which had hitherto enjoyed

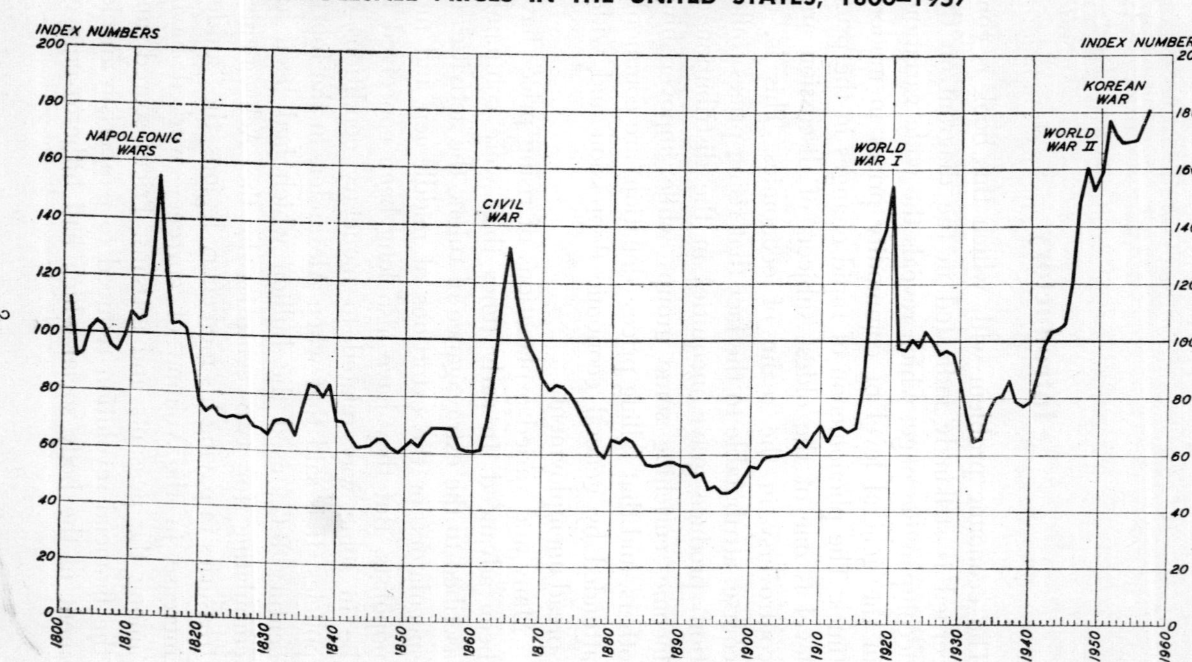
WHOLESALE PRICES IN THE UNITED STATES, 1800–1957
INDEX NUMBERS
200
180
160
140
120
100
80
60
40
20
0
NAPOLEONIC WARS
CIVIL WAR
WORLD WAR I
WORLD WAR II
KOREAN WAR
INDEX NUMBERS
1800
1810
1820
1830
1840
1850
1860
1870
1880
1890
1900
1910
1920
1930
1940
1950
1960

a relative security."[1] Wells describes the situation in Rome in the first century A.D. as follows: "Money was young in human experience and wild; nobody had it under control. It fluctuated greatly. It was now abundant and now scarce. Men made sly and crude schemes to corner it, to hoard it, to send up prices by releasing hoarded metals. A small body of very shrewd men was growing immensely rich."[2]

Throughout the Middle Ages and well into the modern era, discussion of the possible relationship between the supply of money and prices was in abeyance, for two reasons: First, during the Dark Ages money almost completely disappeared from circulation and, except in the Byzantine Empire and parts of the Orient, coinage was suspended. It was not until 1252, when the minting of gold *florins* was resumed in Florence, that European monetary systems began to revive. Second, economic observers were preoccupied with price distortions arising from reductions in the weight of coin by clipping and sweating operations—which tended to obscure the possible influence of the supply of the precious metals.

The great rise in prices in the sixteenth century that occurred more or less throughout Europe, even where currency "tampering" no longer existed, finally directed attention to the question, whether changes in the level of commodity prices might perhaps be associated with changes in the quantity of the precious metals. The first economic writer to ascribe the price revolution of the sixteenth century in large part to the expansion of gold and silver production, especially in the New World,

[1] Arnold J. Toynbee, *A Study of History* (1947), p. 377.
[2] H. G. Wells, *The Outline of History* (1924), 3d. ed., p. 429.

was the Frenchman, Jean Bodin. In 1568 he wrote as follows:

> I find that the high prices we see today are due to some four or five causes. The principal and almost the only one (which no one has referred to until now) is the abundance of gold and silver, which is today much greater in this Kingdom than it was four hundred years ago. . . . The second reason for the high prices arises in part from monopolies. The third is scarcity, caused partly by export and partly by waste. The fourth is the pleasure of Kings and great lords, who raise the price of the things they like. The fifth has to do with the abundance of money, debased from its former standard. . . . It is the abundance of gold and silver, which causes the depreciation of these metals and the dearness of the things priced. . . .[3]

Following the evolution of monetary systems based on gold, changes in the level of commodity prices came to be attributed by professional economists almost exclusively to factors affecting the production of gold. This conception—elaborated in due course to include all forms of money and credit instruments—became a part of the accepted principles of economics.

Crystallization of Thought

Principles once incorporated in formal treatises come to be regarded as established laws, no longer open to question. Indeed, they are sometimes referred to as "received" doctrines, thus taking on a sacerdotal quality. In the words of W. Stanley Jevons, nineteenth century British logician and economist:

> There is ever a tendency of a most hurtful kind to allow opinions to crystallise into creeds. Especially does this tend-

[3] Jean Bodin, "Reply to the Paradoxes of Malestroit Concerning the Dearness of All Things and the Remedy Therefor" from Arthur Eli Monroe, *Early Economic Thought* (1924), p. 127.

ency manifest itself when some eminent author, with the power of clear and comprehensive exposition, becomes recognised as an authority on the subject. His works may possibly be far the best which are extant; they may combine more truth with less error than we can elsewhere find. But any man must err, and the best works should ever be open to criticism. . . . In matters of philosophy and science authority has ever been the great opponent of truth. A despotic calm is the triumph of error; in the republic of the sciences sedition and even anarchy are commendable.

In the physical sciences authority has greatly lost its noxious influence. Chemistry, in its brief existence of a century, has undergone three or four complete revolutions of theory. In the science of light, Newton's own authority has been decisively set aside, after it had retarded for nearly a century the progress of inquiry. Astronomers have not hesitated, within the last few years, to alter their estimate of all the dimensions of the planetary system and the universe, because good reasons had been shown for calling in question the real coincidence of previous measurements. In science and philosophy nothing must be held sacred. Truth itself is indeed sacred, but where is the absolute criterion of truth?[4]

Jevons was concerned with the elusiveness of truth and the deadening influence of seemingly established doctrine. In my view another consideration is equally important in the realm of economics. Here the organism which we study is itself undergoing rapid evolution—leading to profound changes in the very structure of the system by which wealth is produced and distributed. Accordingly, generalizations which may have been true at one stage in economic evolution may become untrue at later stages. Indeed many, if not most, of the economic principles enunciated in the nineteenth century

[4] W. Stanley Jevons, *The Theory of Political Economy* (1871), pp. 265-66.

need reconsideration now simply because of changes in the economic organism itself.

How Knowledge Grows

There are two conceptions as to what is involved in the growth of knowledge. The dominant one is the "tree of knowledge" idea. On the basis of known facts, or assumptions, a central body of doctrine is developed. As new facts accumulate or as the reasoning is improved, the growing tree of knowledge may be refined and proliferated, and the basic principles may be applied to an ever-widening range of related phenomena. This is, of course, the evolutionary theory of knowledge.

A second conception is that knowledge also grows by a revolutionary process, which may involve scrapping much if not all of an established line of thinking. Indeed, many of the greatest advances have come from challenges directed at the very foundations of traditional thinking—such as are found in the works of Galileo, Newton, and Einstein. The new interpretations may be derived from new factual information indicating that the assumptions—the initial premises from which deductions proceed—are in error; from new looks at old conceptions; or they may result from new insights gained from studies in related fields—by a process of cross-fertilization. For example, the dead hand of authority in medical science was eventually removed largely by the infiltration of concepts drawn from the fields of biology, physics, and chemistry. Developments of primary significance have come in recent times through the integration of geology and physics, of physics and chemistry, and especially of physics, biology, and chemistry. Likewise, knowledge of psychology, of technology, and of business organization has contributed greatly to an understanding of the operation of the modern economic system. Above all, vast accumulations of statistical data have made it possible to test the validity of underlying assumptions.

The laws governing the physical universe were regarded in the late nineteenth century as definitely understood. But in the present century profound changes have taken place in underlying ideas. Owing chiefly to the development of the relativity concept and sub-atomic physics—dating back to the discovery of X-rays in 1896—changes in fundamental notions, previously considered axiomatic, have occurred. As summarized by Whitehead, "The stable foundations of physics have broken up. . . . The old foundations of scientific thought are becoming unintelligible. Time, space, matter, material ether, electricity, mechanism, organism, configuration, structure, pattern, function, all require reinterpretation."[5] This, it will be observed, was written before the age of nuclear physics.

The economic structure has undergone revolutionary changes since theories of money in relation to prices were formulated. Instead of a simple economic system in which money appeared in the picture only after the goods had been produced and were in consumer markets awaiting exchange, we now have a complex capitalistic system of enterprise in which money is employed at every stage of production and distribution. As we shall see, this has so profoundly altered the price-making process that traditional conceptions as to the forces responsible for changes in the general level of prices have little relevancy today.

[5] A. N. Whitehead, *Science and the Modern World* (1926), p. 24.

The Objective of the Present Study

This study undertakes a thorough-going reappraisal of the forces responsible for changes in the general level of commodity prices. The conclusions reached differ fundamentally from those expounded in traditional monetary explanations and embedded in most current interpretations of the cause and cure of "inflation." The ultimate question to which the analysis leads is the probable trend of prices in the United States in the years ahead and the problems of control under a free enterprise economic system. The final chapter, IX, shows why inflation cannot be prevented by traditional monetary and fiscal measures.

An essential part of the analysis is an appraisal of both the logic and the evidence on which traditional monetary interpretations have been based. Since much of this is highly technical in character, it has been placed in the appendixes. This device has made it possible in the text proper to set forth the primary issues in brief and relatively simple form. However, the appendix appraisals are essential to full understanding of the origin and development of traditional theories and the reasons why they obscured rather than clarified the forces responsible for changes in the general level of prices.

Background

The method of analysis and the conclusions reached in this study do not represent something new in my thinking. This was my field of specialization at the University of Chicago from 1911 to 1922; and my studies of finance in relation to business operations had led me to question even then the basic assumptions on which current money and price theories rested. Indeed, a book much along the lines of the present volume was projected before I left the University of Chicago in 1922. Because of subsequent commitments and administrative responsibilities at the Brookings Institution, this project had to be deferred indefinitely. In some respects this has of course been advantageous, for the intervening years have furnished abundant new evidence with respect to the factors involved in the price-changing process.

CHAPTER I

Explanations of Changing Price Levels

Most of the economic writers of the eighteenth and nineteenth centuries held that the general level of commodity prices is somehow directly related to the supply of the precious metals which serve as money. But there developed wide differences of view as to the process by which changes in the money supply brought about corresponding changes in commodity prices. Since these diverse conceptions are also found in present-day discussions, it is essential at the outset to outline briefly the several monetary theories that developed. A fuller discussion of the evolution of these varying conceptions will be found in Appendix A.

I. TRADITIONAL CONCEPTIONS

The value of gold approach. Those who emphasize the *value* of gold as the determining factor in price levels start with the fact that under the gold standard a certain weight of bullion is legally defined as the standard, or measure, of values in general. It seemed obvious that any factors which affect the value of the commodity adopted as a standard would automatically affect the prices of commodities expressed therein. In the words of British economist Ricardo: "If the value of money were to fall, the price of every commodity would rise, for each of the competitors would be willing to spend more money than before on its purchase."

The theory that price movements are simply reflections of changes in the value of the commodity, gold, was rooted in observations of primitive barter exchange—in which commodities, including specie, are traded directly one for another. In early gold mining communities, for example, gold dust or nuggets were in fact commonly traded directly for supplies, provisions, and other goods and services. Where miners struck it rich and came to town of a Saturday evening with an abundance of the yellow metal, they would be willing to exchange it on a liberal basis for the goods and services desired. The exchange involved a direct comparison by individuals possessing gold and goods respectively—with each party weighing comparative utilities.

The quantity of money approach. Meanwhile a second approach to the price problem had been developing. In this line of reasoning a *unit* of gold is not compared with a unit of wheat, cloth, or other commodity. Rather, the *total number* of monetary units, or counters, in circulation is compared with the total number of units of commodities being offered in exchange. Instead of thinking in terms of money as a standard, or measure, of values, the thought of these writers runs in terms of another function of money—that is, as a medium of exchange.

In its simplest form the comparison would be only between the quantity of *specie* in circulation and the volume of goods offered in the market places. But as other, supplementary, forms of currency came into use it was seen that the exchange process involved all forms of money, including checks. Moreover, it was reasoned that since the money supply was normally used many times over in the course of a year, the *velocity* of its circulation also had to be taken into account.

Eventually all this was formalized in a so-called *equation of exchange,* which held that the number of monetary units in circulation divided by the number of units of goods equals the price level. In this approach it is assumed that the money supply and the goods supply are in no way connected—that they are independent variables. The money supply is held to be governed primarily by the output of the gold mines while the goods supply depends upon the physical factors governing production—land, labor, capital, and management. Implicit in this analysis is the assumption that money is in no way related to production—that it enters the picture only in connection with the exchange process.

While the price level might be affected by quantity changes either on the money side or the goods side of the equation, it was held that changes in the production of precious metals were the primary *cause* of changes in the level of prices. Thus the price revolution of the sixteenth century was explained by the discoveries of gold and silver in the New World; the decrease in the price level between the Napoleonic Wars and the middle of the nineteenth century by the declining annual production of gold; the ensuing rise in the 1850's by the discovery of gold in California and Australia; the decline in the seventies and eighties by the gradual depletion of gold mines; and the rise beginning in the nineties by a combination of new gold discoveries, in Alaska and elsewhere, and the development of the cyanide process which made possible the profitable extraction of lower grade ores.[1]

[1] For a detailed exposition and critique of the quantity of money theory see Appendixes A and B.

An International Price System

It was early recognized that the forces affecting the prices of commodities transcend the bounds of individual countries. Since gold was produced in many parts of the world and was readily transported from country to country, the value of gold, like that of wheat and cotton, was said to be determined by world-wide conditions of supply and demand. It was reasoned that a fall in the value of gold in consequence of the discovery of rich new mines or a more efficient exploitation of old ones would shortly be reflected in rising prices throughout the world.

Quantity theorists explained the substantial uniformity of prices existing in different countries as follows: If in country A there should be an increase in the quantity of monetary counters relatively to goods, the resulting rise in prices would bring about readjustments in international trade, which would shortly result in shifts in the supply of money. That is, because of the higher prices, country A would become a good market in which to sell but a poor market in which to buy. Hence imports would increase while exports would decrease, resulting in an unfavorable balance of trade which would necessitate an outflow of specie. Thus virtual equilibrium of prices in different countries would be maintained.

This international monetary system reached its culmination in the period just preceding World War I. Most of the world was on the gold standard; exports and imports, together with the service items which help to make up the total of international economic operations, were virtually in balance; exchange rates moved in a narrow range between the gold export and import points and specie flowed in modest amounts in response to temporary needs. Economically speaking, the world could be said to have reached a state of balanced equilibrium.

The money and price theory subscribed to in explaining the maintenance of international economic and financial equilibrium was also at the zenith of its popularity. In no other realm of economics perhaps were the underlying principles and the operating mechanism so widely accepted and extolled by the profession as a whole.

The income approach. More or less contemporaneously there was evolving what has come to be known as the income approach. The focal point of attention with this approach is the flow of money income to individuals. In a pecuniary society the great bulk of individual income is received by participants in the productive process in the form of wages, interest, rents, and profits. Since this stream of money income is more or less concurrently disbursed in payment for the goods and services desired, it promptly moves again through the channels of trade and production until it is once more disbursed in the form of money income. This circular flow is of course continuous—though, to be sure, it may fluctuate in magnitude with changing business conditions. Another term that is now often employed in connection with this approach is *demand*—since the effective market demand for commodities depends upon the aggregate money income in the possession of consumers.

The income approach differs from the value of gold and quantity of money theories in one vitally important respect. The analysis is not anchored in a gold base nor in the existing stock of money. Under the value of gold and quantity of money theories, as we have seen, the price level is supposed to be governed, directly and automatically, by changes in the over-all supply of gold, or money. No thought is given to the possibility that some of the potential money supply might be idle or that the proportion used might fluctuate widely from time to time. The income approach holds that only the actual stream of money income currently being received and expended affects market prices. Fluctuations in such income are governed by the factors responsible for changes in general business conditions, and in the rates of remuneration to those who engage in production. Moreover, longer term price changes may vary widely from the supply of gold and other forms of money.

While the income approach was first outlined as early as the middle of the eighteenth century,[2] it was not until recent times that it gained extensive vogue. As we shall see, it now occupies a prominent position in current explanations of general price movements.

II. THE STATE OF CONTEMPORARY THINKING

The several explanations of changes in the general level of prices which we have been considering were formulated long ago. We shall now attempt to reveal the character of present-day thought. Do the theories briefly outlined above still hold the stage? Has there been any attempt to reconcile the divergent points of view? Have there been any significant changes in emphasis? Have any distinctly new conceptions been advanced?

[2] For a brief summary of the evolution of the income theory see Appendix A.

Postwar interpretations of changes in the general level of prices are so varied in character that it is difficult to present a succinct summary. To convey adequately the divergent interpretations and also the varying emphases, even where the general approach is similar, it will be necessary to quote rather liberally from the literature of recent years. Since we are concerned with points of view commonly held by many authors, we shall in most instances omit personal references. However, inasmuch as price interpretations are made by businessmen, public officials, and journalists, as well as by professional economists, we shall indicate the occupation of each writer quoted. The interpretations of price movements as presented in recent textbooks will be summarized in a special section at the end.

1. Explanations of the Price Revolution Since 1939

We shall consider first the widely varying interpretations of the great upsurge in the level of prices since 1939, as set forth in professional journals and pamphlets. The rise between the outbreak of the war in Europe in August, 1939, and the entrance of the United States into the struggle in December, 1941, was 25 per cent. The advance during the war period proper was 13 per cent; the rise from the end of the war to the end of 1957 was 70 per cent; and the over-all rise from 1939 to mid-1957 was 134 per cent.

Increased money supply. Perhaps the most common explanation of the advance over this period as a whole runs in terms simply of the increased supply of money in circulation.

The doubling of retail prices since 1939 has been primarily caused by the increase in the supply of money and credit. An increase in the supply of money lowers the value of the monetary unit. This is another way of saying that it raises both prices and costs. (Financial Journalist, in 1952)

In mid-1939 we had about 33 billions of money in our economy—currency and check book money (demand deposits). Today we have 118 billions of money. Money is subject to the law of supply and demand just as are commodities. . . . Liquid assets—money in the hands of the American people, including business—rose from 65 billions in 1939 to about 250 billions at present. These liquid assets were chiefly the outgrowth of the deficit spending of the depression and the war periods. Following the North Korean aggression people and business were greatly activated, which is reflected by a great increase in the velocity of money turnover. In this sense all the earlier deficit spending helped greatly to feed the inflationary forces since the summer of 1950. (Economist, in 1951)

The following statement, issued June, 1953, bears the signature of fifty-eight members of the "Economists' National Committee on Monetary Policy."

A very serious situation exists today because of the money and credit "mischief" of the past quarter century. This "mischief" has included departure from the international gold standard, devaluation of the dollar, large-scale monetization of government debt, and huge expansion of loans by commercial banks and government agencies on real estate, on installment and other consumer paper, on commodities, and for fixed capital as well as inventory accumulation needs of many businesses. . . .

The banking system, including the Federal Reserve banks, has created and made available for circulation in the channels of industry and trade many billions of demand deposits (checking accounts) and currency. To the extent that this creation and circulation of purchasing media has outdistanced the production of goods and services to absorb them, inflationary forces have been set loose in the economy.

In fact, in the past quarter century the money supply has increased at a pace not far short of twice the step-up in industrial production.

This over-all result has been made possible largely by the Federal Reserve banks' purchases of United States Government issues, both directly from the Treasury and through open market operations. These purchases were encouraged by the lowering of their legal reserve requirements, the rise in the dollar value of gold, and the acceptability of government securities as assets behind Federal Reserve notes and deposits. But for the excess reserves thus created by the Federal Reserve banks, the commercial banks could not in this way have expanded their assets and deposit liabilities.

A United States senator in 1951 explained to his colleagues precisely how an increase in the money supply changes the general level of prices.

If one pictures a pair of scales on which the amount of money available to buy goods is placed on one side and is balanced against the amount of goods available for sale on the other side, it is possible to get a picture of what is meant when we talk about monetary stability. This picture of what we mean by inflation becomes more clear if we imagine too much money demand on one side of the scales in relation to our capacity to produce goods available for sale on the other side. In that case the value of the money goes down while the price of the goods goes up. That is inflation.

Conversely, if the amount of money on one side of the scales is too small in relation to our capacity to produce the goods for sale on the other side, then the value of the money goes up and the price of the goods goes down. That is what we call deflation.

Let us use an arithmetical example to make this same point clear. If we have \$100 to offer for 100 units of goods, it follows that the average price of each unit will be \$1. Then, if we increase the quantity of money offered to \$200, but the quantity of goods remains the same as before, the average price per unit will now rise to \$2. This is inflation.

If the supply of money is reduced to $50 but the quantity of goods is not changed, then the average price falls to 50 cents. That is deflation.

All this is simple enough. Obviously the purpose of Government should be to help promote as large a supply of goods as possible and to prevent an unbalance in money demand in either direction. What we face today, however, is too much money in relation to available goods.

A report issued in 1953 by the Federal Reserve Bank of Boston, and commended by the Chairman of the Board of Governors of the Federal Reserve System, explains price fluctuations as follows:

> Stability of the average level of prices is fundamentally the result of the over-all relationship between the total supply of money and the available supply of goods, together with the average rate at which the supply of money is spent. Simply stated, too much money chasing too few goods means inflation, usually resulting in higher prices. Too many goods chasing too little money means deflation, usually resulting in lower prices.[3]

The first of this series of quotations, it will be observed, finds the explanation in a reduction in the *value* of the monetary standard. The second likewise stresses the law of supply and demand as affecting the *value* of money, but refers also to the vast increase in the *quantity* of circulating media and the high *velocity* of circulation. The other three interpretations, which emphasize the relative increase in the supply of money as compared with the production of goods, illustrate the *quantity* theory in its purest form. In the second and third quotations the general rise in prices is attributed

[3] "Report on Steps to Maintain Economic Stability," by the Committee on Economic Stabilization of the Board of Directors of the Federal Reserve Bank of Boston, January, 1953.

to government policies reaching as far back as the depression period of the thirties.

Monetization of the public debt. Numerous writers have defined government borrowing from the banks as "monetizing" the public debt. The process is explained by a banker as follows:

> The government borrows from the banks by selling its securities to them, and the banks write up deposit credits for the government to use. This process inflates the banking system, on both the asset and the deposit side of their books. It blows up the system far beyond its natural size. . . . Inflation of the banking system inflates the money supply. The influence of the vast increase in the money supply permeates the whole economic structure and affects all our economic life. . . . We have more dollars than before but they are not so strong.

When the government draws on the deposit accounts resulting from the sale of bonds to the banks, those who receive the government checks promptly deposit them in their banks. Thus this new deposit currency is not extinguished but becomes a permanent part of the nation's money supply. According to this view the money supply cannot be reduced unless there is a subsequent Treasury surplus—the proceeds being used to pay off government bonds owned by the banks. Moreover, there could be no substantial decline in commodity prices unless the public debt were greatly reduced.

The increase in bank deposits resulting from government borrowing at the banks has been held responsible for an artificially low level of interest rates, which further stimulated advances in prices. In the words of a government official:

So long as the public debt continues to be monetized through the purchase of government securities by the banking system, the supply of money will continue to increase, thus tending further to reduce the interest rates on savings and investment funds. The resultant pressure of an increasing money supply and of lower interest rates is bound to have a further inflationary effect upon all capital assets and to increase the difficulty of holding down the cost of living.

The quantity theory is implicit in this line of reasoning. The increase in the money supply relatively to goods is explained simply by the manufacture of additional money through government borrowing from the banking system. The general rise in prices is held to be the inevitable consequence.

Income and demand. Another group of economists emphasizes the increase in mass incomes, and intense demands for consumer goods as the primary cause of the great advance in prices. To be sure, both supply and demand are taken into account but "excessive demand, not deficient supply, is the core of the difficulty." The following statements are illustrative:

"Inflation" has its genesis in an increased volume of spending by consumers, business and government. The increase in spending can ordinarily be matched only in part by an expansion in the volume of commodities and services offered for sale. . . .

With more money to spend and no more civilian goods to spend it on the income receivers of the country would, of course, be apt to bid up prices. . . . (Three Economists, 1943)

The total purchasing power of consumers was greatly swelled, during and after the war, by record employment at generally higher wage rates and an extraordinary rise in net farm income, backed by accumulations of liquid assets roughly equal to a year's disposable personal income, and supplemented by credit resources for acquiring durable consumer goods and homes. . . . War and postwar policies toward veterans, farmers, and wage earners have notably added to the volume of purchasing power in money terms. (Economist, 1948)

The increase in money circulation and money incomes was partly offset by an increase in employment and production—which restrained somewhat the advance in prices. Real earnings of manufacturing workers more than doubled. However, the income effects of the increased wages had been much more important for the increase in prices than effects on production costs. That is to say, the pulling up of prices by way of increased demand has been more powerful than the pushing up by way of increased cost. (Economist, 1948)

These interpretations are, it will be seen, a mixture of quantity theory and income theory. However, the emphasis has been shifted from gold and money supply to the great rise in personal incomes and the consequent bidding up of consumer prices. This point of view is a projection forward of the war-time emphasis upon the "inflationary gap" resulting from the curtailment of the supply of consumer goods at a time when buying power was increasing. It was held that the continuing excess of purchasing power for several years after the war progressively *pulled* prices upward.

Increasing costs. A few writers place primary emphasis upon forces operating from the cost side. Most writers, indeed—even those who attach primary importance to government deficits—often refer to the inflationary "spiral" of rising prices, costs, and again prices. As a rule, however, the spiral is said to begin with increases in demand resulting directly from monetary expansion. But some writers reverse the order as is indicated in the following quotations:

There is a strange contradiction between the insistence of Federal officials on the need for price stability and their failure to deal in a realistic way with the underlying inflationary forces which they and their predecessors have done so much to create. Step by step through many years, a structure of inflation has been built into our economy. . . . Higher wages and higher farm prices have been consistent aims of Federal policy. It would be difficult to find two points in the price structure where political pressure could be applied with greater effect on the general price level and the cost of living. As prices in general have moved higher, Federal pressure in these two fields has become stronger and more direct. . . . There is a similar inflationary interaction between wages and farm prices, especially since the widespread adoption of the escalator clause in union contracts. Higher farm prices mean higher costs of living. Higher costs of living mean higher money wages, which mean higher prices for the industrial products bought by farmers. Higher prices for the things the farmer buys mean higher farm-price parities and higher support prices for farm products. And so on. (Banker, 1951)

The immediate postwar rise in the prices of products, other than foodstuffs, was determined mainly from the cost side and not from the demand side. Prices were related to the respective changes in wages and productivity and also to pricing policies of business organizations. (Economist, 1948)

In discussions of the continued rise in prices in the middle fifties one finds increasing reference to wages as a factor. Rising wages, it is usually held, affect prices by increasing money income and hence the demand for consumer goods. This "inflationary pressure" is held to be the source, or cause, of rising prices. While one now finds frequent reference to wages as a *cost* factor, operating to push prices upward, as a rule this is regarded as merely an additional force. It is sometimes described as a new kind of inflation—*wage* inflation, as distinguished from *price* inflation rooted in monetary expansion.

One finds in British literature a somewhat greater emphasis on cost factors. The term "cost inflation" as distinguished from "demand inflation" is frequently employed. This cost inflation may be ascribed either to rising prices of raw materials or to wage increases. As one writer stated the problem in late 1951:

> Until the summer of 1950 the renewed advance in prices was not such as to suggest *demand* inflation. A general increase in retail stocks indicated that demand was not pressing hard upon sources of supply; nor was the rise in personal expenditure in 1950 great in relation to the increase in national income. . . . The rise in consumer prices was attributable mainly to higher raw-material costs rather than to an increase in domestic costs. By the second half of 1950 the main upward trend had begun. . . . Although the main force of the increase in import prices was by mid-1951 reflected in the prices of consumption goods, a new inflationary influence in the form of rising wages and personal incomes became apparent, and the combined effects of rising costs and rising import prices have yet to be seen. Even with the steadying of the prices of primary products which has taken place in the second quarter of 1951, there is no alleviation of the inflationary problem, which is becoming increasingly one of preventing a cost- and demand-inflation caused by wage demands and higher personal incomes. (A British bank review, 1951)

Both rising wages and rising prices of imported raw materials are cited as significant elements of cost. But the inflationary significance of rising wages still seems to the author to flow chiefly not from wages as costs but from wages as income, and hence demand.

Deficient savings and excessive capital expansion.

A number of European writers, concerned with the problems of postwar reconstruction, have analyzed the forces responsible for price advances in a different way. Instead of finding the cause in an expansion of the supply of money available for the purchase of *consumer* goods, postwar European inflation is attributed chiefly to credit extensions to finance new *capital* growth—public and private:

> The basic disequilibrium, which is at the root of inflationary tendencies . . . is that expenditure on capital account (that is, government loan expenditure, private capital outlay, and additions to stocks) are excessive in relation to the amount of saving. (A Swedish economist)

That is, current money savings were not equal to requirements; hence both government and private enterprise borrowed either from domestic banking institutions or from foreign sources. In either case the expansion of credit for capital development was held responsible for rising prices.

Some American observers also now endorse the conception that a deficiency of savings is a primary source of inflation.

> If the gap between investment demands and available savings should be filled by creating additional bank money, the spiral of inflation . . . would be given further impetus. If the Federal Reserve System were a party to that process, it would betray its trust. (The Chairman of the Federal Reserve Board, U. S. Senate *Hearings Before the Committee on Finance,* 85th Cong., 1 sess., Part 3, p. 1262)

Suggested Remedies

One of the best means of revealing current opinion as to the causes of inflation is to indicate the remedies proposed for its control. Here again one finds wide differences in conception, which will be briefly summarized.

Restore the balance between money and goods. One approach emphasizes increasing production by private enterprise to match the "excessive" supply of money. Another calls for a reduction of the money in circulation. A more comprehensive program, involving both governmental and private policies, is designed to increase the volume of goods as well as to curtail the supply of money in circulation. The following quotations are typical illustrations of these points of view:

Maintenance and expansion of production at home and abroad must be the key objective. High production is the chief antidote to inflationary tendencies. Three sources are open to us in stimulating the expansion of output: restoration of the productive facilities of western Europe; utilization of all available capacity at home, and maintenance of appropriate incentives to the use of such capacity; advancement of productivity in every possible way. This last is of central importance. (Economist, 1948)

(1) Siphon off some of the excess purchasing power by a retail sales tax. (2) Induce larger money savings on the part of individuals. (3) Balance the federal budget. (4) Reduce the volume of industrial spending for capital goods. (5) Abandon the policy of Federal Reserve purchases of newly issued government bonds. (6) Return to free convertibility of currency into gold. (Economist)

(1) We must bend every effort to increase production by greater exertion, greater efficiency, longer hours, fewer leisure people, less of the gracious things of life. (2) We must economize—make sure that no money is spent unnecessarily. (3) As large a share of the necessary expenditures as possible must be met by taxation. (4) The government must borrow what has to be borrowed (in so far as possible) in such a way as to tap income that would otherwise be spent by the

person receiving it. (5) The government should borrow from the banks only the unavoidable minimum. (6) Over-all restraint should be exercised over loans by banks to businesses and individuals. (Economist)

It will be observed that in each of these programs the quantity theory of money is implicitly accepted. However, one finds in the references to consumer spending some of the terminology employed by adherents of the income theory.

Employ fiscal measures. Many writers place primary emphasis on fiscal operations. There are, however, distinct differences as to the scope of fiscal policy deemed necessary. One group would simply balance the budget, thereby eliminating the deficits which give rise to borrowing from the banks. This view is in line with the traditional conception that the Treasury should be concerned only with administering the revenues and expenditures of the government and should not in any way (except as might be imperative in war-time) increase or decrease the money supply of the country.

A second conception is that the government, as the largest single enterprise in the nation, inevitably does, and should, modify the over-all supply of money or purchasing power. In short, by "compensatory" action the Treasury should be a balancing factor in the economy as a whole. In periods of business recession the government should deliberately unbalance the budget, and in periods of active business it should obtain a surplus.

A number of special measures are suggested to achieve the ends sought. In recession periods the Treasury may borrow from the banks and increase the money supply in order to stimulate recovery. In periods of boom a Treasury surplus would dampen inflationary tendencies. Similarly, rates of taxation may be raised or lowered to restrain or increase consumer buying power. And government flotations and refunding operations may be so timed as to assist in stabilizing the money supply. Those who place reliance on fiscal measures emphasize that the volume of money or purchasing power may thereby be *directly* influenced, whereas central banks can, as a practical matter, influence the situation only *indirectly*, by means of credit and interest rate policies.

Rely on control of bank credit. Another school of thought looks to modifications in bank credit policy as the primary means of control. This approach is in keeping with the deeply rooted conception that only the authorities of banking institutions are so situated as to be in a position to feel the pulse of the business community and to gauge credit requirements. In the course of the nineteenth century this idea had gradually become accepted and embodied in the laws of the leading commercial countries of the world: treasuries were deprived of the power to issue money and central banking institutions were freed from government interference.[4]

Those who favor bank credit policy over fiscal measures contend that it is quicker and more dependable. A former high official of the Federal Reserve System compares the two methods as follows:

> [Fiscal policy] is slow, clumsy, and often swayed by many pressures not related to the country's monetary require-

[4] However, in war-time this independent system broke down because of the exigencies of government financial requirements.

> ments. What is raised in taxes and how depends on a complex of political and social considerations. . . .
>
> In contrast to fiscal policy, monetary policy is both feasible and flexible. It can be promptly formulated, vigorously pursued and requires no time-consuming *ad hoc* legislation. As to its effectiveness, there are no times when it is of no consequence and there are periods when it can be the decisive factor in the economy.[5]

One finds differing conceptions as to what is involved in maintaining price stability through credit control. In the view of some, the end can be accomplished in a direct and simple way. All that is necessary is to maintain an exact parallel between the increase in the supply of money and the increase in the supply of goods.

> The positive credit guide here proposed is the normal rate of growth of production. Central banks should aim at so regulating the reserves of the banking system that the outstanding credit built upon those reserves will expand at the same rate as the long-term growth of production. There is enough credit when the curves of credit growth and production growth parallel each other. More than this is too much; less than this is too little. (Economist)

This conception, which has adherents in the business world as well as in professional circles, is in no sense a new thought. It is found in economic literature at least as far back as Sir William Petty (1662); it is implicit in discussions of the responsibility of the Federal Reserve Board to control the price level; and it is reminiscent of the "neutral" money suggestions of the 1930's, which called for 100 per cent bank reserves.

The Committee for Economic Development holds that "the nation should view monetary [that is, bank

[5] E. A. Goldenweiser, address entitled "What Monetary Policy?" *Vital Speeches of the Day,* Mar. 1, 1952.

credit] policy as a principal instrument for preventing inflation and deflation."

We have advocated strong monetary action to curtail inflationary expansion of credit. We recommended a program of general credit controls, supplemented by selective controls on real estate and consumer credit. An appropriate monetary policy in the present inflationary situation should, by restricting bank reserves, limit the ability of the public to borrow from the banks. . . . This general credit control should, we believe, be accompanied by a voluntary cooperation on the part of bankers to limit the granting of inflationary loans and by specific measures to restrict borrowing by the public for home building and for the purchase of consumer goods on credit.

The specific devices counted on for the control of credit, as seen by the Committee, are the following: (1) increasing the interest rate, to discourage borrowers; (2) open market operations, involving the sale of bonds by Federal Reserve banks to member banks, to tighten credit; (3) raising legal reserve requirements, to reduce member banks' lending power; (4) increasing down payments, and shortening the time period, to curtail instalment loans; and (5) increasing "margin," or cash requirements, to restrict the use of credit in stock market speculation. The first three devices rely primarily upon higher costs and closer scrutiny of loans to restrain the over-all amount of credit extended to business. The last three involve outright restrictions on the amount of credit that can be extended for certain specific purposes.

Restore the gold standard. A large group of economists still regard the restoration of the gold standard as the only means of controlling inflation. In their view the gold standard acts as the people's automatic brake on their banks and government, placing limits on the speed and recklessness with which the government may spend money. In the words of the chief spokesman of the Economists' National Committee on Monetary Policy:

> Redeemability gives every individual with dollars the opportunity to get the standard metal if he prefers. This enables him to exercise some control over the use by his government and banks of the amount of promises these agencies may issue. If the supply of currency is increased to an extent that it invites lack of confidence, every individual can express his lack of confidence by demanding redemption in gold. His demand for redemption is a red flag of doubt. If many red flags appear, the banks, the Treasury, and Congress receive warnings and must call a halt or exercise greater restraint in their use of the people's money.
>
> The gold standard, with provision for redemption, in effect, provides a system of golden wires to every individual with dollars, over which he can send messages of approval or disapproval to the central signal board. When our government took the people's gold and thrust irredeemable promises to pay on them, it cut all these wires to the central signal box. . . . The spending orgy is the result. Government spending and bureaucracy are out of control. Apparently this course cannot be brought to a halt except by restoring to our people control over their purse. That can be done only by the institution of redeemability of the promises to pay of the Treasury and banks.[6]

In the view of some writers, the operation of the gold standard in maintaining economic equilibrium and sound financial conditions is virtually automatic. Others, however, recognize that the system depends upon action that must be taken by central bank officials; and that the application of brakes in a period of inflation involves economic and financial readjustments result-

[6] W. E. Spahr, *Monetary Notes*, Vol. 12, No. 8, Aug. 1, 1952.

ing in price deflation and unemployment. Such readjustments, which it is contended need not be severe, are regarded as the price which must be paid for the restoration of healthy conditions. With all forms of currency convertible into gold, it is held that long-term price movements would be governed solely by changes in the value of gold as a standard commodity, and that such changes, in the future as in the past, will be gradual in character.

III. THE PRINCIPLES AS EXPOUNDED IN CURRENT TEXTBOOKS

The foregoing statements have been drawn chiefly from current periodicals and pamphlets and they have been focused on the extraordinary price revolution of recent times. Accordingly, one finds in them little reference to factors governing price trends under more normal conditions. For such discussions one has to turn to textbook literature where the problem of price changes is placed in a broader and longer-term perspective. In the light of the developments of recent decades what changes have occurred in contemporary teaching with respect to the principles governing prices?

Systematic discussions of the factors governing price levels are found both in general introductory texts in Economics and in special texts on Money, Banking, and Finance. The following generalizations are based on examination of more than a score of textbooks which have appeared since World War II.

Expositions of monetary theory almost universally begin with a section entitled "The Value of Money." This implies that if one can ascertain the causes which determine the value of the monetary unit he will automatically have found the causes of variation in the general level of prices. This is the traditional value approach employed by classical writers. Sometimes the discussion is focused on the value of the standard commodity, *gold*—price changes being regarded as merely a reflection of changes in the value of the standard in which prices are expressed. More often, however, attention is centered on the official money unit (dollar, pound, etc.) without reference to any intrinsic value in the money itself—which might be either metal, government paper money, or bank paper money.

The value of money is usually said to be determined by supply and demand. As one text puts it:

> In a broad, general sense it is quite proper to state that the value of money, like the value of any economic good or service, is determined by the demand for it in relation to its supply or quantity. The factors that determine the demand for as well as the supply of money are, however, substantially different from those that determine the demand for and supply of the general run of economic goods.

Demand for money arises from the volume of transactions requiring the use of money. The supply of money includes gold, substitute forms of currency, and credit—multiplied by velocity of circulation. The conclusion always is that an increase in the quantity of the media of exchange relatively to the demand for money will raise prices; and *vice versa*.

The *quantity* theory is also commonly expounded—though it is sometimes not sharply differentiated from the *value of gold* theory. Nevertheless, the quantity of the medium of exchange is usually emphasized as the significant factor in the determination of prices.

Most contemporary writers are not strict adherents

of the older form of the quantity theory. They use the term *transactions* rather than *trade* in recognition of the fact that money is used in exchanging not merely finished goods but all forms of goods, property, and services. Again they emphasize that money is important for *holding* purposes as well as for *spending*. Moreover, they regard the *equation of exchange* as too rigid in its conceptions: specifically they point out (1) that the volume of credit commonly bears no fixed relationship to the gold base; (2) that velocity fluctuates under changing business conditions; and (3) that price changes may themselves have important repercussions upon production and trade and hence upon the volume of currency in circulation.

The *income* approach is commonly presented as merely an extension or refinement of the traditional theories. It is usually discussed in connection with analyses of business fluctuations. Sometimes it is not presented in the section devoted to prices but is placed in a chapter dealing with business cycles or theories of employment. The significance of the income approach is held to lie in the fact that it emphasizes certain factors that had hitherto not been given adequate consideration, such as fluctuations in consumer spending and the occasional withholding of cash for speculative or security purposes.

Only three of the general texts reviewed ignore both the value of gold and the quantity of money explanations of price changes. The authors of one text content themselves with explaining price changes by general fluctuations in the demand for and supply of commodities. Perhaps they are unconscious adherents of the income approach. The two others confine themselves almost entirely to an exposition of the income theory, making only the most casual reference to the quantity of money and not treating it as a causal factor in price changes.

Recapitulation

In the opening paragraph of this section we asked (1) whether the theories outlined in the preceding discussion still hold the stage; (2) whether there has been any reconciliation of the divergent points of view; (3) whether there have been any significant changes in emphasis; and (4) whether any distinctly new conceptions have been advanced. Our answers to these questions may now be briefly stated.

1. Traditional theories certainly still occupy a dominant place in most current thinking. That is to say, the conception that the price level is basically a reflection either of the value of the standard money, or of changes in the quantity of circulating media as compared with the volume of goods, permeates most of the literature of recent times. The value of gold theory is implicit in the proposals for the restoration of the gold standard; and there are survivals of it in the textbook literature. The quantity theory pervades the discussions of deficit financing and "monetization" of the public debt; it is inherent in statements about velocity of circulation; and it is the heart of discussions of credit policy as a means of controlling the price level.

2. Some attempt has been made to reconcile divergent points of view with respect to monetary theory. Most textbook writers find harmony rather than discordance in the several theories, and hold that there is an underlying consistency running through all of them.

Such differences as appear are held to arise out of the varying time periods on which they are focused. The quantity theory of money is held to be a sound explanation of long-term price trends, while the income approach furnishes a more adequate explanation of short-term price fluctuations.

3. Some shifts in emphasis are discernible. Gold is now seldom regarded as the fundamentally controlling factor in the money situation. Indeed, since the suspension of the gold standard, most writers ignore gold as a potent force in current price movements—though to be sure the *restoration* school still looks upon gold as the primary regulator of prices. Discussions of velocity are now usually centered on changes in the tempo of business, withholding cash, and the rate of spending rather than, as formerly, on the normal amount of pocket and till money required to meet the practical exigencies of every day life.

4. The income approach occupies a larger place in current thinking. This theory originated, it may be recalled, in the idea that the amount of money available for spending is governed by current income in the form of wages, interest, etc., rather than by the over-all supply of gold and credit currency. Increasing preoccupation with business depressions—with idle men, idle machines, and idle money—intensified interest in the bearing of fluctuations in current money income on prices—at least in the short run. Similarly, the great expansion of consumer income during war periods centered attention on *demand* as a primary cause of war and postwar inflation. Moreover, over longer periods of time an expanding flow of money income has come to be regarded by many as the essential basis for

expanding production. At the same time it is contended that if the flow of money income increases faster than the flow of goods the result will be a bidding up of prices by consumers.

5. During this period there *has* developed what may perhaps be called a new theory of prices—though so far as the present writer can discover it has never been formulated in explicit terms. The new conception is an outgrowth of the income approach. Since the flow of money income is regarded as of controlling importance, the key to economic stability is to be found in the stabilization of national income. The problem, therefore, appears to be to maintain at all times a high level of employment and a sustained flow of money income and expenditure.

In such a program primary reliance would not be placed upon control of the gold supply or on traditional central bank management of credit. While the banking authorities might help by easing or tightening credit, it is held that the Treasury would have to play a role of decisive importance. Whenever private business enterprise fails to maintain a high level of employment and income, the Treasury should fill the breach by borrowing funds to finance public works, and by decreasing taxes to sustain consumer purchasing power. Similarly, in periods of boom a reduction of Treasury deficits would serve to check further advances. Thus both inflation and deflation, it would seem, might be avoided.

This line of analysis is focused on business cycle phenomena and is directly concerned only with short-term fluctuations. The point of interest is the prevention of depression and the maintenance of full employment. But, the question presents itself—if this program succeeded in stabilizing the flow of income would not stability of prices also be assured? In short, if the alternating periods of inflation and deflation were eliminated, would not long-term price stability thereby be achieved? Few, if any, writers have in fact followed through to this conclusion. Long-term price trends are still commonly explained in terms of traditional monetary theory.

It should be noted, finally, that the high existing price level is commonly accepted as here to stay. Indeed, a general deflation is regarded as highly undesirable because of the inevitable repercussions upon business and employment during the process. Moreover, the federal legislation which has set the maintenance of "full employment" as a national goal implies a maintenance of prices at or near existing levels. Thus, the principal problem at present appears to be not how to reduce prices but how to prevent still further advances in the years ahead.

CHAPTER II

How Money Gets Into Circulation

The traditional theories of money in relation to prices gave little attention to the process by which money enters into, or is withdrawn from, the channels of circulation. The *value of gold* reasoning, as we have seen, was concerned only with money as a standard, or measure, of commodity values; if gold became more abundant, more dollars were demanded for goods; that is, prices rose. In the *equation of exchange* reasoning it was simply assumed that the entire money supply was somehow automatically in circulation. In short, the analysis began with a static conception—an existing volume of money on one side of an exchange and an existing volume of goods on the other side: divide the money supply by the goods supply and the quotient is the price level.

Present-day explanations of rising prices also commonly run in terms of an increasing supply of money as compared with the supply of goods, without any attempt to explain how this phenomenon comes about. Many writers have used the expression "pumping additional money into the channels of circulation"; but the pipe lines through which the stream of new money is assumed to pass are not indicated. Others have employed the term "injecting money into circulation"—as though it were somehow *forced* into the hands of the public by bankers or government officials.

The problem has been further obscured by the unhappy use of the word "inflation" in connection with money. The term inflate is derived from the Latin *inflare*—to blow; and according to Webster it means "swell with air or gas; expand; distend; puff up; elate." Webster, familiar with popular usage of the term in relation to prices, went on to define inflation as "an abnormal or imprudent expansion—as to inflate currency or credit; disproportionate and relatively sharp and sudden increase in the quantity of money or credit, or both, relative to the amount of exchange business. Inflation always produces a rise in the price level." Thus the original concept was not only extended to a different realm, but *causal* connotations were introduced into the definition itself. The underlying conception of inflation as a blowing up process is carried over. The money supply is assumed to be independently expanded—without regard to the requirements of production and trade, and without association with the financial operations of business.

I. THE MOLD OF THOUGHT FROM WHICH MONETARY THEORY EMERGED

The restricted character of the conceptions or assumptions on which traditional monetary theories rest is explained by the economic circumstances of the age in which they originated. The value of gold theory was rooted in observations of primitive barter exchange—in which commodities, including specie, are traded directly one for another—as in early gold mining communities. Under such conditions the theory clearly had validity.

Some writers explained the *value of gold* in terms

of the cost of producing the precious metals; others stressed its utility; while still others discussed more broadly the factors governing the supply of and demand for gold as a commodity. In any case, it was held that if the supply of gold increases, other things equal, the prices of commodities, expressed in gold, will rise; and *vice versa*. The value of gold theory, thus expounded, sounded reasonable; as Professor J. Laurence Laughlin was wont to say, "It is just as plain as a pikestaff." Once incorporated in textbook literature as a fundamental principle, it was readily accepted as axiomatic.

The *quantity* theory also involved the same basic assumption—namely, that the supply of money and the supply of goods are governed by wholly independent factors. The money supply was determined by the productivity of the mines of gold and silver, or by the amount of paper money manufactured by governments or banks. The supply of goods was determined by the effectiveness of production.

This assumption, that the supply of money and the supply of goods are in no way related, is explained largely by the general framework of classical economic analysis. For purposes of simple exposition the older economic treatises usually divided the subject matter into several distinct parts: Production; Valuation; Exchange; and Distribution—that is, the division of the output among those who participate in production.

The section on *Production* considered the fundamental resources which determine or limit output:—the quantity and fertility of land, the number and quality of the labor force, the amount and quality of capital instruments, and management and organization. The analysis was cast wholly in terms of physical resources and physical units of output. In opening the discussion of *Valuation* it was observed that once production had become specialized in character it was necessary for each person to exchange all or the greater part of his product for commodities produced by others. Before this could take place it was essential to determine the *relative values* of the commodities to be exchanged. After discussing the principles governing commodity *values* the author then turned to *Exchange*. Under primitive economic conditions the exchange of commodities was accomplished by direct barter—often with something "to boot," to offset value differentials. When money came to be used as an intermediary, each commodity was first compared with the money object, and was priced accordingly.

In this framework of thinking, it will be seen, money came into the picture only after the production of goods had been completed; the productive process itself appeared to be in no way connected with financial operations. There entered the market places a certain number of units of commodities which met there a certain number of units of money, the amount of each being governed by wholly independent factors.

It should be noted that in the development of the theory of commercial banking it was assumed that credit was in no way related to production proper. This is readily understandable in view of the fact that in the eighteenth century nearly all productive operations were carried out on a small-scale handicraft basis and that only in commercial or marketing operations were extensive financial resources required. As the term "*commercial*" banking implies, bank credit operations were supposed to be confined solely to commerce, or marketing. Credit was extended merely to facilitate "the movement of goods between producer and consumer." In the view of pure banking theorists, credit was obtained from the banks only to carry or move goods whose values had already been determined, and governed the amount of credit extended; hence it was held that credit would normally not affect prices. In the view of others, however, this credit, or deposit currency, constituted a net addition to the supply of money being offered in exchange for a given volume of goods.

The framework of thought and the underlying assumptions were thus rooted in conditions of the pre-industrial age—when the producing and manufacturing process was largely conducted on a non-monetary basis, and when in the main it was only final consumer goods that were exchanged through the use of money. But under the conditions of capitalistic industry, money, and credit, are utilized in connection with every stage of the complex productive process.

Indeed, all our financial institutions have been called into existence by opportunities for service, and financial reward, in providing essential funds for the *conduct* of business enterprise. With the growth of large-scale capitalistic enterprise there developed a wide range of financial agencies which, taken together, constitute a complex, inter-related financial system by means of which the entire process of production is organized and operated.

The monetary theories which originated before the capitalistic age have little relevance in the *economic* world of today. Whereas in primitive communities gold was exchanged directly for commodities, and hence some comparison of relative utilities was involved, today gold coins are akin to museum pieces and no one has occasion to compare a unit of gold with units of other commodities. Whereas in the pre-industrial age commodity prices were largely determined at public auctions in central market places provided by the great fairs[1], in the modern world most commodities are *priced* by manufacturers before they reach the channels of trade.

The price-making process, with few exceptions, is now directly connected with, and is an integral part of, the productive system itself. The conception of an equation made up of a goods side and a money side, each independent of the other, has no reality. The wide combination of factors operating in the productive system which affects prices under varying conditions will be discussed in subsequent chapters.

Early exponents of the *income* theory made a great forward step when they observed that the money supply available for purchasing consumer goods is derived by its owners from services rendered in the productive process; and received by them in the form of wages, rents, interest, and profits. Unfortunately they did not go on to consider whether there was any direct connection between gold supplies and credit potentials and the level of money income. Later income theorists believed that the level of money income, or effective demand (purchasing power), governed both business activity and price movements. They were, however, preoccupied with short-term cyclical fluctuations. So

[1] See discussion of the role of Spanish fairs, Appendix B, pp. 258-59.

far as long-term price trends were concerned, they usually remained orthodox quantity theorists.

II. THE FLOW OF MONEY INCOME

To give concreteness to this discussion it is essential to survey briefly the actual flow of money income in a modern nation. The money of the people is received by them as compensation for work performed or as rewards for ownership of property. The productive system requires labor, land, capital, and management—which give rise, respectively, to wages and salaries, rents, interest, and profits. The income of unincorporated business and professional men and farmers is composite in character: that accruing from the ownership of land or capital is akin to rent and interest; that resulting from the individuals' labor is personal wages; and that attributable to management is profits.

The aggregate money income[2] received by the American people in the year 1956 is shown by the table on page 46.

Out of this total of 343 billions, taxes must be paid by wage and salary earners, professional men, corporations, individual and partnership enterprises, and the receivers of rents, interest, and dividends. So-called *disposable personal income* (after taxes) was 287 billions in 1956.[3]

Mention should be made here of certain minor additions to these primary sources of money income such as relief payments to individuals, certain forms of pen-

[2] It should be explained that the figures include some minor payments in kind and adjustments of inventory values.

[3] U.S. Dept. of Commerce, *Survey of Current Business,* July, 1957, p. 10.

NATIONAL INCOME BY DISTRIBUTIVE SHARES, 1956[a]
(billions of dollars)

	AMOUNT		PER CENT
Compensation of employees:			
Wages and salaries	$227.2		
Supplements[b]	14.1	$241.3	70.2
Income of unincorporated enterprises:			
Business and professional	28.0		
Farm	11.6	39.6	11.5
Corporate profits:			
Tax liability	22.0		
Dividends and undistributed profits	21.0		
Inventory valuation adjustment	–2.6	40.4	11.8
Rental income of persons		10.3	3.0
Net Interest		11.9	3.5
TOTAL		$343.6	100.0

[a] U. S. Dept. of Commerce, *Survey of Current Business*, July, 1957, p. 27.

[b] Includes employer contributions for social insurance, private pensions, welfare, etc.

sions, and subsidies to farmers and others. Moreover, the money supply available for current expenditure may be augmented by consumer credit operations. Since such credit advances call for repayment in the not distant future, it is obviously only the net increase in the amount outstanding over a given time period that enhances buying power. Since such increments to spendable income are commonly less than 1 per cent of aggregate wages and salaries, they are of negligible importance.

Aggregate money income naturally fluctuates with changing business conditions. In periods of acute depression all types shrink, though in varying degrees; in periods of prosperity all tend to rise, though far from uniformly. The fluctuations reflect both changes in the volume of business activity and rates of pay.

III. HOW CAN MONEY INCREASE FASTER THAN GOODS?

We come now to one of the crucial questions with which this study is concerned—*How* does it come about that money income does in fact often increase faster than the supply of goods? The answer is that in normal business operations an increase in the ratio of money income to goods produced occurs only when higher rates of remuneration are given for the same amount of service. When higher wage rates are paid for the same output, the quantity of money entering the channels of circulation increases while the supply of goods remains the same. Similarly, if rental or interest rates rise, the owners of land and capital receive more money income without increasing output. If in 1956 wage and salary rates had averaged 10 per cent higher, the aggregate flow of money would have been increased by 22.7 billion dollars; a similar increase in interest rates would have augmented the money flow by roughly 1.2 billion dollars.

An increase in the supply of gold or an expansion of bank credit can increase the flow of money income to the people only if there is occurring an increase in rents, wages, interest, and profits. Since there are no other circuits than these pay envelopes there can be no independent "inflating" or blowing up of the money supply; no automatic "pumping" or "injecting" money into the channels of circulation. It follows that the aggregate money income available for expenditure can be expanded, appreciably, only by an increased flow through pay envelopes.

Thus we arrive at the conclusion: *The supply of money as compared with the supply of goods is governed by the ratio of rates of pay to productive output.* Accordingly, if we are to understand the price-changing process we must analyze the forces operating within the productive system to increase or decrease rates of pay as compared with output.

The analysis thus far has related only to the basic question: How does the increased money supply get into the *ultimate* channels of circulation, that is, into the hands of the consuming public? It should be noted now that an increase in the supply of money relatively to goods may occur at an earlier stage in the productive process. This is often the case in an incipient boom when businessmen greatly expand orders for raw materials—paying for them with the proceeds of bank loans. If prices of materials rise in consequence the producers receive more money than before for a given quantity of material. Such bulges in inventory purchases are, however, commonly followed in due course by a period of subnormal buying, which brings about at least a partial readjustment of prices; and as the loans are paid off bank deposits automatically decline. Such short-term fluctuations in business loans and deposits do not *directly* affect long-term levels of money income in the hands of consumers. For a specific illustration of this type of price distortion, see page 150.

IV. TREASURY DISBURSEMENTS AND THE MONEY SUPPLY

The foregoing discussion has related solely to the operation of private enterprise. It remains to consider whether the situation is essentially different when the increased currency supply is disbursed through Treasury operations rather than by way of the banking system. We are not here interested in deficit financing as such; we are concerned only with the question: Through what channels do Treasury disbursements reach the hands of the public?

The great bulk of Treasury outlays, like those of business corporations, represents payments for services rendered. These include salaries for government employees, interest payments on government securities, rents on leased properties, and payments for commodities purchased for civil or military purposes. In the case of purchases, the disbursements are, of course, in the first instance made to business enterprises and they pass into the hands of the general public through the disbursements made by such enterprises. The government also pays out money for retirement pensions, old age insurance, and relatively small amounts go for subsidies and miscellaneous types of relief. (Only in the case of the Works Progress Administration of the depressed 1930's were the sums disbursed for relief purposes substantial.) In virtually all cases, Treasury disbursements are made in accordance with contracts or statutory provisions; and the amounts cannot be altered without changes in governing legislation.

Consideration must be given at this place to the so-called "monetization of the public debt." As the quotations given on page 20 indicate, the conception is that when the Treasury borrows from the banking system the process "blows up the system far beyond its natural size . . . and inflates the money supply. . . . We have more dollars but they are not so strong." When the Treasury draws checks against this deposit account in favor of business X, the latter will normally deposit the Treasury's check in its bank deposit account; and in turn when X draws checks against this deposit, the recipients thereof will deposit them in their respective banks. Thus deposits in the banking system as a whole continue to be enlarged.

This process is, however, in no way different from what occurs when a private corporation borrows from a bank. The company receives a deposit credit on the bank's books, against which it draws checks which are promptly deposited in some bank. It could as well be said therefore that private business debts are thus "monetized," with a resulting blowing up of the banking system and the money supply.

The initial increase in deposits resulting from Treasury borrowing from the banks is not an increase in money in actual circulation. The money can get into the ultimate channels of circulation only as it is paid to the public for services rendered—either directly by the Treasury or indirectly by business enterprises from which the Treasury is procuring goods or services. Thus the flow of this deposit currency into the hands of the people is also governed primarily by existing rates of remuneration.

It follows from the foregoing that under conditions of full employment the Treasury cannot increase the aggregate national money income simply by spending more or reduce it by spending less. There are no independent circuits through which it may pump money directly into the hands of the people. The total money income disbursed is governed simply by rates of pay for services rendered—private and public.

V. ASSUMED STEPS IN THE INFLATION PROCESS

Thus far we have been considering only the simple assumptions underlying most current discussions of "inflation" and also the old formal "equation of exchange." It must now be noted that numerous writers have endeavored to show the steps in the process by which an increased supply of gold or available bank reserves automatically *leads* to higher prices of consumer goods.

Writers who have given specific consideration to the process by which additional money supplies find their way into circulation hold that it is through the medium of higher wages. This, for example, was the view of Cantillon, whose interpretations were based on conditions found in the early days of capitalistic evolution. As he observed the situation, business enterprisers simply used their newly available monetary resources to hire laborers who had hitherto not been employed as money wage earners—thereby increasing aggregate money income in the hands of the people.

As the capitalistic system became more complex, new supplies of gold were usually desposited in banking institutions, where they might be borrowed by businessmen generally. As gold production increased, the banks would have abundant funds to lend at low rates of interest. It was believed that businessmen would thus be induced to borrow additional money with which to expand their operations, thereby providing more employment and—through increasing the demand for labor—raising wage rates. Money income available for expenditure would thus be increased.

The later income, or demand, theorists went on to explain a succession of steps by which increased bank reserves were supposed to bring about higher prices of consumer goods. According to Keynes, "The primary effect of a change in the quantity of money on the quantity of effective demand is through the interest rate." Induced by a sufficiently favorable interest rate, the enterpriser borrows from the bank and uses the money in bidding for labor in the market. So long as unemployment exists, Keynes notes that "An increase in the quantity of money will have no effect whatever upon prices . . . and employment will increase in exact proportion to any increase in effective demand brought about by the increase in the quantity of money"; but "as soon as full employment is reached, it will thenceforth be the wage unit and prices which will increase in exact proportion to the increase in effective demand."[4] In short, the increased income of the laboring population results in a bidding up of the prices of consumer goods.

In the reasoning just presented, the line of motivation runs as follows: (1) increased bank reserves and lending power; (2) lower interest rates; (3) increased business borrowing; (4) bidding up wage rates; (5) increased money income; and (6) bidding up the prices of consumer goods. The validity of this analysis may be tested by studying the factual records pertaining to the order of events in periods of rising prices, and also by appraising the principal factors which govern business decisions. This will be done in ensuing chapters.

[4] See John Maynard Keynes, *The General Theory of Employment, Interest, and Money* (1936), pp. 295-340.

CHAPTER III

Is the Interest Rate Significant?

In this chapter we examine the underlying assumption in the inflation process outlined at the end of the preceding chapter. This basic assumption is that large bank reserves—resulting from an increase in gold production, an inflow of gold from abroad, or reduced reserve requirements—lower interest rates; and that low interest rates will induce businessmen to increase their loans from the banks. Since the interest rate is regarded as of controlling importance—the motivating force—this primary assumption requires thorough-going appraisal.

This thesis—that the short-term interest rate directly affects the volume of bank borrowing and thus the supply of credit currency and the level of prices—is deeply embedded in economic literature. It has long been the view of many bank officials as well as professional economists that both fluctuations in business activity and in prices may be prevented by controlling the rate of interest at the central banks. It is merely necessary to raise interest rates when business is buoyant, thereby checking loan expansion, and to lower rates when business is dull, thereby inducing increased borrowing. It was contended that even a slight advance in the discount rate—such as one-eighth or one-fourth of 1 per cent—would immediately check or restrain loans, and similarly that in dull times loan expansion would quickly be stimulated by ever-so-modest decreases in the cost of borrowing.

It is necessary to bear in mind throughout this analysis that two distinct, though related, problems are involved: The first pertains to the effectiveness of the interest rate in checking expansion in boom times and in stimulating recovery in periods of depression. The second relates to its usefulness in stabilizing the general level of commodity prices.

In the earlier years of the Federal Reserve System the Board held that its function was merely to restrain credit for speculative purposes and to help banks over acute financial crises, and that the Federal Reserve law did not intend that the Board should undertake the task of controlling the price level. Following an extensive review of its problems and policies, the Federal Reserve officials evolved a "broadened credit policy," which was made public in 1923.

Here it was conceded that they should not be content merely with restraining speculative activities, but should endeavor through credit policy to keep the entire economy on an even keel. But the Reserve authorities still did not concede that it was their function to control commodity prices, or that it would be possible in any case to do so. They expressed themselves on this issue as follows:

> The price situation and the credit situation, while sometimes closely related, are nevertheless not closely related to one another as simple cause and effect; they are rather both to be regarded as the outcome of common causes that work in the economic and business situation. . . . The demand for credit is conditioned upon the business outlook. Credit is created in increasing volume only as the community wishes to use more credit—when the opportunity for the employment of credit appears more profitable. Sometimes borrowers want to borrow more and sometimes they are content

with less. Sometimes lenders are ready to lend more and at other times less. Why this should be so depends on all those multifarious conditions and circumstances that affect the temper of the business community. . . . When the business outlook is inviting . . . new business commitments are made in increasing volume. But only later will these commitments be reflected in the possible rise of prices and an increase in the volume of credit provided by the commercial banks of the country. The Federal Reserve banks will not to any considerable extent feel the impact of the increased demand for credit until the whole train of antecedent circumstances which has occasioned it is well advanced on its course; that is, until a forward movement of business, no matter from what impulse it is proceeding, has gained momentum.[1]

In 1939 the Board of Governors made the following statement:

Experience has shown . . . that (1) prices cannot be controlled by changes in the amount and cost of money; (2) the Board's control of the amount of money is not complete and cannot be made complete. . . . There have been times when the amount of money and prices have changed together; but usually they have not. . . . Usually other things have a greater influence on prices than has the amount of money.[2]

However, in recent years Federal Reserve officials have not expressed themselves with equal pessimism. On the contrary, there has been a strengthening of the view that the Federal Reserve, through wise and timely action, may not only exert a stabilizing influence on business conditions, but control the price level as well.

Bearing in mind this twofold objective of interest rate control—to stabilize business and to stabilize prices—we turn to the lessons of experience. Since the effec-

[1] *Tenth Annual Report of the Federal Reserve Board* (1923), pp. 31-32.

[2] *Federal Reserve Bulletin*, Apr. 13, 1939, pp. 255-59.

tiveness of the interest rate in stimulating recovery from business depressions may be rather summarily treated, it will be considered first.

I. LOW INTEREST RATES IN DEPRESSION PERIODS

The facts show conclusively that the low interest rates prevailing in periods of recession have never stimulated an expansion of loans. For example, in the long depression from 1873-79 interest rates, both in the United States and Great Britain, remained at unprecedentedly low levels. In 1877 Professor Bonamy Price of Oxford University wrote as follows:

> One per cent has now reigned supreme in the market for discount for the space of a whole year. . . . One per cent has been only an average for the twelve months. For a considerable time the rate for lending went to one-half per cent: and even on such infinitesimal terms the bankers have at times found it hard to reap any profit from their deposits.[3]

In fact, many banks closed their doors for want of customers.

American experience in the great depressions of the 1890's and the 1930's was similar. In the latter case, as the depression deepened the Federal Reserve authorities made every effort to arrest its decline and stimulate recovery. Discount rates were reduced to very low levels, but with no effect. The Federal Reserve then sought to push additional money into circulation by offering direct loans to borrowers on especially favorable terms. But borrowers did not respond.

Throughout the decade of the thirties, interest rates

[3] "One Per Cent," *Contemporary Review*, Vol. 29, April, 1877 (London), pp. 778-81.

both in the Federal Reserve banks and at member banks remained unprecedentedly low; and yet business remained stagnant. The aggregate loans of all banks were as follows: 41.1 billions at the peak of the boom in mid-1929; 21.9 billions at the low of the depression in mid-1933; and 22.2 billions at the end of 1939. Commercial banks, unable to expand commercial loans, were increasingly becoming investors in U. S. government and corporate securities, the holdings of which came materially to exceed the loans outstanding. Lending power meanwhile remained superabundant. In order to reduce the "excess" reserves, the legal minimum requirements were raised by law from 13 to 26 per cent in Central Reserve city banks, from 10 to 20 per cent at Reserve city banks, from 7 to 14 per cent in the so-called country banks. Even so, there remained great unused credit potentials.

After 1940, under the stimulus of war and postwar developments, bank loans naturally increased enormously in keeping with the expansion of production and the rising level of costs. However, the reserves available throughout this period were adequate to support a vastly greater expansion than in fact occurred. Minimum reserve requirements were maintained with slight variations at or near the new high levels authorized in the late thirties. Even so, we continued to have substantial excess reserves of lending power.

II. HIGH INTEREST RATES AS A RESTRAINT

Historically, efforts to restrain credit expansion and rising prices have been fruitless. In the boom stage of the recurring business cycles of earlier years higher rates of interest did not curb loan extension, either in the

United States or in European countries. It is true that raising the bank rate in one money market often attracted funds from other markets; but it never proved an effective means of stabilizing business and prices—of controlling the so-called business cycle.

Sponsors of the interest rate theory were long disposed to ascribe its ineffectiveness not to any inherent defect in the reasoning involved, but rather to a failure on the part of the banking authorities to use the instrument wisely. The failure to check booms was sometimes charged to tardiness in applying the brake and sometimes to failure to raise the rate sufficiently. Whatever the harassed officials did appeared to be wrong, because it did not bring the results anticipated by the theory.

The Role of Open Market Operations

Mention should be made at this place of so-called "open market" operations by the Federal Reserve banks. When this conception was first advanced in the 1920's, such operations were extolled by some as a great new mechanism of control whereby business and prices could be stabilized. The idea was that by buying securities in the financial markets, the Federal Reserve banks would be putting money into the channels of circulation and that by selling securities they would be withdrawing money from circulation.

Such operations, however, do not *directly* affect the volume of currency in the hands of businessmen or the consuming public. Purchases of securities by Federal Reserve banks may increase the reserves of the banks from which the purchases are made; and, conversely, sales of securities held by Federal Reserve banks may reduce the reserves of the member banks which bought them. While these inter-bank transactions may thus ease or tighten credit conditions and affect interest rates at the member banks, it is still necessary for businessmen to decide to borrow more if the volume of money in the channels of circulation is to increase. Again the question is whether higher, or lower, interest rates will be effective.

We have used the words *may,* and *might,* in referring to potential effects of open market operations on member bank reserves and interest rates, because in practice this expected result has commonly been nullified by shifts in bank assets. In former times, when member banks were regular borrowers from the Federal Reserve, they offset open market operations by increasing, or decreasing, their loans at the Federal Reserve. Under present conditions, when the banking system has vast holdings of government securities in its portfolios, the member banks need merely sell, or buy, governments to maintain their reserve position.[4]

The Test of 1955-57

The interest rate theory still permeates the thinking of the financial community as well as that of professional economists. A poll of financial experts conducted by an investment house in the autumn of 1955 gave first place among the top ten business-news events of the year to the Federal Reserve credit restraint policy, designed to check rising commodity prices. The actions of the Federal Reserve were summarized as follows:

> Starting in April 1955 the rediscount rate was raised an unprecedented four times during the year from 1.5 per cent to 2.5 per cent, an increase of two thirds. The Federal Re-

[4] See p. 60.

serve's open market operations also put steady pressure on the commercial banks' ability to lend as it sopped up excess funds. . . . As a result . . . interest rates on commercial paper, prime business loans, short-term U. S. Treasury obligations all went up repeatedly. Most rates are now at the highest levels since the early Thirties.

It is apparent that this time the Reserve authorities were alert and forehanded. In 1956 and the first half of 1957 a series of further advances brought the rate on short-term commercial paper to 3.88 per cent.

What effect did this vigorous Federal Reserve policy have upon bank lending operations? The official figures show that the loans of all commercial banks increased steadily throughout this period—from 70,619 millions at the beginning of 1955 to 87,720 millions on June 27, 1956—a greater increase than in the three preceding years combined.[5] By the end of 1956 the total reached 90,302 millions;[6] and the expansion continued in 1957.

During this period the Federal Reserve not only raised the interest rate again and again but also sought to tighten credit conditions at the member banks by engaging in extensive "open market operations"—which obliged the member banks to buy securities sold by the Federal Reserve banks. How then was it possible for the member banks to continue to expand loans for business purposes? The answer is chiefly through the sale of their holdings of United States' government obligations—to business corporations and individuals and to other financial institutions. Bank holdings of United States' government issues decreased in the 18-months' period, December 31, 1954-June 27, 1956, from 68,981 to 56,360 millions. Cash assets during the period decreased by

[5] *Federal Reserve Bulletin*, August, 1956, p. 855.
[6] *The same*, July, 1957, pp. 754 and 788.

2,839 millions. Meanwhile, the excess reserves of member banks showed little change.[7]

The Federal Reserve interest rate policy did not prevent further advances in commodity prices. The authorities expressed satisfaction over the fact that in the calendar year 1955 the wholesale price index for all commodities increased less than 2 per cent. But this favorable showing was due almost entirely to the adverse agricultural situation. The prices of agricultural products as a whole fell 3.4 per cent, while in other lines prices rose during the year by more than 5 per cent. The rise was most rapid during the second half of the year at the very time that the higher interest rates were supposed to be achieving results. The rise was greatest in raw and semi-manufactured metals—over 14 per cent—and least in chemical products. The rate of the price rise accelerated in 1956 and the first half of 1957. By this time "inflation" had come to be regarded as the "number one issue" facing the country. Farm prices had ceased to decline—thus eliminating the offset factor existing earlier.

The reader should bear in mind that in this section we have been considering only the effect of changes in the rate of interest. Another phase of Federal Reserve policy involves an outright positive restriction of bank loans. This will be considered in Section IV.

III. INTEREST AS A COST FACTOR

What is the origin of the conception that the interest rate is a factor of primary importance in business operations? Under the so-called commercial system of the eighteenth century the business of commercial banks was confined largely to financing purchases of raw ma-

[7] *Federal Reserve Bulletin,* August, 1956, p. 859.

terials for domestic manufacture under a household system of production. The sums borrowed usually made up the greater part of the enterpriser's capital; and because of the dearth of money savings and of bank credit facilities, interest rates were extremely high. At the same time other elements of cost were of minor importance; little in the way of plant or equipment was involved, and wages were mere pittances—often paid in kind. Under such conditions the interest item was the all-important factor in the calculations of businessmen—almost the sole element of risk. It is understandable, therefore, why early economic analysts should have found the interest rate an engaging instrument for regulating business activity.

Under modern conditions interest has become an insignificant item in business costs. The relative importance of wages and salaries and interest outlays in principal groups of industries in 1954 is shown by the following table.[8] Manufacturing industry is of primary importance—the leading influence in general business expansion or contraction. But in manufacturing as a whole the interest item is inconsequential. Indeed, in

	WAGES AND SALARIES[9]	NET INTEREST
Manufacturing	$71,304 millions	$194 millions
Transportation	12,447 "	344 "
Contract construction	11,863 "	85 "
Communications and public utilities	6,481 "	697 "
Mining	3,743 "	32 "
Wholesale and retail trade	36,113 "	208 "

[8] Data from U. S. Dept. of Commerce, *Survey of Current Business*, July, 1955, pp. 14, 15, 17.

[9] The figure includes supplements.

some years the net interest item has been a minus quantity—interest paid out on bank loans and bond and note obligations being exceeded by interest received from investments.

Other elements of cost besides wages and salaries are also highly important in business operations—notably materials and supplies, depreciation, advertising, and engineering, legal, and other fees. The relative importance of these various items varies widely in the different industries. For example, in manufacturing, raw material costs make up a large portion of the total, while in service activities such as transportation, public utilities, and communications, materials and supplies are much less important and the wage and salary component is very high.

The interest item in modern industrial corporations is often non-existent and is always so unimportant that a separate figure or reference to the item is seldom found in published corporate reports. We have, however, obtained interest figures from five large corporations chosen at random and representative of the oil, harvester, food, cement, and automotive industries. The following consolidated figures show the interest item together with other elements of cost. The wage and salary item includes deductions and bonuses.

Wages and salaries	$3,278,298,000	53.0 per cent
Materials and supplies	1,134,800,000	18.4 " "
Taxes—other than income	1,063,353,000	17.2 " "
Depreciation	298,526,000	4.8 " "
Administration	207,541,000	3.4 " "
Advertising	162,243,000	2.6 " "
Rents	21,677,000	.3 " "
Interest	17,622,000	.3 " "
Total	$6,184,060,000	100.0 per cent

It is obvious from these figures, which are characteristic of all industrial corporations, that any conceivable increase in the interest rate would be an inconsequential factor in the over-all situation. Business decisions do not revolve around changes in the least significant element of cost.

It should be noted, finally, that if the interest cost were significant, it might readily be passed along in the form of higher prices. In discussions of rising wage and raw materials costs it is always taken for granted that in a period of prosperity such increases will be added, in whole or in part, to selling prices. But interest rate theorists implicitly assume that higher interest costs must be absorbed by the producer. In fact, the price advance required to offset any customary increase in interest rates would be negligible. Concretely, using the figures in the preceding table, a doubling of the interest rate would have increased total costs only about three-tenths of one per cent.

Attention is also directed to the fact that the financial position of modern American corporations is often such that it is not really necessary to *borrow* money. At any given time large funds for expansion purposes may be available because of preceding depreciation charges. The ratio of quick assets to current liabilities is commonly at least two or three to one; even cash and immediately marketable securities may be well in excess of short-term obligations. Moreover, where large-scale expansion programs are contemplated, there is usually an alternative to borrowing at fixed rates of interest through the medium of common stock flotations.

It is sometimes contended that the impact of higher

interest rates is certainly felt in *marginal* situations. In other words, high-cost producers would be forced to curtail operations—which would be sufficient to stem the tide of expansion and bring about corrective readjustments. With reference to this argument three comments may be made: First, the interest item among marginal establishments is a minor element of cost; such companies are much more vulnerable to increases in the cost of wages and raw materials. Second, the interest rate would be raised in a period of prosperity—that is, at the very time when even the least efficient companies make good profits, thanks to high volume and favorable prices. Third, even if marginal establishments should be seriously affected by higher interest rates, they are of such minor importance in the industrial structure that their failure would have slight effect upon the over-all business situation.

Again, the housing field is sometimes cited as one in which the interest item is of especial importance. Because of the general economic significance of a high rate of construction, it is argued that an advance in interest rates in this sector might turn the general tide of business. So far as the building *contractor* is concerned, the interest item is negligible in relation to total costs. Wages and salaries make up 56 per cent and interest two-tenths of one per cent of the costs. Thus a change in wage rates or in the cost of materials would be of incomparably greater importance.

For the individual home owner, also, the rate of interest is not a prime consideration. Where houses are financed out of accumulated savings, the interest item obviously does not bulk large in the figuring; one sacrifices interest on savings accounts or securities in order to save rent. Where houses are purchased on the installment plan, interest is included in the aggregate monthly payment. The simple question in the mind of the potential buyer is whether he can meet the combined monthly payments for interest, insurance, taxes, and amortization of the loan. Any moderate increase in the rate of interest would be much less important than an increase in the down payment required or in the rate of amortization of the loan. In fact, in controlling housing construction and installment purchases the government has come to rely on restriction of the amount of credit (by requiring a larger down payment and a shorter term) rather than on increasing the cost of credit.

Short-term or Long-term Rates?

In concluding this discussion attention should be called to the fact that until well after World War I the theory under review was conceived solely in terms of short-term interest rates on loans from commercial banks. But the ineffectiveness of the short-term rate eventually led to a shift in emphasis from short-term to long-term rates. As late as 1924, Keynes expressed complete confidence in the efficacy of the short-term rate, contending that business could be completely stabilized by well-timed increases and decreases in the discount rate on commercial loans. But, by 1931, events had led him to abandon the short-term rate in favor of the rate on long-term loans in which he expressed great confidence.[10]

[10] This statement of Keynes' position is based on personal conversations in 1924 and 1931, respectively. While in his later writings Keynes appears at places to have lost confidence in the effectiveness of the interest rate, it nevertheless remains embedded in his basic theory. See for example the quotation on p. 52 above.

It may be argued that a high long-term rate would be more effective simply because of the longer commitment. But in view of the negligible sums involved, and the possibility of passing higher interest costs along through higher prices, the longer time period is not a significant factor.

We have discussed the interest rate at some length because of its central position in the theoretical explanation of the process by which increasing supplies of money get into circulation and affect commodity prices. The entire theory rests on the validity of the assumption that the level of interest rates is a primary factor in business decisions to expand the scale of operations. Our analysis leads to the conclusion that under modern conditions the interest rate, an inconsequential and often non-existent element of cost, has no appreciable effect on business calculations.

Hence increased supplies of gold, abundant bank reserves, and low interest rates do not result automatically in an expansion of loans and a consequent bidding up of wage rates by business enterprisers. Thus the initial assumption in the reasoning summarized on page 53 above is not valid.

IV. POSITIVE CONTROL OF THE VOLUME OF CREDIT

There remains for consideration the possibility of controlling the money supply, and the level of prices, by direct means. That is, instead of relying upon increases or decreases in the *cost* of credit through changes in the rate of interest, cannot the banking authorities accomplish the end desired by exercising outright control over the volume of bank loans? This suggestion has often been advanced;[11] and it is a part of the present control program of the Federal Reserve authorities.

Experience has shown that in periods of depression it is impossible to inject additional credit money into the channels of circulation if borrowers do not need or wish the money. As one administrator grimly remarked in the early thirties, when strenuous but unavailing efforts were being made by the Federal Reserve system to force money into business use—"It is difficult to push on a string." In short, at a time when business corporations have idle financial resources of their own they will neither request nor accept additional loans from the banks.

In a boom situation the problem is fundamentally different. Further expansion of credit could indeed be checked by a general moratorium on bank loans. Moreover, it could be restrained somewhat by more conservatism in the granting of loans, by greater discrimination between good and mediocre credit risks, and by refusal to take on new accounts. The latter method was, in fact, employed in the middle 1950's. The meager result achieved has been indicated on pages 59-60 above.

An outright restriction of commercial bank credit is obviously difficult to administer under a private banking system. If a borrower's credit position is satisfactory, he is entitled to additional accommodation to meet legitimate requirements; and a banker cannot well turn him down simply because all borrowers—good, bad, and indifferent—are also applying for additional credit.

[11] See, for example, the proposal on page 29.

Moreover, if banker A should perchance refuse the loan, he might lose a valued customer since the borrower might obtain the accommodation from banker B.

As a measure of cooperation with the Federal Reserve authorities the individual banker may indeed refuse to take on new borrowers. But unless loans to good credit risks and regular customers are also restricted, the general expansion of business will not be checked appreciably; such restriction as may occur in connection with new borrowers and the weaker companies may be offset by continued expansion in the strongly entrenched companies. The most that can be expected is a lessening in the *rate* of business expansion.

As a practical matter the banking authorities dare not declare a general moratorium on extensions of bank credit. This is because of the fear that such a policy would upset the equilibrium and precipitate a depression. The business situation is the result of interacting forces delicately adjusted. A further expansion in the volume of production would require additional monetary expansion even if the level of costs were stable. And if the cost of materials, labor, etc. is rising, more money will be required to finance each unit of output. Thus to clamp a moratorium on credit expansion without freezing costs would force business contraction and precipitate far-reaching readjustments.

It should be noted here that restriction of *consumer credit* is not beset with similar complications. Increased down-payment requirements or shortening the time periods involved in installment contracts restrict buying at the consumer end without directly affecting the cost-price structure of business. With this method the hope is that a moderate restriction on consumer buying will ease demand sufficiently to restrain the tempo of business without forcing extensive readjustments.

Credit restriction in a period of general expansion cannot prevent rising prices. This is proved by the experience of 1955-57 referred to above. So long as the level of wages continues to rise, costs of production will continue to rise; and at the same time the ratio of money income to the supply of goods will continue to increase. Since the banking authorities have no control over wages—the primary element in cost of production and in spendable income—they cannot control the market prices of commodities. By a moderate restriction of credit they may possibly ease immediate tensions; but a vigorous curtailment policy may readily upset the economic equilibrium.

CHAPTER IV

The Role of Money Income

Modern adherents of the income *theory* stress consumer demand as the determining factor in price movements. In short, the flow of money income governs spending power, and spending power, or demand, governs prices. While it is recognized that supply must be taken into account, changes in demand are regarded as of controlling importance. "Inflationary pressures" are held to be rooted in an excess of buying power in the hands of the public, resulting in a bidding up of the prices of consumer goods. For illustrations of this point of view, reference is made to numerous quotations given in Chapter I; to the discussions of war-time price theory presented in Chapters VI-VII; and to the reasoning of Keynes as summarized in Chapter II.[1]

Two assumptions underlie this reasoning: The first is that wage rates rise prior to the advance in prices, thus increasing the real income of the laboring population. The second is that the price rise begins in retail markets as a result of competitive bidding by consumers armed with enhanced buying power. The validity of these assumptions may be tested by data pertaining to the relative movements of wage rates and prices, and the relative movements of retail and wholesale commodity prices.

[1] P. 21; p. 51; pp. 110-12; p. 138, and p. 147, respectively.

I. MOVEMENTS OF WAGE RATES AND RETAIL PRICES

What light does available evidence shed on the assumption that wage increases lead the procession—advancing ahead of retail prices, thus providing consumers with extra money income with which to bid up the prices of consumer goods? The order of events, as we shall see, has not always been the same. Numerous cases are to be found where the rise in retail prices preceded the rise in wage rates while in other cases wage increases kept ahead of the advance in retail prices.

In the American Revolution, the French Revolution, and the Civil War, wage rates appear to have advanced much less rapidly than prices. While precise statistical series are not available for the earlier war periods, contemporary economic discussions commonly cited the "well-known lag" of wage rates behind retail prices, and pointed out that the wage-earning population suffered in consequence. The "high cost of living" quickly became a major source of public discontent.[2] In the World War I period the rise in wage rates in manufacturing closely paralleled the rise in *retail* prices.[3] But in nonwar lines wages lagged well behind retail prices, prior to the establishment of war-time controls. In the postwar boom of 1919-20 retail prices rose ahead of wages.

In contrast to the foregoing, the following cases may be cited: (1) During the price revolution in sixteenth-century Spain the advance in wage rates over the century as a whole, according to Professor Earl J. Hamilton's comprehensive investigation, appears to have kept pace with, and in the second half of the century

[2] See discussion in Chap. 5.
[3] See Chap. 6, pp. 120-21.

to have kept ahead of, the advance in *wholesale* prices. While retail price data were not available, the commercial practices in vogue suggest that retail prices closely paralleled wholesale prices.[4] (2) During the Canadian boom period from 1900 to 1914, according to data presented by Professor Jacob Viner, wage rates rose roughly twice as fast as wholesale prices;[5] and it seems probable, therefore, that they rose faster than retail prices.

Since 1900, especially since 1920, wage and price data are reasonably satisfactory for manufacturing industry. The accompanying chart shows the relative movements of hourly earnings and retail prices over the long period from 1900 through 1957. It will be seen that in the expansion period prior to World War I, it appears that hourly earnings in manufacturing rose a little faster than retail prices. Since the great depression of the early thirties, the wage index has progressively outstripped the cost-of-living index.

Thus the evidence shows that there has been no set pattern. Sometimes—in earlier history as well as in later years—wage rates have advanced ahead of prices, while at other times they have lagged behind. Accordingly, the primary assumption that the inflation process always begins with an increase in buying power in the hands of labor is not sustained.

Nevertheless, the fact that during the last 25 years wage rates have persistently advanced much faster than retail prices is challenging. It appears at first thought to support the view that expanding consumer income has

[4] For analysis and appraisal of the Spanish price revolution, see Appendix A.

[5] See table in Appendix B, p. 292.

HOURLY EARNINGS AND RETAIL PRICES, 1900–57[a]
1926 = 100

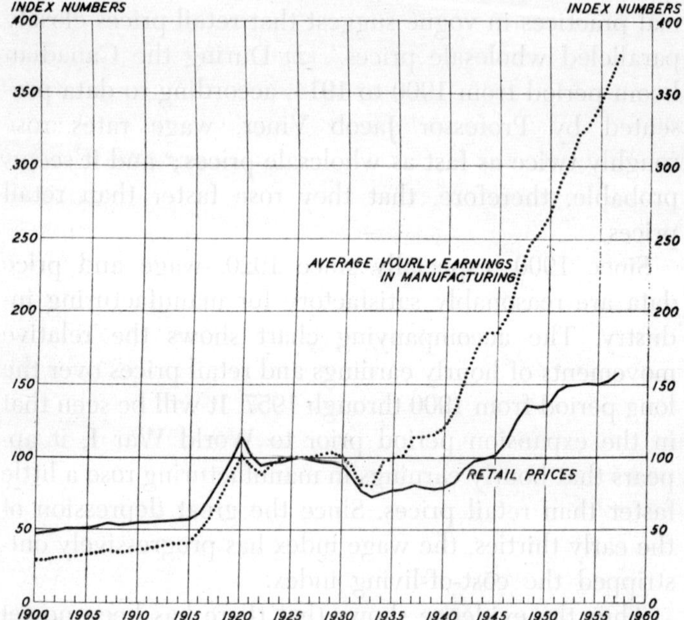

[a] Bureau of Labor Statistics. The wage figures here used are average annual hourly earnings, and thus take account of both the standard wage rates and the extra rates involved in overtime.

in recent times become the propelling force in the upward trend of commodity prices. This issue will be considered in ensuing sections.

Before concluding this section, a brief discussion of the forces responsible for rising wages appears desirable. In Keynes' analysis, summarized on page 52, the rise in wages is assumed to be the result of competitive bidding for labor by business enterprisers. This point of view also underlies the appraisal by Arthur F. Burns of the postwar wage increases in the United States.[6]

It is something of a phenomenon that any observer should conclude that the rise in wage rates in the last 25 years is *chiefly* the result of employers' efforts to lure workers away from other companies. The great bulk of the labor population cannot readily pull up stakes and move; the costs and sacrifices involved are prohibitive. Moreover, the workers come to have a sort of vested interest in the company with which they are associated as well as in the community in which they live. Union leaders regard the relationship of labor and management as a sort of partnership in the business enterprise; and company officials encourage this point of view. The shifting of jobs and locale occurs chiefly among the higher paid salary workers.

It is common knowledge that wage advances for the entire union are periodically demanded by labor leaders and become the basis of negotiation in the making of wage agreements. It is of course traditional that labor officials demand more than they expect to get and that employers offer initially somewhat less than the expected compromise figure. This is the typical process both in ordinary private wage contracts and in those where arbitration is involved.

It seems apparent that the great advance in wage rates during this recent period is attributable primarily to the power of labor organizations, backed much of the time by the sympathetic support of government. Businessmen have largely acceded to labor's demands as the necessary price for industrial peace and the achievement of capacity operation.

[6] See *Prosperity Without Inflation* (1958), Chap. 1.

II. RETAIL AND WHOLESALE PRICE MOVEMENTS

If the motivating factor in a general increase in prices were competitive bidding by consumers armed with abundant buying power, one would expect to find retail prices advancing ahead of wholesale prices. What light does available evidence shed on this assumption? In the following discussion we shall draw in part upon factual material found in other chapters of this volume pertaining to the movement of wholesale and retail prices.

In Chapters V, VI, and VII data are presented showing the time order in which changes in wholesale and retail prices have occurred during periods of great inflation. The price charts on pages 101, 120, and 148 reveal that in war-time wholesale prices have always begun to rise considerably earlier than retail prices and continued to lead the procession throughout the inflation period. In the downward movements wholesale prices have also led the way, and the extent of the decline has been much greater than in the case of retail prices. However, an exception is noted in Chapter VII: the 1920 price break began at the retail level, though, as usual, the extent of the decline was very much greater in the wholesale area.

A picture of retail and wholesale price trends over a long period of time is presented in the chart on the accompanying page, which reveals the relative trends of wholesale and retail prices of finished commodities from 1900 to 1956.

Retail price movements have almost continuously lagged behind wholesale price trends, and been much

RETAIL AND WHOLESALE PRICE MOVEMENTS, 1900–57[a]
1926 = 100

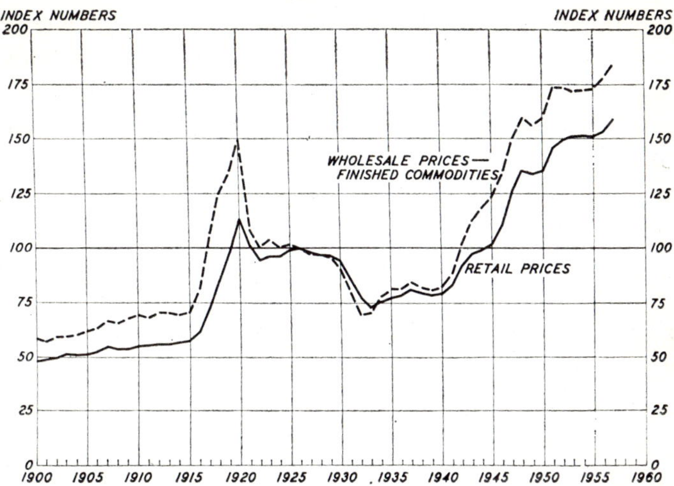

[a] Data from U. S. Bureau of Labor Statistics.

less pronounced. Over the period as a whole the spread between wholesale and retail prices has widened.[7]

The relative trends thus recorded are well known to students of American economic and financial history. It is, indeed, a commonplace in economic literature that retail price movements lag behind wholesale price movements. The surprising thing is that this fact should have been so often forgotten in discussions of changes in the general level of prices.

[7] For a more detailed analysis of the relative movements of wholesale and retail prices, and wages, see Chaps. 6 and 7 dealing with the price-changing process in time of war.

III. THE PUSH OF COSTS OR THE PULL OF DEMAND

The disbursements made by business enterprisers in connection with the employment of labor, the purchase of materials and supplies, the borrowing of capital, etc., constitute money costs of production. On the other side, the money income received by the various participants in the productive process provides the means by which the goods produced may be purchased in the markets. The aggregate money incomes received by the participants in the productive process are of course identical with the aggregate money costs of production (profits included).

Wages are thus both costs of production and income available for expenditure. They are financial costs to the producing enterprises which disburse them; they are money income to the individuals who receive them. In concentrating attention upon the flow of money available to consumers, the income school all but lost sight of money costs. It was seen that an advance in wage rates increases the buying power of workers. It was forgotten that the higher wages also operate to increase the cost of production.

The crucial question now to be considered is whether the primary motivating force in price advances proceeds from the cost side or the demand side. When costs of production rise in consequence of an increase in wage rates (without corresponding changes in productive efficiency), the business enterpriser has no alternative except to recoup the added costs by raising selling prices. In short, he must either raise prices or sooner or later retire from business. The pressure from the cost side is real, insistent, and inescapable.

On the other hand, there is no *pressure* toward higher prices emanating from the demand side, following a rise in wages. The wage earner is under no compulsion to spend his increased money income for consumer goods. Unlike the businessman whose costs have risen, the wage earner possesses alternatives—inviting ones. He may elect to increase his insurance, enlarge his savings deposits, buy securities, or reduce his indebtedness. Similarly, if he does not dissipate his higher wages in bidding up prices he is able to buy more, or better quality, goods. This is, of course, the way progressively higher standards of living are realized.

The consumer may properly be said to *bid up* prices only in cases where some basic necessity is so scarce as to induce panicky buying. Under normal circumstances consumers resist advancing retail prices as best they can: they grumble, they buy less, and they hunt bargains elsewhere.

The situation confronting consumers is thus in sharp contrast to that faced by manufacturers. If consumers bid up prices they have less income left for other purposes. But businessmen may bid up the prices of raw materials without suffering any loss; they may recoup by passing the higher costs of materials along to the purchasers of their products. It should be pointed out at this place that in periods of intense boom, such as occur in war-time, the advance in commodity prices commonly begins with raw materials. This fact is strikingly illustrated in the charts in Chapters VI and VII.[8]

It should be noted, finally, that wage increases nowadays commonly appear as *costs* before they become available as purchasing power. A wage contract to ex-

[8] See pp. 101, 120, and 148.

tend over a year or more instantly creates a new cost level which quickly becomes the basis for new price quotations. On the other hand, some time may elapse before the increased money wages become available for expenditure. In view of the common need of catching up on over-due bills, it may well be months before all the increased wage income is available for additional purchases of consumer goods. Meanwhile, prices will already have been marked up because of the push from the cost side. This order of events is strikingly evident after every important wage contract calling for higher rates of pay.

The validity of the foregoing analysis is evidenced by the parallel movements of wage rates and the wholesale prices of manufactured products. This is revealed by the chart on page 162, showing the average hourly earnings in manufacturing and the wholesale prices of finished commodities from 1900 to 1956. The analysis is also attested by the time sequence in wholesale and retail price movements discussed above: Prices at the manufacturing level rise first and prices in the retail stores rise subsequently. The time lag before the higher costs are passed down the line to consumers is shown in all the price charts in this and other chapters.

IV. THE MODERN PRICING PROCESS

The conception that inflation proceeds from competitive bidding at the consumer level appears to be rooted in the general theory used in explaining changes in the prices of individual commodities. The demand and supply curves employed to illustrate the process of price determination proceed from the assumption that a given supply of commodity X meets a given supply of purchasing power in a market place—akin to that found in medieval fairs. There is a "higgling" process, as the early economists called it, in which buyers and sellers, after bids and offers, finally reach a price acceptable to both. Thus if total purchasing power should increase relatively to the supply of goods in the market, prices of goods in general would automatically rise. It will also be noted that this is strictly in line with the reasoning underlying the quantity theory of money.

Under modern conditions, however, only the merest fraction of commercial operations is carried out under the conditions assumed. To be sure, perishable farm produce and Christmas trees are disposed of under circumstances not unlike those just described. Moreover, wheat and cotton and other staple products are sold in organized markets—the price arrived at reflecting traders' estimates of the general supply and demand situation, actual and potential. In a sense, auction sales of livestock, or of household effects, or of surplus stocks of commodities held by dealers, are somewhat analogous. Also, there is a certain amount of "horse-trading" pertaining to allowances on second-hand cars to purchasers of new models, or of second-hand equipment to purchasers of new farm machinery.

But with the overwhelming proportion of commodities passing through retail channels there occurs no such bargaining process. The goods are priced *before* they reach the hands of merchants and dealers. Groceries, hardware, dry goods and clothing, house furnishings and home appliances are produced in a complex economic system involving capital commitments, raw material outlays, wage and salary payments, depreciation charges on plant and equipment, taxes, and advertising and selling expenses—all of which must be covered by the selling price if the business is to succeed. It is, therefore, necessary for the producers to establish prices which will cover costs and leave a necessary margin for profits. This does not mean that competition is eliminated; for there is the constant effort of each producer to gain a larger share of the market by means of lower prices, better quality, or superior service.

This pricing process does not, of course, imply that buying power is unimportant. It is always necessary for producers, before making final commitments, to take account of the market outlook. This involves estimating the potential sales volume at given prices—which depends primarily on the buying power of consumers. If the general demand situation appears favorable, the quoted prices may be edged up somewhat; and, similarly, if the market outlook is none too good, they may be shaded on the down side. The price established may represent an attempt to charge all that the traffic will bear at the moment; or it may be set somewhat lower in the hope of attracting additional customers and expanding markets in the future. But, in any case, the price is determined long before the consumer enters the retail store. There is no "higgling" between customer and salesman; and there is no bidding by the former.

The great bulk of the commodities which flow through the distributive channels enters the market with price tags attached. In present-day manufacturing industry, characterized by large-scale enterprise, prices for the season ahead are set, or at least "administered," by the managers of manufacturing establishments. They are based primarily on the cost of production of a *standard* volume of output, which it is believed can be sold at the prices set. While these prices may be modified somewhat in the light of changing conditions, they are the quoted prices which merchants and dealers must pay.

In fact, the prevailing system of quoted prices long antedated the development of large-scale business enterprise. Throughout the nineteenth century the traditional manufacturing and distributing system involved the setting of prices at the manufacturing level and the allowance of a succession of mark-ups to jobbers, wholesalers, and retailers, respectively. Since the mark-up in each case was computed on the basis of the cost at that stage, the price advance was cumulative in character. In the old days of unfettered competition this system was more universal and more stereotyped than it is at the present time.

The data presented in the foregoing pages thus afford no support for the thesis that consumer demand is the *propelling* force in price advances—that the sequence of events is enlarged bank reserves, low interest rates, an expansion of business loans, a bidding up of wages, and, finally, a bidding up of consumer goods' prices. Rather the line of motivation runs from the cost side. Rising wage and other costs lead to compensating advances in wholesale prices, which in turn lead to mark-ups through distributive channels to the ultimate retail outlets.

The True Significance of Demand

It should not be inferred from the foregoing analysis that the author deems effective demand, or mass purchasing power, as of little economic significance. On the contrary, in a long series of studies dating as far back as 1918[9] he has stressed the vital importance of expanding mass income in stimulating economic progress. This was, indeed, the primary conclusion of the Brookings Institution studies on *Income and Economic Progress,* published in the early 1930's. Without expanding markets, currently or in very early prospect, there is scant inducement for so-called *venture* capital.

The point at issue here is not whether economic progress depends upon expanding consumer buying power, but rather whether rising prices are directly stimulated by competitive bidding in consumer markets—whether the so-called *inflationary pressures* flow from the side of demand, or the side of costs. Our conclusion, already stated, is that rising costs constitute the only *pressure* toward higher prices.

[9] In "Commercial Banking and Capital Formation," *Journal of Political Economy* (1918) it was held that a restriction of consumption retards capital formation, that a significant expansion of plant and equipment occurs only when consumer demand is also expanding.

CHAPTER V

War-Time Price Phenomena: I Under Paper Money Regimes

The most violent price distortions have been those occurring in war periods. The diagram on page 2, showing American price movements over a century and a half, reveals the great peaks reached in the Napoleonic era and the War of 1812, in the Civil War, in the two World Wars, and during the lesser Korean struggle. The American price level roughly doubled in each of the world wars, while in the Korean conflict the rise was not much greater than that which sometimes occurs in a period of business boom.

These war-time price distortions have sometimes been associated with inconvertible paper money regimes, while in other cases no change in the monetary standard was involved. In the first of three chapters we review briefly four episodes which involved the abandonment, wholly or in part, of a specie standard: (1) The "bills of credit" of the American Revolution; (2) the paper currency of the Confederate States; (3) the irredeemable "greenback" notes issued by the United States Treasury during the Civil War; and (4) the German mark episode following World War I. In the second chapter we analyze the price-changing process during World War I. During this struggle the United States did not resort to irredeemable paper money and remained to all intents and purposes on the gold standard. In the third chapter we study the price disturbances produced by World War II and the ensuing Korean struggle. Inasmuch as the United States abandoned the gold standard in the 1930's and there has been no change in the official definition of a dollar since 1935, no tampering with the monetary standard occurred during these conflicts.

In these three chapters we shall review the available evidence relating to the price-changing process in time of war. Only thus can one appraise the validity of traditional conceptions pertaining to war-time inflation and reveal the governing factors in the complex price-changing process. It should be stated at this place that the evidence shows that despite many similarities the process is not always precisely the same.

The use of inconvertible paper money in time of war is sometimes complete and sometimes only partial. Under the partial system, a substantial part of the funds needed is derived from taxation and bond flotations, with paper money in a supplementary role. Even so, the irredeemable notes constitute a new form of money, forcing a departure from specie as a standard. A third type involves substituting land for specie as security for the paper currency. Each type is illustrated in the cases which follow.

I. THE "BILLS OF CREDIT" OF THE REVOLUTION

At the outbreak of the American Revolution the several colonies were operating on a specie basis. But the central government possessed no monetary system of any kind. Accordingly, the only means of meeting its exigent financial requirements was by the issue of paper promises to pay; and within six weeks after the Continental Congress convened, bills of credit were authorized as a "temporary expedient." The several states were requested to impose taxes in order to redeem their respective quotas of the bills. But, for practical reasons, the states failed to comply; indeed, they were soon finding it necessary to issue paper money on their own account.

Despite legal tender acts, regulation of prices, and drastic penalties for refusing to accept Continental bills in payment, the paper money rapidly depreciated in value as compared with specie. By 1781 a dollar was worth less than 2 cents in specie and before the end of the war the bills had become virtually worthless. Hence the opprobrious phrase, "not worth a Continental."

The way in which the paper money reacted upon commodity prices may be summarized as follows: Sellers of goods, knowing they would be paid in paper bills of dubious value, naturally demanded a higher price in order to cover the risk of a further fall in the value of the paper before it could be passed on to someone else for commodities. So long as there was expectation, or hope, of ultimate redemption in specie, the mark-ups were modest in character; as the outlook grew dimmer the more rapid became the price adjustment.

The process, once begun, was cumulative. The higher the prices of raw materials, foodstuffs, and manufactured products, the greater the pressure for higher rates of pay, both in civilian occupations and in the armies. Progressive increases in costs both in private and public enterprise necessitated ever-increasing issues of paper money; and with each new issue the prospect of ultimate redemption declined. In the case of war supplies, speculative activities contributed to the process.

The general advance in commodity prices did not flow from increased buying power in the hands of the consuming public and competitive bidding by consumers for scarce commodities. While statistical data are not available, there is abundance of other evidence indicating that the general public was squeezed because of the lagging upward adjustment of wages; mass buying power appears to have fallen steadily.

II. THE LAND-SECURED CURRENCY OF THE FRENCH REVOLUTION

The revolutionary government of France in 1790 issued paper currency secured by church lands. It was argued that since land is "an imperishable national asset" the stability of the currency is assured. In the words of Mirabeau, "It is in vain to compare assignats, secured on the solid basis of these domains, to an ordinary paper currency possessing a forced circulation. They represent real property, the most secure of all possessions, the land on which we tread." It was recognized that stability could not be maintained unless the supply of money was limited. A solemn pledge was made that the volume of such currency issued would not be permitted to exceed the real value of the underlying property.

Talleyrand in vain opposed the issuance of such paper currency, contending that:

> Assignat money, however safe, however solid it may be, is an abstraction of paper money; it is consequently but the free or forced sign, not of wealth, but merely of credit. . . . You can arrange it so that people shall be forced to *take* a thousand francs in paper for a thousand francs in specie,

but you never can arrange it so that the people shall be obliged to *give* a thousand francs in specie for a thousand francs in paper.

The process by which the rise in prices was brought about was as follows: Doubt with respect to the practicability of the plan, and hence of the value of the paper currency, quickly led traders to mark up the sales prices of goods paid for in paper currency. Once the process of depreciation in terms of specie was under way and confidence waned, the rise in prices accelerated rapidly. The higher prices became, the greater was the quantity of currency needed to meet the requirements of trade. Thus the volume of notes—backed by the same land acreage—had to be continuously increased.

The sequel proved that a constitutional government, no less than a king or a dictator, was quite unable to make good on the solemn pledge to limit the supply.

> What the bigotry of Louis XIV, and the shiftlessness of Louis XV, could not do in nearly a century, was accomplished by this tampering with the currency in a few months. . . . In the spring of 1791 no one knew whether a piece of paper money, representing 100 francs, would, a month later, have a purchasing power of 100 francs, or 90 francs, or 80, or 60. The result was that capitalists declined to embark their means in business. Enterprise received a mortal blow. . . . Commerce was dead; betting took its place.[1]

Faced with disaster, the government next offered to redeem the *assignats* on the basis of 30 to 1 for *mandats*, a new form of paper money which entitled the holder

[1] Andrew D. White, *Paper Money Inflation in France* (1876), pp. 30-34.

to take immediate possession of any of the pledged lands. Because of the practical difficulties involved in seizing parcels of land, this device proved no more satisfactory; in a short time the *mandats* passed for only one-thousandth of their face value.

The government of France resorted to many vain expedients to maintain the value of the paper currency. The use of coin was prohibited; the purchase of specie was forbidden under penalty of imprisonment in irons for six years; and the sale of *assignats* below their nominal value was forbidden under penalty of imprisonment for twenty years in chains. The whole experiment ended in 1796 when the government finally swept away the entire mass of paper money by a simple decree authorizing everybody to transact business in any money he chose. No one chose paper.

III. THE CONFEDERATE CURRENCY

In the newly organized Confederacy there was no already existing monetary or fiscal system. While some slight tax levies and minor bond flotations were employed to raise money for the Treasury, the issue of irredeemable paper money was from the first looked to as the primary financial resource of the government. It was also hoped that loans might in due course be procured from sympathetic foreign governments.

The paper promises carried an inscription that "six months after the ratification of a treaty of peace the Confederate States of America will pay the bearer ——— dollars." But the prospect of a successful conclusion of the war was never sufficiently promising to maintain the value of the paper currency. Depreciation began early and progressed rapidly. As the tide of war turned against the South, virtually all possibility of ultimate or even partial redemption vanished. At the end of the war it was worthless—though the slogan "Hold your Confederate currency; the South will rise again" suggests that for many years a lingering hope survived.

The impetus to advancing prices, as in the cases cited above, came from the uncertainty with respect to the future value of paper. Sellers of goods marked up prices to compensate for an anticipated further depreciation of the paper money in which they would be paid. The price rise thus did not begin as a result of bidding in retail markets by consumers armed with war-born purchasing power. In fact, the advance in wages lagged much behind the advance in prices. The mark-up of prices by producers and distributors, for the reason mentioned, came quickly and more or less universally while the increase of wages, made necessary by advancing prices, was a slow and uneven process.

IV. UNITED STATES NOTES, OR "GREENBACKS"

At the beginning of the Civil War, the United States was on a specie basis—theoretically gold and silver but in practice only gold. The pressing financial needs of the federal government in the early months were met by short-term borrowings, chiefly through Treasury notes, payable on demand but not vested with a legal tender attribute. In fact, it was expected that these notes would shortly be redeemed from the proceeds of taxes and long-term loans; and it was assumed that there would be no derangement of the monetary system.

But there were delays in the levying of additional taxes and in the development of machinery for marketing long-term bond issues. Late in 1861 financial conditions became critical and gold stocks were being depleted by exports and by internal hoarding. Accordingly, the New York banks found it expedient to suspend specie payments on December 30, 1861. As soon as the banks ceased paying the Treasury in specie, the latter was also obliged to cease meeting its obligations in coin.

Meanwhile the financial requirements of the Treasury were becoming increasingly pressing, and the argument for the issuance of legal tender Treasury notes more cogent. There was a full-dress congressional debate on the dangers and evils involved; but in the end the contention that "necessity knows no law" won the day. Successive acts of February 25, 1862, July 11, 1862, and March 3, 1863, each authorized the issuance of 150 million dollars of non-interest bearing United States notes. These green-backed notes were declared to be lawful money and legal tender in payment of all debts, except duties on imports and interest on the public debt; and it was understood that they would be redeemed after the war was over. In due course a great increase in taxation and in methods of selling bonds to the public so relieved the financial pressure that on June 30, 1864, Congress passed an act which fixed the limit of greenback issues at 400 million dollars, plus 50 millions for the purpose of paying a temporary Treasury loan.

The way in which the United States legal tender notes affected commodity prices may be indicated with greater precision than was possible with the Continental bills of credit and the Confederate currency. This is because the suspension of specie payments was followed by the development of what amounted to a *Gold* Exchange, or market. Here importers and exporters, bankers and traders, and also professional speculators, bought and sold the precious metal. The price of gold was thus determined much as the prices of stocks are determined on the Stock Exchange. The extent to which the paper currency depreciated was reflected in the so-called *premium* on gold. Dealings in gold began on January 13, 1862, and the operations continued during the whole period in which greenbacks were irredeemable.[2]

The extent of the premium on gold reflected current opinion with respect to military and financial trends. In Mitchell's words—"failures and successes of the Union armies were recorded by the indicator in the gold room more rapidly than by the daily press."[3] However, it also reflected changes in fiscal policy and in the financial position of the federal Treasury; and at times such considerations, as we shall see, had greater weight than current war news.

The main fluctuations in the value of the greenbacks may be summarized as follows: (1) In the early months of 1862, a very moderate decline; (2) from May to February, 1863, an almost steady fall to a level of about 62 cents on the dollar; (3) from February to August, 1863, a recovery to 79 cents; (4) from August, 1863, to July, 1864, a progressive decline to a low of approximately 35 cents; (5) a sharp rise from July, 1864, to about 74 cents at the end of the war. It will be observed that the great depreciation in 1864 came after ultimate victory for the Union forces seemed reasonably assured. This surprising movement is attributed by Mitchell in part to oc-

[2] The Gold Resumption Act of 1875 provided for the convertibility of United States notes into gold, to become effective Jan. 1, 1879.

[3] Wesley C. Mitchell, *A History of the Greenbacks* (1903), p. 203.

casional military reverses but mainly to the slowness of Congress in passing essential financial legislation.[4]

The daily quotations of the price of gold on the Gold Exchange provided businessmen with an index by which to adjust prices promptly and in some conformity with the realities of the changing situation. Prices in wholesale markets were the first to be increased when the gold premium rose; then in due course retail prices were advanced in accordance with the prevailing system of mark-ups.

Mitchell attributed the general advance in prices, during the course of the war, primarily to the depreciation of the greenback currency, as expressed by the premium on gold. He pointed out that prices remained fairly stable through the year 1861 and that the rise did not begin until the suspension of specie payments and the appearance of a premium on gold. He concluded that "there is a general correspondence between the relative prices of specie and of commodities in greenbacks."[5] He notes that, when the value of the paper in relation to gold was falling, commodity prices advanced, though somewhat belatedly; but that, when the paper rose in value, prices, instead of falling, usually continued to advance. However he did not grasp the full meaning of the failure of prices to fall when the paper currency rose in value as compared with gold.

The rise in prices was in fact practically continuous throughout the war. During the last nine months of the struggle, after victory for the Union was assured, the greenback quotations in terms of gold rose more than 100 per cent. But instead of a downward readjustment

[4] *The same*, pp. 221-22.
[5] *The same*, p. 276.

of prices, there was a continued rise to the very end of the war. This suggests that once the price rise was well under way the influence of rising costs became of paramount importance. The progressively higher cost structure clearly served to prevent any downward price readjustment and to force further advances.

The rise in prices of consumer goods during the Civil War cannot be attributed to a general increase in buying power on the part of the masses and a consequent bidding up of retail prices. As already shown, the rise began at the wholesale level and was gradually passed along through the channels of distribution.[6] Moreover, statistical studies of the period show that wages and salaries rose less rapidly than retail prices. "If our figures give a fair picture of the situation, the period of advancing prices must have forced painful economies upon the vast majority of the working-men's families."[7]

The conclusion with respect to the Civil War experience is that the depreciation of the paper money as compared with the gold was an initiating and powerful force in the price rise in the early part of the war; but, as time passed, the changing value of the greenbacks in terms of gold became of minor importance. The not uncommon lag in the advance of prices when the greenbacks were depreciating and the continuing advance in prices when the greenbacks were appreciating clearly show that commodity prices in the later stages of the war were not being adjusted with reference to the changing value of the greenbacks in terms of gold.

[6] *The same,* p. 260.

[7] Mitchell, *Gold, Prices, and Wages Under the Greenback Standard* (1908), p. 245.

Rather they continued to be pushed upward by the cumulative effects of rising costs even when the paper currency was rising rapidly toward parity, as in the last year of the war.

V. THE GERMAN MARK EPISODE AFTER WORLD WAR I

During the conflict the German government had exercised direct control over both prices and wages. With the gradual release of these controls after the war, prices were again free to adjust themselves in the light of changed, and still changing, economic conditions.

Germany had used up most of her gold reserves during the war and there was no early prospect of a restoration of the gold standard. The situation was complicated by two facts: (1) It was necessary to obtain large imports of raw materials and foodstuffs at a time when gold reserves were inadequate and proceeds from foreign trade were meager. (2) The country was obligated to make large reparation payments for war-time damages.

Acute difficulties did not arise until after the so-called London Settlement of 1921, which fixed a definite schedule of reparation payments. Current reparation payments were being met by Germany in three principal ways: (1) by mobilizing remnants of investments and assets owned in various parts of the world; (2) by negotiating loans in Holland, England, and the United States; and (3) by selling paper marks abroad to naive speculators. The funds obtained by these expedients were, however, far from sufficient to meet the requirements; and accordingly the value of the paper mark fell rapidly in the foreign exchange market. The repercussions upon the internal German price structure proceeded as follows:

The depreciation of the mark, registered in the foreign exchange quotations, provided an index by which merchants and others increased the prices of commodities. At first this was a gradual process; but in due course prices came to be marked up automatically from day to day in proportion to the depreciation of the mark. Indeed, ultimately they were often marked up more than proportionally in the hope of staying ahead of the procession. In the later stages the price advances became so rapid and so extreme that wage earners rushed to the stores to buy goods before the buying power of the paper mark should evaporate completely. To prevent impoverishment and grave unrest among the masses, it became the practice to adjust wage rates almost daily by reference to changes in the cost-of-living index.

Thus the order of events was (1) a fall in the value of the paper mark in the foreign exchange market; (2) a corresponding upward adjustment of prices; (3) a corresponding, though lagging, increase in wage rates; and (4) an increase in the internal currency supply made necessary by the higher level of monetary costs.[8] In the end the imminent collapse of Germany led the creditor countries to devise a reconstruction program based on a restoration of the gold standard, made possible by foreign loans.[9]

[8] For chart showing rates of foreign exchange, the wholesale price index, and currency circulation for the period 1919-23, see James W. Angell, *The Recovery of Germany* (1929), p. 27.

[9] For discussion of the theory of international price adjustments as related to the German reparation problem, see pp. 235-38.

Summary and Interpretations

The paper money currencies resorted to under wartime conditions, which have been briefly summarized in this chapter, produced grave economic and social consequences. With the exception of the Civil War *greenbacks*—which, fortunately, were limited in amount—each episode ended in complete loss of confidence in the value of the currency. Hence financial collapse and repudiation were inescapable. In short, it was necessary to start over again and construct a new monetary system and a new structure of prices.

None of the cases reviewed in this chapter can adequately be described as a mere arbitrary increase in the currency supply as compared with the quantity of goods. In every case the "inflation" worked itself out through a series of interrelated operations involving costs as well as prices. The steps were as follows: (1) a depreciation of the irredeemable paper as compared with specie; (2) a mark-up of prices at wholesale to compensate for the depreciation of the paper offered in exchange; (3) advances in retail prices in accordance with the established system of mark-ups; (4) demands for increased wage rates to offset the rising cost of living; (5) further issues of currency to meet the expanded monetary needs of the economy—followed by another round of price and wage advances. The tempo in each successive interrelated series of events constantly accelerated.

CHAPTER VI

War-Time Price Phenomena: II
In World War I

For the wars of the present century available price and wage data make it possible to reveal with some precision the successive steps by which prices moved upward and the motivating forces which were at work within the financial system by means of which the nation's resources are mobilized. The method employed is to study the price movements of specific types and groups of commodities, together with the trend of costs, in order to determine insofar as possible the seqence of events and the motivating forces involved in the complex financial structure.

The American monetary system during World War I differed from that obtaining in the Civil War in one important respect. The United States did not issue irredeemable paper money, forcing a departure from the gold standard. Although as a matter of practice the Treasury discouraged efforts to redeem other forms of money in gold, there was at no time a formal suspension of specie payments; and all forms of money, in fact, remained at par with gold. Still, as the chart on page 2 indicates, the advance in prices was similar to that which occurred in the Civil War.

The great price advance in the United States began long before this country entered the conflict. Hence, in reviewing the rise in prices during the period of World War I, it is essential to divide the discussion into two time periods: (1) the thirty-two months prior to the entrance of the United States into the conflict in April, 1917; and (2) the twenty months of active participation.

I. PRIOR TO AMERICAN PARTICIPATION, AUGUST, 1914–MARCH, 1918

Prices had been comparatively stable through 1913 and the early months of 1914. The chart on the following page shows the movements of wholesale prices of *all commodities* and of *thirty basic commodities;* the movement of retail prices (cost-of-living index); and the trend of wages in manufacturing industry. We shall have occasion to refer to this chart repeatedly in the ensuing discussion.

With the outbreak of war in Europe in mid-summer 1914 there was a slight advance in the general wholesale price index of all commodities in August and September; but this flurry was short-lived and the year ended with the index back at the June level. During the first nine months of 1915 there was virtually no change in the level of wholesale prices. The rise began in the last quarter of 1915 and by December the wholesale price index stood at 110. Throughout 1916 and the early months of 1917 the rise was continuous and by March, 1917, just before the United States entered the war, the index stood at 160.

The wholesale price index of thirty so-called basic commodities showed a trend similar to that of the wholesale index for all commodities during 1914 and 1915. But the rise in these commodities, chiefly raw

PRICE AND WAGE TRENDS, 1914–21[a b]

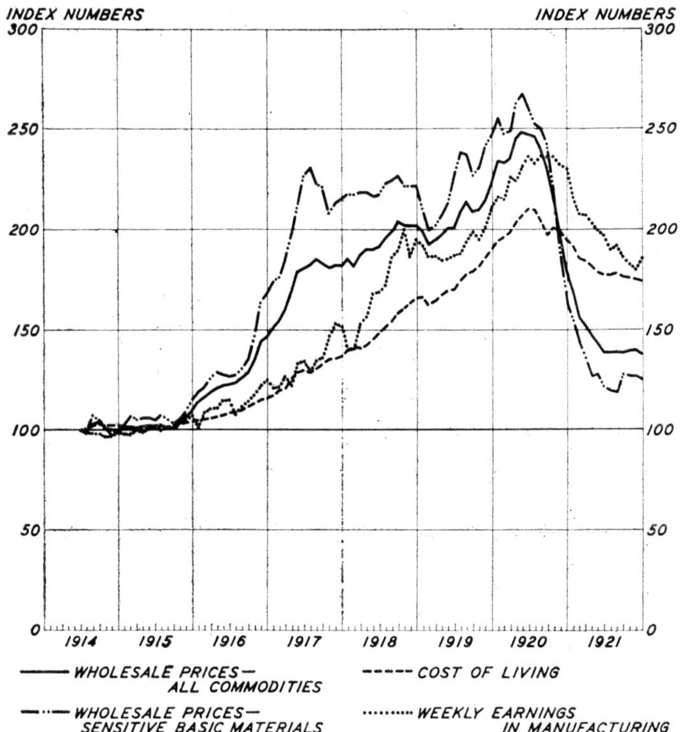

[a] Indexes of wholesale price, cost-of-living, and wages are from U. S. Dept. of Labor, *Monthly Labor Review*, Vol. 53 (November, 1941), Witt Bowden, "Wages and Cost of Living in Two World Wars," pp. 1122-24.

[b] The wholesale price index of sensitive or basic commodities is that of Warren and Pearson, "Wholesale Prices for 213 Years, 1720 to 1932," Memoir 142, November, 1932, Cornell University Agricultural Experiment Station, Table 29, p. 75.

materials, was somewhat more rapid in 1916 and early 1917, and reached 180 in March.

The advance in retail prices revealed by the cost-of-living index was slightly belated and lagged continuously behind the movement of wholesale prices. Through March, 1917, the advance was only 21 per cent.

The increase in weekly earnings in manufacturing was slightly greater than the rise in the cost of living. In March, 1917, the index stood at 127 per cent. The weekly wage figures, it should be noted, include overtime work and pay. An increase in the length of the working week would of course serve to increase sharply the weekly wage. The rise in wage *costs* in manufacturing was substantially greater than the rise in weekly earnings. This is attributable to the fact that in most industries the length of the standard work week was substantially reduced during the war period. It remains true that in non-manufacturing lines and in other occupations wage and salary adjustments were belated.

The forces responsible for the great price advance which occurred during this period can be discovered only by examining the data relating to certain special commodities and classes of products. First, the slight price rise at the outbreak of the war in Europe is explained almost entirely by speculative advances in the prices of sugar, hides, wheat, and chemicals. Within the broad field of chemistry some items were unaffected but others rose sharply—notably alum, glycerin, opium, and quinine, which it was thought would be in immediate demand by the European belligerents.

It should be recalled here that in 1914 it was generally believed that the war would be of short duration. Not until the repulse of the Germans at the Marne, and the beginning of trench warfare did it become clear that the struggle would be one of attrition. In the early months it was assumed that the war would be fought largely with *existing* supplies of materials; but after mid-1916 both Germany and the allied powers recognized the necessity of greatly expanding their production of war materials and of obtaining vast quantities from other countries. Not until then did the United States begin to feel the real impact of European demands.

The extent of the price rise in major groups of commodities from August, 1914, to March, 1917, was as follows:[1]

Farm products	57 per cent
Food, etc	54 " "
Cloth and clothing	65 " "
Fuel and lighting	98 " "
Metals and metal products	134 " "
Lumber and building materials	13 " "
Chemicals and drugs	66 " "
House furnishings	33 " "
Miscellaneous	47 " "

The greatest percentage increases were in metals and metal products, fuel and lighting, chemicals and drugs, and cloth and clothing. The rise in prices of certain individual commodities, particularly susceptible to the war influence over the same period, was roughly as follows: cotton, 46 per cent; hides, 63 per cent; wheat, 140 per cent; copper and lead, 100 per cent; glycerin, 180 per cent; steel, 247 per cent; and soda ash, 400 per cent.

The striking feature of this period is, of course, the extraordinary rise in the prices of war materials. The initiating force with such products as wheat, hides,

[1] U.S. Dept. of Labor, B.L.S. *Bulletin #296*, pp. 20-23.

steel, and certain chemicals was obviously an intense new demand for limited supplies. In due course European nations sacrificed their gold and other liquid assets, and mortgaged their future in buying essential products in the United States; and in the period of our neutrality both allied governments and central powers competed for war goods, which went to the highest bidder.

Interacting Forces

Traditional monetary theorists agree that exceptional demands for specific products will raise their prices, but they insist that such increases in individual prices would be offset by corresponding decreases in the prices of other commodities—unless the over-all money supply were being allowed to increase. Such arithmetical reasoning fails to take account of the interrelations of the complex price structure of modern society. In fact, the sharp rise in the prices of war materials had wide repercussions and exerted pressure toward higher prices throughout the economy. The prices of basic industrial raw materials such as copper, lead, steel, coal, hides, wool and cotton were high in domestic trade as well as in foreign trade. Hence the cost of manufacturing such materials into finished goods for American consumption rose; and the resulting higher prices at the manufacturing level were passed along to consumers. So, also, the rising prices of such foodstuffs as grains and livestock resulted in due course in higher prices of bread and meat.

In turn the progressive price advances of necessitous commodities led to widespread clamor for wage and price increases to offset the "high cost of living." In the war industries, to be sure, competitive bidding for workers had raised wage rates sharply in 1916. In manufacturing industry as a whole, weekly earnings were keeping well abreast of the rise in retail prices, thanks in part to overtime work at extra rates of pay.[2] But most other wage and salaried groups fared badly; and by the spring of 1917 the lag in wage and salary adjustments was resulting in real privation for large sections of the population.

The insistent demands for compensating wage rate increases were successful and in late 1916 and early 1917 there were widespread advances. Thus higher wage rates became in due course an almost universal factor operating from the cost side to push upward the prices of non-war goods.

In short, the interacting forces to which we have referred generated a progressive, if uneven, advance throughout the economy. A spiral of rising prices, costs, and again prices was operating strongly throughout 1916 and the early months of 1917.

Financial Aspects

That government fiscal policy was not responsible for the price rise during this period is evident from the fact that the United States government was not a purchaser of war supplies and hence it was unnecessary for the Treasury to borrow money or increase taxes. In fact, the expansion of business in 1916 resulted in a substantial Treasury surplus.

The initial rise in the prices of war materials, as we have seen, was simply the result of an exceptional de-

[2] See U. S. Dept. of Labor, *Monthly Labor Review*, Vol. 53, Nov., 1941, Witt Bowden, "Wages and Cost of Living in Two World Wars," pp. 1122-24.

mand for special products; and the rise became general, though uneven, because of interactions within the complex economic structure. It is true European governments used their gold, liquid assets, and borrowing power in purchasing war materials in the United States; but this did not increase American purchases of civilian goods. Within the United States, as the cost repercussions gradually spread throughout the economy, it became necessary of course to use more money to meet the financial requirements of business. This was borrowed from the banking system by individual enterprises as and when it was needed.

At this point we must consider the traditional view that *if* the over-all supply of money had not been allowed to increase, the price level as a whole *could not* have risen—that the prices of non-war goods would have had to fall sufficiently to offset the price rise in war lines. This is easy arithmetic. But because of the interacting forces to which we have referred, especially the rise in the cost of basic materials and wage rates, it was impossible, as a practical matter, for the prices of civilian commodities to be reduced. The bread, clothing, equipment, drugs, etc. required by the civilian population were in the main made from the same materials as the war goods, and by workers whose wages had increased materially, if not as much as those who transferred to munitions plants.

So long as we were operating under private enterprise conceptions, relying upon the price and profit mechanism to bring about the necessary shifts in productive operations, a progressive increase in the supply of money was necessary. Businessmen, armed with war contracts, were prime credit risks, and it was the business of the banks to grant the essential credits. Those producing for the civilian market were also satisfactory credit risks so long as selling prices could be increased to cover advancing costs. Wage earners were entitled to demand, and if necessary, strike for higher rates of pay. The newly created Reserve System—thanks to lowered reserve requirements and a large inflow of gold from abroad—possessed abundant lending power; and it was a primary function of the banking system to provide an elastic currency, responsive to the needs of business.

But even if this had not been the case and the Federal Reserve authorities had possessed the legal power to freeze the volume of loans at the existing level, they could not have done so without: (1) simultaneously freezing the cost of raw materials and labor; or (2) completely disrupting business operations.

II. DURING AMERICAN PARTICIPATION, APRIL, 1917–NOVEMBER, 1918

Once the United States entered the war the government became an enormous purchaser of war supplies. The increased demands for war materials naturally gave a further impetus to rising prices of war materials, which was helped along by competitive bidding among the military services for limited supplies. At the same time the government officially favored high prices as a means of stimulating the production of war goods—both foodstuffs and munitions. The existing policy and the results were summarized at the time by the present writer as follows:

> It was recognized that if a maximum of war supplies . . . was to be induced it would be necessary that high prices be

guaranteed. It was recognized that costs would be high, that the risks involved in new enterprises would be unusual, and that unless producers were assured a reasonable return above costs, the additional production required would not be forthcoming; hence the system of contracts, arranged on a cost plus percentage basis, or on modifications of this principle. . . . The controlling factor in this price determination was expenses of production in marginal establishments. . . .

The fixing of prices of iron and steel and kindred war materials at a high level promptly caused an increase in the expenses of production in all establishments using such materials. . . . This increase in the cost of raw materials substantially increased the expenses of production of manufacturers in non-war as well as in war lines. These increased expenses of production obviously required the manufacturers to sell to wholesalers at an increased price, and the wholesaler and retailer in turn were accordingly compelled to advance their prices.[3]

The cost-plus profit principle was nefarious in its effects. Since the higher the cost the greater would be the profit, there was no incentive to keep costs down; indeed, the system encouraged bidding high for needed materials and labor.

It is not surprising, therefore, that in the early months of America's involvement in the war wholesale prices should have risen at an accelerated pace. (See chart, page 101.) In the first five months, April-August, the wholesale price index of *all commodities* rose 16 per cent, as compared with 8 per cent in the preceding period. But there was a slight decline thereafter for a few months, and the wholesale index showed relatively little advance during the remainder of the war period. The *sensitive commodity* wholesale index, which rose

[3] "War Finance and the Price Level," *The Journal of Political Economy*, Vol. 27 (1919), pp. 697-98.

sharply in the autumn and winter of 1916-17, reached a peak for the whole war period in July, 1917.

Retail prices showed an advance, during the war months as a whole, of roughly 25 per cent. Unlike wholesale prices there was no stabilization in the summer of 1918 and the rise in the latter months of the war was somewhat more rapid than in the early months. Wages also rose throughout the twenty months' period—most rapidly in late 1918. The index of *weekly earnings* in manufacturing industry (see chart, page 101) shows an over-all advance of as much as 64 per cent—reflecting, no doubt, an increasing volume of overtime work at extra rates of pay. Workers in manufacturing lines continued to fare much better than those employed in other occupations.

The Influence of Price Controls

Why was the wholesale price rise less rapid during the war years than it had been earlier, especially in view of the continuous rise in wage costs? The answer is that many prices were in due course effectively controlled. After mid-1917 various war boards, and eventually the Price Fixing Committee, began setting the prices which producers might charge the government, and in many cases the public. An index number covering 573 commodities brought under price control showed a reduction from 209 in July, 1917, to 189 in June, 1918; thereafter minor increases were permitted. Meanwhile, 793 commodities which remained uncontrolled rose from 160 in July, 1917, to 201 in October, 1918.[4]

[4] Wesley C. Mitchell, "Prices and Reconstruction," *The American Economic Review*, Supplement, Vol. 10, No. 1 (March, 1920), p. 142.

It is thus obvious that the prices of war goods had been increased in the first seven months of 1917 beyond any necessity imposed by rising costs. The economies inherent in operation at full capacity were apparently offsetting in substantial degree the increase in direct costs. Profits were excessive; and the regulating agencies in due course performed a national service of first importance in pegging prices at substantially lower levels. The principle on which the price control authorities operated was to permit reasonable, but not excessive, profits. In fact, the profit margin permitted still afforded ample inducement, and essential war production was not jeopardized.

Financing Methods

Shortly after the United States entered the war, a memorandum on methods of financing the war, subscribed to by a large number of professional economists, was submitted to the government. In brief, it was contended that stability of prices could be maintained if "proper" methods of war financing were employed. It was held that if all the money required by the government were raised by taxes on income or from the sale of bonds to individuals who pay for them out of savings, there would be no increase in the supply of money as compared with the supply of goods, and hence no rise in the price level. On the other hand, to the extent that the Treasury borrowed the money required, either from banks or from individuals who borrow in order to invest in government securities, the resulting increase in the supply of money would inevitably produce a general rise in prices. It was recognized, of course, that pressing immediate cash needs might necessitate temporary borrowing. But it was held that such loans should be liquidated as rapidly as revision of the tax laws and the organization of bond-selling programs permitted; at the most there need be only a brief lag in the collection of taxes and the mopping up of savings.

The policy pursued by the government was in fact quite the opposite. The popular slogan was "Money will win the war"; and the sources of such funds were apparently deemed of little importance. Treasury bonds and notes were sold in great volume direct to banking institutions and the public was encouraged to borrow and buy government bonds—the bonds to serve as collateral for the loans. In fact, a substantial portion of the public sales were thus financed by bank credit.

This method of finance was clearly open to a valid criticism: The primary need was to shift from the production of non-essential civilian goods to indispensable war goods—as rapidly as possible. To the extent that the required money was not drawn from personal savings, the ability of the people to purchase consumer goods was not curtailed; hence there was less pressure on businessmen to shift quickly from peace to war activities.

But financing the war from current savings could not by itself have prevented a great rise in prices. So long as the government adhered to a cost-plus contract system, so long as there was competitive bidding for labor by war industries, and so long as we continued to rely upon the price and profit mechanism, the prices of war goods would inevitably have risen.

For reasons indicated above, the view that prices would have been proportionally reduced because of the decline in consumer demand fails to take account of the interactions within the price structure as a whole. It is true, of course, that a restriction of civilian buying power would have depressed the prices of goods already produced and in stock. But necessities had to be continually replaced, and in view of the progressive advances in the cost of raw materials and labor, the replacements would be on a constantly rising cost basis. Luxury goods, to be sure, would have been largely eliminated—a national gain in war-time; but since such goods have little weight in the index, the effect on the general level of prices would have been negligible. The most that can be said is that the rise in prices of civilian commodities would have been somewhat restrained had the war been financed wholly out of savings.

It should be remembered that, notwithstanding the Treasury deficits of the war period proper, the rise in wholesale prices was distinctly less than in the comparable period from late 1915 to the spring of 1917 when there was no deficit. In fact the period of greatest deficit financing coincided with the period of virtual stabilization of wholesale prices. This result must be credited to the price control authorities who, despite the methods of finance employed, and the existing momentum of the cost-price spiral, almost completely checked the rise.

III. THE POSTWAR RISE OF 1919–20

In the first few months after the end of the war, commodity prices remained comparatively stable. The wholesale index of all commodities declined about 3 per cent from November through February; and the index of basic materials about 10 per cent. The cost-of-living index and the level of weekly earnings fluctuated but slightly.

In government circles, these were months of indecision and of strongly opposing views as to the policies that should be pursued. On the one hand, the various war-time price regulatory agencies were rapidly dissolved, "leaving prices free to seek their natural level." In February the Federal Reserve Board suggested that "those countries which first succeed in readjusting their costs of production and restoring their industries to a normal level of values will be most successful in developing their exports and securing a foothold in the markets of consuming nations the world over."[5] Then President Wilson cabled from Paris his approval of plans for readjusting prices downward and authorized an Industrial Board of the Department of Commerce to suggest practical measures. This board proposed substantial reductions in the prices of steel; but when the Railroad Administration, then the greatest purchasing agency of the government, attacked the recommendation as wholly inadequate, the Industrial Board resigned.

On the other hand, many government officials were deeply concerned over the possible consequences of competitive price cutting. While the more efficient firms would do well enough, the less efficient might be forced into bankruptcy leading to widespread unemployment. It was this fear of industrial disorganization that had led the Industrial Board to fix the price of steel at a level which would protect the high-cost producers.

Meanwhile the price of wheat continued to be pegged at war-time levels. And the Division of Public Works and Construction Development of the Department of

[5] *Federal Reserve Bulletin*, February, 1919, p. 104.

Labor, armed with Professor Fisher's thesis referred to on page 235 below, urged businessmen to recognize that the new price level is permanent, and that it would be futile to wait for a return to the former level.

The business community was equally divided and uncertain. In the early months most businessmen argued that a return to former price levels was indispensable, and were in accord with the aphorism of Vice President Marshall that "what this country needs is a good five-cent cigar." However, practical difficulties were involved in "getting down to earth." Prices might be reduced somewhat by ruthless competition involving the elimination of inefficient producers; but it was evident to businessmen that prices could not be reduced to anything approaching prewar levels without "liquidating labor"—that is, drastically reducing wage rates.

By April, 1919, the tide of business opinion was turning in favor of stabilization at existing levels. There was deep concern over the consequences of wholesale price and wage reductions and unemployment, occurring at the very time the armed forces would be returning home. Moreover, there was increasing support for the view that business might go forward without an antecedent liquidation. There was urgent need for replacement of depleted inventories of many types of consumer goods; there was an acute shortage of housing facilities; and there were exigent European requirements for refilling empty larders and replacing inventories, and for rehabilitation and reconstruction of industrial plant and equipment of every kind. The pegging of the price of wheat, still a dominant factor in the agricultural situation, ensured prosperity for a substantial portion of the agricultural population. Finally, demobilization of the armed services would presumably mean a quick pick-up in consumer spending.[6]

In the spring of 1919 a plan was worked out, in co-operation between business leaders and the Department of Commerce, which was designed to get the economy off dead-center and to start a forward movement. In brief, the plan called for a stabilization of the prices of steel and certain other key commodities for a six-months' period—long enough to carry through the first round of peace-time contracts. But before this plan could be consummated, the United States Steel Corporation announced that it was going forward on the present level of costs. Almost immediately industry generally followed suit.

Reduce Consumption and Expand Production?

We pause here to consider briefly a conception held by some monetary theorists that prices could gradually be reduced to former levels simply by restricting consumption and expanding production. As the Federal Reserve Board put it:

> The way in must be the way out. . . . Prices will fall as savings accumulate and liquidation of the war-loan accounts of the banks ensues. . . . The whole volume of outstanding bank credit would thus contract itself, and the same causes that brought about the contraction would result in a lowering of prices. . . . The effect of increased production will be to place a larger volume of goods against the greatly enlarged volume of our purchasing media, and thus to reduce prices.[7]

[6] For further discussion, see Wesley C. Mitchell, "Prices and Reconstruction," *American Economic Review*, Supplement, 1919, pp. 143-47.

[7] *Federal Reserve Bulletin*, October, 1919, p. 913. For a concurrent analysis of this thesis, see Harold G. Moulton, "Will Prices Fall?" *Journal of Political Economy*, Vol. 27, January-December, 1919.

It will be noted that the emphasis here is not on increased productive *efficiency* as a means of reducing unit costs, thus making price reductions possible; the thought runs simply in terms of total volume of production as compared with total quantity of money.

In this line of reasoning two vital aspects of the process by which currency increased and prices rose are forgotten. The "way in" had involved a great increase in production and a progressive rise in wage rates and other elements of cost, as well as an expansion of credit. A "reversal of this process" would thus seem to involve a great reduction of business activity, a decline in wage and other costs, and, finally, a shrinkage in credit outstanding. But the Board contemplated no such reversal as this. On the contrary, it was assumed that wages would be maintained, if not increased, and that there would be a great increase in production. In short, the existing cost structure was overlooked, and at the same time it was forgotten that it would be impossible to expand production on the existing level of costs without an expanding currency supply.

The Sharp Price Rise of 1919–20

When in the spring of 1919 business operations were resumed on an expanding scale, prices began to rise—notwithstanding the attending increase in the volume of production. The price advance was moderate in the first few months. But from the late summer of 1919 to May, 1920, the rate of increase was faster than it had been in the war period proper, though still not quite as sharp as that which occurred in the months immediately preceding America's entrance into the war.

As the chart on page 101 indicates, there was less divergence in the degree to which the several indexes advanced than was the case in the war period. The over-all rise from the low of early 1919 to the peak month of 1920 was 32 per cent for the *basic commodity* group, 29 per cent for the *all-commodity* index, and 23 for the retail (cost-of-living) index.

In manufacturing, weekly earnings just about kept pace with the rise in the cost of living. But in the regulated industries—railways and public utilities—and in the unorganized and unskilled trades, wage rate adjustments were much belated; and salaries, as usual, lagged far behind the procession. In consequence, large sections of the population suffered severe reductions in real incomes; and there was widespread clamor over the "high cost of living."

A striking feature of the 1919-20 boom was the vast accumulation of inventories, especially by manufacturing industries. Once the price advance was well under way, purchasing agents rushed to place orders in advance of actual requirements. This doubling up of orders made supplies on hand appear scarce relative to immediate demands. At the same time, the inordinate demands made it necessary to ration customers—each being awarded only a percentage of the amount ordered; and when this became the practice the buyers sought to offset the expected reduction in allotments by ordering proportionally more. As a result, there was a vast volume of *fictitious* ordering. This multiplication of demand for certain classes of goods led to sharp advances in the prices of raw materials. Since the prevailing practice among manufacturers was to raise their selling prices *proportionally*, the increased cost of materials was promptly passed along to wholesalers, retailers, and consumers.

The expansion was financed chiefly with funds borrowed from the banks. In accordance with traditional bank credit policy, the banks were willing to make loans to established customers so long as the general standing of the borrower was good and the ratio of quick assets to current liabilities was satisfactory. Moreover, warehouse receipts on goods held in storage were, in accordance with accepted banking principles, regarded as especially satisfactory because each loan was backed by a specific consignment of goods which the bank could seize, if necessary, to protect the loan. Similarly, two-name paper—the acceptance—was regarded as superior because it grew out of a *specific* sale of goods. In general there was little concern in private banking circles over the situation since each loan appeared well protected by assets.

Nor did Federal Reserve officials express any grave apprehension over the situation. The rediscount rate at the Reserve banks was indeed raised progressively in the autumn and winter of 1919-20 in the belief that the increased cost of borrowing would restrain speculative activities and stabilize the economic situation generally. Meanwhile, each succeeding *Federal Reserve Bulletin* emphasized the expansion of production that was occurring as of basic importance—auguring well for the future. However, as we shall presently see, the over-all situation was highly vulnerable.

The price "inflation" of 1919-20 cannot be attributed to government fiscal operations. The period of the great price rise coincided closely with the fiscal year 1919-20.

The government deficit for the fiscal year ending June 30, 1919, had been $13,363,000,000. In the ensuing fiscal year it was completely eliminated and replaced by a surplus of $291,000,000. Meanwhile, the debts of state and local governments increased only about $600,000,000. In sum, "the net contribution of government to purchasing power" decreased by more than 12 billion dollars.

The Limit Imposed by Reserve Requirements

A special factor in the 1919-20 situation was the rapid decline in unused lending power at the Federal Reserve banks. In every boom period prior to the establishment of the Federal Reserve System, as loans—and hence deposits—increased, reserve percentages gradually declined to the limits imposed by banking legislation. But it was believed that the concentration of reserves in the Federal Reserve banks, together with the withdrawal of gold from circulation and the huge inflow of gold from abroad, had so greatly expanded the reserve base that a dearth of credit facilities was never likely to exist again. But, as the expansion of business at ever higher prices proceeded in the autumn of 1919, it soon became clear that the reserve limits established under the Federal Reserve System might soon be reached. As the situation appeared to the writer in December, 1919:

> The reserves of our Reserve banks are less than 45 per cent of note and deposit liabilities—with 40 per cent the virtual deadline. The total volume of credit could still be expanded by nearly a billion dollars before the reserves of the system as a whole were reduced to the final limits prescribed by law. An increasing volume of business conducted on an ever-rising price basis will inevitably bring us to the limit of expansion in our banking system within a relatively

short time. . . . The breaking point in finance is not far distant; and, regardless of other contingencies, if the financial system breaks on the rock of exhausted surplus reserves, there will be precipitated a general economic collapse.[8]

Since a sharp increase in Federal Reserve discount rates could at best only temper the boom, without reducing the prevailing level of costs, and since any positive reduction of bank loans would inevitably force a curtailment of business activity, the conclusion seemed to be that:

The only means by which a substantial fall in the level of prices, and a replenishment of bank reserves can be brought about is through depression. And such a reduction of prices and bank currency in circulation must be brought about if the economic and financial structure is to be so adjusted that an era of constructive development may be inaugurated. A great period of construction cannot possibly be started from a high cost basis, when at the same time banking reserves are at or near the irreducible minimum. We should therefore welcome a depression and the resulting shrinkage of values as a necessary prelude to better days.[9]

The end of the boom came in May, 1920. But the break was not, in fact, occasioned by the impending shortage of bank reserves; and there was nothing resembling a banking panic. In this instance, contrary to former experience, the price break began at the retail end. The high cost of living and the imminent "buyers' strikes" led certain large retail establishments to announce substantial price discounts on a wide range of consumer goods. These price cuts led almost immediately to a vast cancellation of orders back

[8] "Banking Policy and the Price Situation," *The American Economic Review*, Vol. 10, No. 1, Supplement, March, 1920.

[9] *The same.*

through the channels of trade. The cancellations involved both the fictitious and the regular; a greatly abnormal mass of unfilled orders was replaced by a greatly subnormal volume of orders.

The accompanying decline of prices and curtailment of output left business establishments with swollen inventories and the banks with promissory notes of dubious value. Warehoused goods were in many cases taken over by the banks, which now found themselves, in effect, in the mercantile business. Unfortunately, this shift in ownership did not restore the shrinking values. To cite the extreme case: The price of sugar which had increased between May, 1919, and May, 1920, from 7.3 cents a pound to 20.9 had, by December, 1920, fallen to 5.3 cents, with the bankers still holding the bags of sugar. The only recourse for either bankers or merchants was to wait for an eventual recovery of business and increasing demands to provide market outlets at possibly better prices.

As the chart shows, the decline was greatest in the sensitive basic materials, and least at the retail end. Between May, 1920, and July, 1921, the index for basic materials fell 56 per cent; and the all-commodity wholesale index 43 per cent. The cost-of-living index, however, declined only about 17 per cent. Thus, wholesale prices generally were back to the levels of 1916.

As soon as the price decline was under way and unemployment appeared, wage cuts became general in the unorganized trades. Where unions were strong there was, of course, stout resistance; but in the end wage rate reductions became virtually universal. As the chart indicates, the decline was moderate in 1920 but sharp in 1921. At the end of the period, however, wages in manufacturing were still at the level prevailing when the post-war boom began. Labor's relative position was thus distinctly improved.

In general, the liquidation process had greatly reduced money costs of production. With the prices of raw materials back to pre-war levels, with the cost of labor substantially lower, and with operating efficiency increasing, it was apparent that the greatly needed business expansion could now be carried out on a *relatively* low cost and price basis. In fact, over the ensuing eight years of reconstruction and expansion the level of prices remained comparatively stable. (See chart, page 2.)

The Process of Deflation

We may now consider briefly the process by which the volume of money in circulation was decreased. Existing loans were of course expected to be paid. There were, to be sure, many business failures and accompanying defaults on credit obligations; and, in most cases, loans were extended in order to give hard-pressed borrowers time to "work things out"—that is, to dispose of stocks of goods on hand.

As loans were gradually paid off they were not immediately replaced by new loans of equal amount, for two reasons: (1) The volume of business had shrunk and (2) the level of costs had shrunk. Even after business recovered, the second factor continued to operate; it was not necessary to use as much money as before to purchase a given volume of materials or a given amount of labor. In short, more goods could be produced for the same money. The credit currency eliminated from the productive and exchange process by these reductions in costs of production had returned to the banks whence it came.

In terms of banking operations and accounts, the process involved is as follows: Loans are paid off by checks drawn against deposit accounts; that is, loans are liquidated by a reduction of deposits. When in due course business recovery leads to a resumption of borrowing, the new loans—and deposits—are smaller than those which they replace because of the intervening decline in costs of production. In consequence of this decline in deposits, the reserve ratio, that is, the ratio of cash to deposits, increases. The extent of the financial liquidation that occurred in 1920-21 is indicated by the increase in the reserve ratio at the Federal Reserve banks from less than 45 per cent in early 1920 to 70 per cent by the end of 1921.

Summary and Interpretation

On the basis of the evidence assembled, the facts pertaining to the great advance in the level of prices during the World War I period may be summarized and interpreted as follows:

The greatest rise occurred during the period of our neutrality—at a time when the Treasury had a large surplus rather than a deficit.

The advance in wholesale prices was virtually checked in 1918 by the price control authorities—during the period of greatest deficit financing.

The general advance in prices varied widely both in the case of individual commodities and groups of commodities—reflecting differing intensities of demand and differing levels of cost.

The upward movement of *all* types of commodities,

civilian as well as military, was the inevitable outcome of interactions between prices and costs in the complex financial system.

The price rise occurred first and was much the greatest in raw materials and it was last and much the least in finished consumer goods—indicating that the motivating force could not have been competitive bidding by the consuming public. In fact, the buying power of large sections of the population was depressed.

In the postwar "inflation" of 1919-20 the divergence in the several indexes was less marked than in the war years, but wholesale prices still led the way and retail prices lagged somewhat.

The persistent concern over the high cost of living and the ultimate buyers' strike indicate that the 1919 price advance was not rooted in excess consumer buying power.

The fact that a huge Treasury deficit was replaced by a surplus proves that the postwar inflation was not due to fiscal deficits.

The increasing money supply required to finance business expansion on an ever-increasing cost basis throughout the period 1915-20 came from bank credit expansion; but the extensions of credit followed rather than preceded the rise in prices.

CHAPTER VII

War-Time Price Phenomena: III The World War II Period

In this chapter we shall review the major price upheaval produced by World War II and the less pronounced distortion which followed the outbreak of the Korean conflict. Since a great rise in prices also occurred between the two wars, the data presented will cover the entire period from 1939 to the middle 1950's. During this period, as a whole, we have had what is often referred to as a veritable price revolution.

The first phase of World War II began with the German attack on Poland in 1939. Thus a period of 28 months elapsed before the United States officially entered the war in December, 1941. Accordingly the movement of prices, as in the case of World War I, must be studied in two stages: (1) Prior to active participation in the war by the United States; and (2) after this country entered the conflict. Again we shall review the evidence pertaining to the sharp rise in prices that occurred shortly after the end of the war.

I. THE FIRST PHASE, 1939-41

When the war in Europe began in 1939 the United States was still in the throes of depression. The wholesale commodity price index was lower than in any year since 1934, though somewhat above the levels reached in the early thirties. Industries were operating far below capacity and the volume of unemployment was in the range of 8 to 10 millions. Thus, in the view of monetary theorists, a great industrial expansion could occur without strong "inflationary" tendencies—the increase in production serving largely to offset any increase in credit that might occur.

The accompanying chart shows the movements of: the wholesale price index for "sensitive" basic ma-

PRICE AND WAGE TRENDS, 1939–49[a]
(August, 1939 = 100)

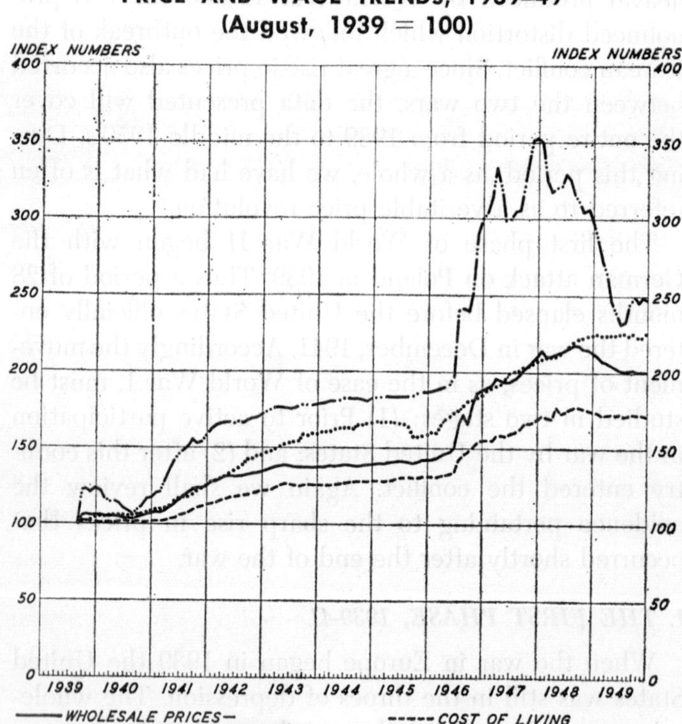

[a] Basic data from U. S. Bureau of Labor Statistics.

terials; the general wholesale price index; the retail, or cost-of-living index—which includes rents; and hourly earnings in manufacturing industry.[1]

The price advances were of moderate proportions during 1939-40, but pronounced in 1941. The index of the "sensitive" group, chiefly raw materials, rose 58 per cent between August, 1939, and December, 1941; and the index of all commodities rose 25 per cent. There was a substantial lag, however, in the cost-of-living index, the advance aggregating only 13 per cent. The index of hourly earnings showed a continuous rise and by December, 1941, was 25 per cent above the level of August, 1939.

Among major groups of commodities the rise was greatest in farm products and least in metals and metal products. On the farm side the greatest advances were in hogs, cotton, wheat, corn, and wool. In the mineral field the only sharp increases were in imported products, such as manganese and zinc.

The rise in farm prices was due primarily to government policy. There was, to be sure, a substantial increase in domestic demand for farm products; but as offsets there was a 50 per cent decline in exports, and some increase in farm output. *Surpluses* continued throughout this period. The government's program for raising agricultural prices to and above parity involved the use of three methods: (1) acreage restriction for certain major staples; (2) government loans on commodities stored in warehouses; and (3) outright purchases of food and clothing materials—for lend-lease

[1] In the chart showing World War I trends, weekly earnings were used because hourly earnings, on a monthly basis, are not available for that period.

operations and for stock-piling, to meet anticipated postwar European needs. When in due course farm prices rose above parity, the administration still withheld supplies from the market.

The sharp rise in the prices of farm raw materials was quickly reflected in advances in the prices of processed foodstuffs and textiles. For example, an 80 per cent rise in the price of cotton brought a rise of 52 per cent in cotton goods. Similarly, a rise of 47 per cent in the price of wool was promptly followed by a rise of 29 per cent in wool and worsted goods.

The steady rise in wage rates was due to a combination of factors. Without attempting to assess their relative importance, the following influences may be enumerated: (1) the rising cost of living, resulting in demands for compensating wage increases; (2) a disposition on the part of employers to accede readily to demands for wage advances at a time when profits were rising; (3) growing shortages of certain types of skilled labor and a scarcity of labor in certain geographic areas following the launching of the defense program of 1941; and (4) government policy pertaining to labor.

Government policy manifested itself in a variety of ways: First, the administration accepted the principle of the 8-hour day and the 40-hour week, with payment of time-and-a-half for all overtime. Second, higher wage rates were encouraged in order to raise mass purchasing power; and the National Defense Mediation Board in the great majority of cases coming before it decided in favor of advances in hourly rates of pay. Third, government contracts contained clauses conducive to wage advances. While the cost-plus system of World War I was abandoned, provision was nevertheless made in both negotiated and fee contracts for subsequent price adjustments due to rising labor costs; thus the war industries, when necessary, bid high for scarce labor.

The most striking fact of this period is the improvement of real incomes among two classes of people, farmers and laborers. The prices of farm products rose very much more than the prices of the things farmers had to buy; and wages rose very much more than the cost of living. The rise in *hourly* earnings by no means fully reveals the situation because the number of hours per week increased, employment was steady throughout the year, and more members of the family worked.

The data presented show that the order of events was (1) rising prices of basic materials, especially farm products; (2) rising rates of wages, especially in manufacturing; (3) rising wholesale prices; and (4) slowly rising retail prices. The rise in the prices of raw materials was substantially greater than that of semifinished manufactured articles, and more than double that of finished manufactured products. The extraordinary increase in raw material and wage costs was absorbed, in substantial part, by the economies inherent in capacity output.

The great increase in employment, the overtime work and pay, and the increase in wage rates combined to provide an enormous expansion of consumer buying power. Yet retail prices of consumer goods through November, 1941, rose less than half as much as wholesale prices.

The fiscal situation underwent no great change during this first phase. The Treasury cash deficit for the fiscal year ending June 30, 1939, had been $3.4 billions while in fiscal 1940 it was reduced to $1.7 billions. In fiscal 1941 there was an increase to $5.4 billions. However, government borrowing operations for war purposes did not assume major importance until after the United States entered the war in December, 1941.

II. DURING AMERICAN PARTICIPATION, 1942–45

Before considering the factual record it will be useful to review the state of contemporary thinking with reference to the sources of inflation and the problem of price control. Price control discussions in World War II revolved around widely differing conceptions. At the beginning the prevailing professional view was again rooted in the quantity theory. Fiscal policy was again regarded as the primary key to price stability. Banking policy was also deemed important but supplementary. With severe restrictions on government and private borrowing, it was held that there could be little advance in the general level of prices.

On the other hand, there were some who contended that a system of direct controls should be immediately established. It was held that there should be a virtual freezing of wage rates and raw material prices—which constituted the basic elements in manufacturing costs. With the underpinning fixed and ceilings established in relation thereto, it was believed that virtual stability of prices could be achieved. In the words of Bernard M. Baruch: "Wages form the biggest component of all price structures. To attempt to fix price levels without thorough consideration of this element would be as abortive as to try to cure a sick man of all his ailments except the one that is most dangerous—the one that is likely to be fatal to him."[2] While Mr. Baruch was in favor of high taxes and bond sales to investors rather than to banks, he held that such indirect controls can never hold the price line—that direct control of costs is indispensable.

Monetary theorists as a rule opposed direct controls as unnecessary and impractical. "The price ceiling method fails to reach the heart of the inflationary process. . . . The essence of inflation is the expansion of money income which results from an unsound fiscal and credit policy—a policy that puts a constantly increasing supply of liquid funds in the hands of the public . . . [which] will draw prices upward."[3] At the most, direct control was regarded as a sort of handmaiden to indirect control—for "any procedure which keeps down the cost to the government of goods and services . . . will lessen the pressure on the Treasury for the creation of more and more new money."[4]

A publication of the National Bureau of Economic Research found the sources of inflation primarily in the "(1) more active use of currency and bank credit, (2) creation of new money by the government directly or by the banking system on behalf of the government, and (3) creation of new money for business and consumer spending through the expansion of bank credit."[5]

[2] "Preventing Inflation," containing statements before Rules Committee of House of Representatives, 1941.

[3] Charles O. Hardy, *Wartime Control of Prices* (1940), pp. 94-95.

[4] *The Same*, pp. 93-94.

[5] W. L. Crum, J. F. Fennelly, L. H. Seltzer, *Fiscal Planning for Total War* (1942), p. 77.

In accordance with this point of view little importance was attached to wage rates operating through costs as a cause of price increases. The study just referred to devoted but a single page to wages. While it was recognized that increasing wage rates might in time raise costs and bring pressure on prices, the authors placed primary emphasis on the effect of increased wages as purchasing power:

> Whatever effects an advance in wage rates may have on costs and prices, it tends to swell labor income and, in time of shrinking supplies of goods and services, acts as a positive force in bidding up prices and, hence, in raising the general price level. Since labor income accounts for more than 70 per cent of national income . . . there can be little doubt that pushing up wage rates . . . augments this major share of the national income and adds to the potency of this inflationary force.[6]

During the course of World War II a new term—the "inflationary gap"—was invented to describe a well-known phenomenon. The diversion of effort from the production of consumer goods to the production of war goods lessened the supply of goods in consumer markets—without reducing consumer incomes available for their purchase. Concretely, if instead of producing 200 billion dollars' worth of consumer goods, we produced only 150 billion dollars' worth, the balance being war goods, 200 billions of money income would be available with which to buy 150 billions of goods; hence the gap would be 50 billions. It was contended that unless this amount were diverted to the government to pay for war goods, the prices of consumer goods would inevitably rise. It was held that the direct price control and ration-

[6] *The same,* pp. 116-17.

ing system simply prevented this excess of purchasing power from producing its normal market effects. Inflation was said to be merely *suppressed.*

Eventually, though not until the spring of 1943, a program of direct control—known as the "hold-the-line" policy—was adopted. This involved a stabilization of the prices of farm and mineral products and wage rates. Some flexibility was permitted—to take care of belated adjustments—and subsidies were authorized for hardship cases.

This direct method of control had in fact been adopted by Germany at the very beginning of the Hitler war mobilization program. The prices of agricultural products were stabilized at levels slightly above those prevailing in the depth of the depression; the wage structure was frozen; and the prices of imported foodstuffs and raw materials, which bulked very large in the German economy, were rigidly controlled. It was believed that with these basic elements of cost stabilized, commodity prices generally would remain stable; and such proved to be the case. Somewhat similar, though less complete and rigid, methods of control were instituted in other European countries.

The period during which the United States was an active participant in the war divides itself into two parts—before and after the establishment of price control in the spring of 1943. During the first period all the indexes show a rapid rise from December, 1941, through April, 1943. The several price indexes, as the chart indicates, moved up more or less together—roughly 10 per cent. Among the groups of commodities, farm products still led the way with a rise of 33 per cent. Processed foods rose 20 per cent and textiles 6 per cent, while metals and metal products remained practically stationary.

Of greatest interest is the fact that the wage index was well in the lead throughout this period—the over-all advance from December, 1941, through April, 1943, being nearly 22 per cent. This is the reverse order from that found in World War I. While the wage figures given pertain only to manufacturing industry, other evidence indicates that wages in general kept fully abreast of the rise in the cost of living during this period.

In summary, the sequence of events during this period was: (1) rising farm prices, aided by government policy; (2) rising wage rates; (3) rising prices of raw materials; (4) and finally, rising wholesale and retail prices. It is noteworthy that during this period the cost-of-living index nearly kept pace with the general wholesale commodity index.

As the chart on page 126 indicates, the control system established in the spring of 1943 proved reasonably effective during the remainder of the war. However, the fact that the index of hourly earnings in manufacturing showed a further rise of about 6 per cent indicates that the control of wages was not unyielding.

The Increase in Money Supply

We may now consider the causes of the extraordinary increase in the money supply that occurred between 1939 and the end of the war. During the war period unemployment was eliminated, the average length of the standard work week increased somewhat, and there was very extensive overtime work in the war industries.

At the same time the vast existing industrial slack was taken up and there was a great expansion of productive capacity in war industries. The number of employed persons, including those in the military services, increased from 55,600,000 in 1939 to 65,140,000 in 1945.

These developments, even with no change in rates of remuneration, would naturally require a vast increase in the volume of money in use. At the same time, as we have seen, there occurred a great increase in wage *rates;* a great increase in farm income; and a great increase in profits. What transpired may best be indicated by the data showing the increase in national money income from 1939 to 1945.

NATIONAL INCOME, 1939, 1945[a]
(In millions of dollars)

	1939	1945	PERCENTAGE INCREASE
National Income	72,753	181,248	148.8
Compensation of employees	48,108	123,181	156.1
Income of unincorporated businesses and professions	7,293	19,011	160.0
Income of farmers	4,317	11,824	173.9
Corporate profits (before taxes)[b]	6,403	18,977	196.4
Rental income of persons	2,742	5,634	105.5
Net interest	4,604	3,185	—30.8

[a] U. S. Dept. of Commerce, *National Income* (1954 ed.), p. 162. In this income table inventory valuation adjustments are omitted.

[b] The peak of corporate profits before taxes was reached in 1943, when they aggregated 24,554 million dollars.

That an increase of employment and production required an additional volume of money is of course readily understood. The troubling question has been: *Why* did the money supply increase faster than the supply of goods? The primary explanation is that more money was being paid labor and other producers for the same services. As the table just presented indicates, the additional money supply was received by the people as compensation for services rendered and the amount was governed by the terms of the contracts. A 10 per cent increase in wage rates in 1945 would have meant that employees received 12.3 billion additional dollars for the same output. Similarly, a rise in farm price supports would have meant that more money was being paid farmers for the same output than formerly. This was what was occurring prior to the spring of 1943. After the hold-the-line policy was adopted this process was largely checked. If it had been completely checked the increase in money paid out henceforth would have been just proportional to the increase in employment and production.

Could the increase in money supply have been halted by avoiding government deficits and meeting the financial requirement solely from taxes and borrowings paid for out of savings? The answer is no—so long as wage rates and farm prices were not stabilized. Every increase in wage rates meant paying out more money for the same output; every increase in the price of farm products meant more money for the farmer for the same volume of production.

In concluding this discussion of price movements during World War II, it is of interest to make certain comparisons with the trends in World War I. As the charts show, there was a general similarity. In both cases the greatest price advances occurred before the United States actually entered the war. In both cases the rise in wholesale prices was eventually checked or retarded by controls directed at the stabilization of costs and profits. In both wars the price rise began and was much the most pronounced at the wholesale level. In both cases there was a substantial and continuous lag in retail prices.

One significant difference is to be noted: In World War I wages in manufacturing lagged behind wholesale prices and moved upward but little faster than the cost of living, whereas in World War II the wage index rose more rapidly than the cost of living index—more rapidly even than the general wholesale commodity index.

It is worth recalling at this place that during World War I the United States remained formally on the gold standard, though as a precaution against possible hoarding the presentation of paper money for gold was discouraged. At the outbreak of World War II the United States was operating on a "managed currency" basis—and there was no official policy calling for a restoration of the gold standard in the future.

III. AFTER THE WAR

The immediate question at the end of the war was whether the price control machinery should be continued, at least during the period of readjustment from war to civilian activities. Whereas in 1919 President Wilson had favored a quick demobilization of all wartime controls, the Truman administration urged the retention of most of them; and it was promptly announced that price control would be continued, at least to June 30, 1946, in order to prevent a further rise in the cost of living.

Conflicting Conceptions

Opinions as to impending price movements were sharply contradictory. On the one hand, it was contended by many that the "inflationary gap"—the vast, unspent, purchasing power accumulated during the war, but held in leash by the price control and rationing system—would result in a great new advance of prices the moment controls were abandoned. In short, consumer demand, hitherto "suppressed," would quickly bid up the prices of commodities. People "couldn't have all that hot money rolling around in their pockets without spending it and forcing prices up."[7] This group favored: the continuance of price control to prevent prices from going through the ceiling, and the roof; increased taxation to mop up purchasing power; and tight credit controls.

Others, principally in labor and government circles, were convinced that demobilization would bring deflation and acute depression. This conclusion was based on the assumption that the elimination of overtime work, at time-and-a-half rates of pay, together with the reduction of the labor force as demobilization proceeded, would involve a quick shrinkage in aggregate current purchasing power. To this group a price and business debacle appeared inevitable unless the prospective deficiency in purchasing power was promptly made good. They urged a two-fold program: first, an increase in standard wage rates to offset the loss of overtime pay; and second, a public works program de-

[7] Chester Bowles, Administrator of the Office of Price Administration, *Extension of Emergency Price Control Act*, Hearings before the House Committee on Banking and Currency, Vol. 2, 78 Cong. 2 sess., pp. 2272-73.

signed to sustain employment at or near war-time levels.[8]

In line with this thinking, the Director of the Office of War Mobilization and Reconversion had announced before the end of the war that: "We must be prepared to make some upward adjustments [in wage rates] to compensate for severe declines in take-home pay."[9] Then almost immediately after the end of the war, on August 18, 1945, the President issued an executive order in furtherance of this conception. The order alluded to the desirability of maintaining purchasing power, and provided that employers might increase wages or salaries without obtaining the approval of the War Labor Board—upon condition that such increases should not be made the basis for compensating price adjustments. It was also stated that the War Labor Board should be terminated as soon as possible after the conclusion of the forthcoming Industry-Labor Conference. These developments opened the door to wholesale increases in wage rates, not only to correct inequities but also to sustain over-all purchasing power.

The Breakdown of Postwar Price Control

The death knell of postwar price control had unwittingly been sounded in the President's executive order, which read as follows:

> With the return to a peacetime economy and the elimination of the present temporary wartime agencies and procedures, we must look to collective bargaining, aided and supplemented by a truly effective system of conciliation and

[8] For other conceptions as to the requirements of the situation, the reader is referred back to Chap. 1, pp. 25-32.

[9] *The Road to Toyko and Beyond,* 3d Report to the President, the Senate, and the House of Representatives, July 1, 1945, p. 38.

voluntary arbitration, as the best and most democratic method of maintaining sound industrial relations.[10]

This order, in effect, abolished government control over wage rates, which had been a crucial part of the hold-the-line policy.

This early abandonment of wage control was, no doubt, inevitable because of political considerations, and also perhaps on grounds of constitutionality. In any case demands for increased wage rates quickly became general. In August, 1945, some 130,000 workers in the lumber industry asked for a substantial wage increase and the War Labor Board directed the interested parties to settle the matter by collective bargaining. The CIO requested the War Labor Board to raise wages in the construction industry in order to prevent a retardation of expansion in construction activity. The CIO United Automobile Workers demanded of General Motors a 30 per cent increase in wage rates, arguing that "the profit and reserve position of General Motors provides ample margin for the absorption of the wage adjustment without necessitating price increases."[11] Since the authorized postwar price for General Motors cars was based on the assumption that existing wage rates would continue, it is obvious that if the wage increase were granted the price schedule would be subject to revision.

Despite these developments the Administrator of the OPA remained hopeful that the situation could be controlled, expressing himself as late as July 7, 1946, as follows: "As our peacetime production is stepped up, supplies will gradually come in balance with demand,

[10] *New York Times*, Aug. 17, 1945.
[11] *Evening Star* (Washington, D.C.), Aug. 19, 1945.

first in one field then another. As quickly as this occurs, price controls in that area will be eliminated."[12] Here the basic principle on which the price regulatory system had hitherto been based was apparently forgotten—namely, that prices should cover costs and permit a reasonable profit. The implication of the statement is that the cost level at which the new supplies would be produced could be ignored—that supply and demand would automatically ensure stable prices, regardless of wage rates and other elements of costs, as soon as the accumulated shortages in all lines were eliminated.

It should be observed, moreover, that if during the period of acute shortages the price control machinery should succeed in preventing the accumulated purchasing power from dissipating itself in the process of bidding up prices, such purchasing power would continue to overhang the markets after the positive shortages were eliminated. And since current postwar production would presumably generate new purchasing power at least proportional to the value of the goods produced, the accumulated carry-over would *not* gradually be absorbed. Thus it would appear necessary to continue price control indefinitely.

It became impossible, in fact, to administer the price control system once wage control was given up. Every increase in wage rates admittedly affected, directly or indirectly, the whole structure of prices. Since in the nature of the case no general formula could be applied in a wide range of varying circumstances, each application had to be studied on its individual merits—which often required weeks or even months of time. Because

[12] Memorandum to Newspaper Editors, Columnists, and Radio Commentators.

of rapidly changing conditions involving readjustments in volume of output, reductions in cost due to the elimination of overtime work and rates of pay, changes in raw material prices, and rising wage rates, the price control authorities were confronted with an insurmountable administrative problem. Before one case could be decided, a host of new ones pressed for consideration.

All that the Price Administration could accomplish in these circumstances would be to retard price advances by delays in granting price relief or by applying "the squeeze" somewhere along the line. An announced policy of requiring distributors to absorb increased costs of manufacture greatly magnified the difficulty of price control at the retail end. War experience had indicated that rationing was essential to the control of retail prices in lines where there were acute shortages; but retention of a rationing system for consumer goods in peace-time was admittedly not to be tolerated. As matters stood, it was impossible to readjust individual prices to meet the requirements of a rapidly changing situation. Inevitably, therefore, the attempt to continue price control could only impede essential business readjustments to meet the needs of the peace-time economy. Congress reached this conclusion and refused to renew legislative authority.

The Succession of Events

The war was not followed by a serious economic crisis resulting in deflation, nor was it followed immediately by "wild inflation." As the chart on page 126 indicates, the postwar price rise was slight for the first eight months; the real advance began in mid-1946, accelerated through 1947, and reached its peak in mid-1948. Before attempting to appraise the motivating forces, it is essential to review the facts as to the *relative* advances in the several indexes.

The over-all rise in the general wholesale price index from the end of the war to the peak month in 1948 was 55 per cent; while the "sensitive" commodities rose 92 per cent. The prices of raw materials, semi-manufactured, and finished products showed an almost parallel rise—56 per cent, 60 per cent, and 57 per cent respectively. Among the major groups of products the greatest advances were: petroleum products, 100 per cent; foods, 77 per cent; hides and leather products, 67 per cent; and building materials, 67 per cent. Farm products as a whole rose only 53 per cent, but the livestock group advanced 108 per cent.

The wage index declined slightly during the closing months of 1945—in contrast to the price indexes. This decline was due not to a decrease in the standard wage but to the reduction in overtime rates of pay as production in the war industries was curtailed. Thereafter, the wage advance was greater than the rise in the cost of living throughout the postwar inflation period. Indeed, through 1947 and 1948 wages in manufacturing industry nearly kept pace with the rise in wholesale prices. A feature of this period was the series of so-called "across the board" increases in wage rates. In transportation and public utilities, in banking, and in wholesale and retail trade, the upward adjustments in wages and salaries were somewhat slower.

Retail prices lagged continuously and substantially behind wholesale prices—this despite the exceptional rise in the retail prices of foods which were strongly influenced by government purchases. It was during this period that farm prices were sharply enhanced by government purchases for foreign relief and aid programs, especially under the Marshall Plan.

It should be noted that the peak of the postwar rise was reached first in the "sensitive" commodity group—as early as December, 1947. The ensuing decline was also more drastic for this group and by late 1949 the differential had largely disappeared. The decline in the general wholesale index was also less than the decline in the cost of living—8 per cent as compared with less than 4 per cent.

The Motivating Forces

What conclusion may be drawn from the foregoing data with respect to the factors chiefly responsible for the great postwar advance in prices? The natural first question is: Does not the outcome support the views of those who had forecast a great advance in prices in consequence of the release of accumulated war-time purchasing power at a time when many kinds of consumer goods were scarce? It is true that a large volume of spending money was accumulated during the war period. Moreover, this carry-over purchasing power was soon greatly enhanced by two developments, already noted—the rise in the incomes of farmers and the increase in wages. Finally, consumer credit was available on easy terms. Did not this increase create an intense "inflationary pressure" forcing prices upward?

Notwithstanding the superabundance of purchasing power in the hands of the public, the data assembled do not indicate that spending of "hot money" by consumers was the initiating impulse in the general advance of prices. As the chart clearly shows, retail prices lagged continuously behind wholesale prices. Moreover, the retail trade data do not support the view that there was a great bulge in consumer buying. Women's wearing apparel and accessories would be one of the commodity groups where extravagant buying would presumably first manifest itself. This is a good class of commodities to consider because inventories can be replenished quickly in the textile field. The dollar sales figures for December (Christmas month) ran as follows:

Dec. 1944	407	million dollars
Dec. 1945	421	" "
Dec. 1946	454	" "
Dec. 1947	495	" "

A substantial part of the modest dollar rise from year to year is accounted for by the gradual rise in prices which occurred.

The trade trends were similar in other lines. There was to be sure a gradual increase in dollar sales through 1946 as servicemen returned, as supplies became more available, and retail prices increased. But as the chart so clearly shows, the postwar rise in prices was not precipitated by a skyrocketing of prices of consumer goods, resulting from excess buying power.

What became of the accumulated purchasing power that was not absorbed by higher prices? Much of it was used as time passed in buying additional quantities of consumer goods as they became available in the markets. Some of it was used for the construction and improvement of homes. Some of it went for the purchase of urban or farm real estate. Some of it went to liquidate mortgages, to buy insurance policies, to increase savings deposits, and to purchase securities in the market.

The postwar price advance was touched off by industrial, and speculative, buying of basic materials and by rapidly rising wage rates in manufacturing industry. There followed the usual spiral of rising costs and wages through the successive steps of production and distribution. The rise was last and least at the retail end.

It remains true that adequate consumer buying power, actual and prospective, was an essential for postwar business recovery and expansion. During the war period there had occurred a veritable revolution in the distribution of national income—a factor of much greater enduring significance than the carry-over of war-time earnings. The favorable market possibilities afforded the essential inducement to businessmen to proceed with replacement and expansion activities—despite the high and rising level of costs.

What, finally, was occurring in the realm of public finance during this postwar boom period? Did deficit financing play a significant role? In the last fiscal year of the war period, ending June 30, 1945, the cash deficit had been 49.5 billion dollars. In the ensuing fiscal year this was reduced to 7.4 billions; while in the fiscal years 1947 and 1948 there were cash surpluses of 19.4 billions and 7.3 billions respectively.[13] Thus at the period of greatest advance in prices the huge government deficits were being eliminated and replaced by very substantial *surpluses.*

[13] These data are from *Annual Report* of the Secretary of the Treasury on the State of the Finances for the fiscal year ended June 30, 1952, p. 750.

IV. THE KOREAN WAR

The most common explanations of the rapid advance in prices which occurred in the second half of 1950 was a new expansion of the money supply and panicky buying by the consuming public. People were said to be influenced by (1) the fear of acute shortages later, and (2) the desire to get ahead of the impending rise in prices.

With respect to control, primary emphasis was, as heretofore, placed on fiscal and credit policy—upon a balanced budget and private credit restrictions. However, certain direct controls were generally regarded as necessary and helpful. An allocation system for strategic material was quickly adopted; and the Defense Production Act gave the President power to impose ceilings upon prices and to "stabilize wages, salaries, and other compensation." In due course, price and wage stabilization boards were appointed to serve under the leadership of an Economic Stabilization Administrator. However, the wage stabilization plan was killed by the protest withdrawal of the labor members of the Board.

The chart on page 148 shows the comparative movements of the several price indexes and hourly earnings in manufacturing. From May, 1950, to February, 1951, the index of sensitive commodities rose 52 per cent; the wholesale index of all commodities, 17 per cent; and the cost-of-living index only 8 per cent. During this 8-month period the upward movement of hourly earnings in manufacturing closely paralleled the rise in the cost of living.

The arresting fact in this price advance is its shortness. The peak in wholesale prices was reached as early

PRICE AND WAGE TRENDS, 1950–55[a]
(January, 1950 = 100)

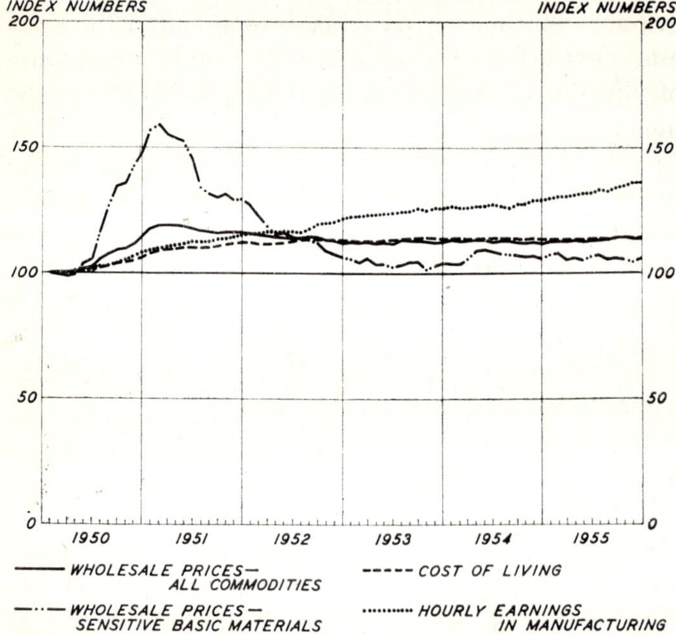

[a] Basic data from U. S. Bureau of Labor Statistics.

as February-March, 1951, although the fighting in Korea did not cease until 1953. By February, 1953, the index for sensitive commodities was back to the level of June, 1950. The general wholesale index declined but remained some 10 per cent above the pre-Korea level. Meanwhile, however, the cost-of-living index continued to creep slowly upward. By the end of 1955 wages and salaries in manufacturing were nearly 25 per cent above the level of early 1951. The wage trend in other lines was similar to that in manufacturing.

A striking feature of the price data is the comparatively slight advance in the consumer goods index. It is evident that there was no competitive bidding at retail establishments. If consumer buying had been the cause of the price rise following June, 1950, one would expect to find a sharp increase in the dollar value of retail sales —reflecting both increased quantity and advancing prices. However, the dollar value of retail store sales remained practically stable during this 8-months' period. The monthly data are as follows:[14]

June 1950	11.96	billion dollars
July 1950	12.31	" "
Aug. 1950	12.74	" "
Sept. 1950	12.50	" "
Oct. 1950	12.08	" "
Nov. 1950	11.61	" "
Dec. 1950	14.46	" "
Jan. 1951	12.19	" "

Since there was some advance in retail prices during this period, it would appear that there must have been an actual reduction in the quantity of goods sold.

Fiscal data again do not support the theory that the sharp advance in prices between June, 1950, and February, 1951, was due to deficit financing. In the fiscal year ending June 30, 1950, there had been a cash deficit of 2,207 million dollars. In fiscal 1951 there was a surplus of 7,593 millions.[15]

[14] U. S. Dept. of Commerce, *Survey of Current Business*, February, 1951, and February, 1952. These figures are not adjusted for seasonal variations.

[15] These data are from *Annual Report* of the Secretary of the Treasury on the State of the Finances for the fiscal year ended June 30, 1957, p. 400.

The Motivating Forces

The price-motivating forces at work during this period are revealed by the relative changes in the several price indexes. The extraordinary rise in the sensitive commodities index and the very substantial rise in the general wholesale index is directly attributable to extensive business buying for inventory purposes. Purchases of materials by manufacturers had averaged 11.1 billions in the early months of 1950. After June they rose rapidly, reaching a total of 15.3 billions in February, 1951. The rapid accumulation of inventories indicates that manufacturers were laying in stocks in order to be ahead of the price rise—which was, of course, stimulated by such buying. Inventories increased from 29.7 billions in June, 1950, to 35.9 billions in February, 1951. The funds required to finance this vast increase in inventories came in part from available working capital but chiefly from bank borrowings. Commercial loans outstanding rose progressively from June, 1950, to February, 1951, from 13.5 billions to 18.5 billions.

The excessive accumulation of inventories ended in a relatively short time and was succeeded by a period of subnormal purchases. This served to correct the price distortions which had occurred in the sensitive commodity group. As the chart indicates, the index reached a peak of 159 in February, 1951. By the end of the year it was back to 129; and it continued to fall through 1952 and 1953—reaching a level below that of the early months of 1950. Meanwhile there was a considerable decline in the wholesale price index of *all* commodities—roughly halfway back to the pre-Korea level. This decline was apparently due chiefly to the fact that the sensitive commodity group—chiefly raw materials—is included within the general wholesale index.

The sharp upward thrust of wholesale prices in 1950 left—despite the ensuing downward readjustment—an important impact on the price structure. The advance in prices was promptly followed by demands for compensating advances in wage rates; and wage increases, in fact, soon became general. Thus while the downward readjustment of raw material prices in 1951-52 served to reduce the cost of manufacturing finished commodities, the rising cost of labor worked in the opposite direction. The new higher level of wages became a built-in part of the cost structure. As the chart indicates, the wage index continued to rise in the ensuing years. The significance of this trend will be discussed in Chapter VIII.

General Conclusion on War Price Phenomena

In this and the two preceding chapters we have reviewed the history of war-time price distortions under widely varying monetary conditions: under pure fiat paper money regimes; with paper currency secured by valuable lands; under temporarily inconvertible paper money; where there has been no official departure from the gold standard; and where the gold standard no longer exists. In some cases, the funds required were obtained almost wholly from the printing of Treasury notes; in other cases bank credit currency was substituted for government paper; and in still other instances a substantial portion came from taxation and bond sales to investors. Yet, apart from the pure paper money episodes, which eventuated in complete financial demoralization, the pattern of price movements in the several war periods has been much alike. The similarity is best revealed by the long-term price chart on page 2.

The price rise begins typically in war materials and other commodities of impending shortage, and gradually extends, though in varying degree, to all commodities. Involved in this interacting process are rising costs of materials and foodstuffs, rising wages, and rising costs of finished products, both civilian and military. The continuing round of cost and price advances proceeds irrespective of the character of the monetary system or of the methods of financing employed; and it proceeds whether there is a budget deficit or a budget surplus. Experience has taught that the progressive rise in prices could be checked only by stabilizing wage rates and raw material prices—the two primary elements of cost.

CHAPTER VIII

Long-Term Price Trends

We return now to the ultimate question—what are the forces which govern the level of prices over long periods of time? Leaving war-time distortions and other short-term fluctuations out of the picture, how does one account for the longer term price movements which have characterized the capitalistic era? Is it possible to gauge the trend of prices over the decades ahead?

As we have seen, both *value of gold* and *quantity of money* theorists found the basic explanation in changes in the production of gold, the standard money. Our study has revealed, however, that price movements have shown little correlation with fluctuations in gold production, or with potential supplies of money and credit, which in recent decades could have supported a price level several times that which has in fact prevailed.

The *income* approach differed essentially from the gold theories in that the aggregate money in circulation was held to be determined, not by gold reserves or credit potentials based thereon, but by the factors governing the level of money wages, interest, rents, and profits.[1] However, it resembled the traditional monetary theories in the underlying assumption that the price level is simply a reflection of the volume of money (in-

[1] For a discussion of the history, and incompleteness, of the income approach, see pp. 225-231.

come) available for market expenditures as compared with the volume of goods available for purchase.

Our analysis has shown that the supply of money and the supply of goods are not independent variables but are inextricably connected in the processes of production. In a pecuniary society money is employed, as we have seen, in every stage of production in assembling the land, labor, capital, and managerial talent essential to business enterprise. The supply of money in the channels of circulation at any given time is simply the amount employed in organizing and carrying out productive operations. The magnitude of the money supply thus used is determined by the aggregate volume of production and the level of costs per unit of output.

I. THE COST STRUCTURE OF THE AMERICAN ECONOMY

The money and credit which business operations require is expended chiefly for materials and supplies, transportation service, fuel, electricity, etc., and in meeting interest and rental charges and the wages and salaries of employees. As we have seen, manufactured goods, generally speaking, enter the market places—stores, shops, filling stations, etc., with the price tags already attached. The selling prices quoted at any given time are those deemed necessary for the successful operation of business enterprises. This means that in the long run they must cover costs of production, including depreciation of plant and equipment, and provide a margin for profits. Money costs thus constitute the primary basis of money prices.

To reveal clearly the role of money costs in relation to prices it is necessary to have before us certain data pertaining to the American economy as a whole. First, the relative magnitude of the major divisions of the economic system may be indicated by their respective contributions to aggregate national income—as shown by the following table.

NATIONAL INCOME BY INDUSTRIAL ORIGIN, 1956[a]
(In millions of dollars)

Manufacturing	$108,075	31.5 per cent
Wholesale and retail trade	57,874	17.0 " "
Contract construction	17,704	5.2 " "
Agriculture, forestry, and fisheries	16,084	4.7 " "
Transportation	16,713	4.9 " "
Communications and public utilities	12,499	3.6 " "
Mining	6,050	1.9 " "
Government and government enterprises	40,078	11.8 " "
Services	35,550	10.4 " "
Finance, insurance, and real estate	30,932	9.0 " "
Total	$343,620	100.0 per cent

[a] U. S. Dept. of Commerce, *Survey of Current Business*, July, 1957, p. 16.

Manufacturing industry, and the wholesale and retail trade operations directly associated therewith, account for 48.5 per cent of the total. Contract construction, mining, transportation, communications and public utilities comprise another 15.6 per cent. The addition of agriculture, forestry, and fisheries brings the total to nearly 70 per cent. It is the products of these industries which are chiefly used in compiling price indexes. Manufacturing industry is thus of decisive importance from the standpoint of costs and prices—both because of its magnitude and its permeating influence in the economy as a whole.

Those responsible for setting price schedules as a matter of course base their decisions primarily on the level of costs. In competitive industry the price established at any given time may be somewhat above, or below, the prevailing level of costs—depending upon current market conditions; but in the long run the price trend closely approximates the cost trend.

In the regulated industries, such as railroads and public utilities, the rates (prices) permitted are always fixed in the light of costs. In periods of falling costs, in consequence of technological advances or business recession, the regulatory authorities are besought to reduce rates; in periods of rising costs, every case that is brought before federal, state, and municipal regulatory commissions requests compensating increases in rates.

The price control authorities of World War I and World War II directed their primary attention to cost foundations. It was recognized that so long as wage rates and raw material costs continued to rise, the prices of manufactured products for both military and civilian uses would inevitably rise. Every case considered by the price control authorities involved first and foremost the question of essential costs and profits. The principle employed was to permit prices that would cover costs and ensure a necessary, but not an unreasonable, profit.

Ramifications of the Cost-Price System

Some sectors of the economy, notably agriculture, are not conducted on a strictly cost-accounting basis. While monetary outlays are involved, the prices are not, as in manufacturing, mining, transportation, and public utilities, based directly on costs of production. Historically, the great bulk of farm produce was sold for what it would bring in local or central market places. Thus, supply and demand played a much more direct role than was the case in manufacturing or transportation. In general, the farmer long passively accepted the market price, hoping that the receipts would provide a living. Exceptions are to be noted in the case of such products as fruits and milk where for many years cooperative marketing agencies have endeavored to establish prices at levels which will cover costs and provide a reasonable return.

In modern times, however, the greater part of agriculture has become articulated with the industrial cost-price structure. The *relative* decline of agricultural prices led eventually to federal legislation designed to maintain agricultural prices at levels comparable to industrial prices. In brief, under the so-called parity principle it is the duty of the government to keep the prices of the things the farmer has to sell to urban consumers in line with the things he has to buy from urban producers. The mechanism involves government purchases to the extent necessary to support farm prices at the levels stipulated by the *parity* formula.

Thus agricultural prices are now linked directly with the industrial cost-price structure. Any increase in the level of costs and prices in mining, manufacturing, or transportation requires, under the law, compensating, upward adjustments in the prices of cotton, wheat, corn, and many other agricultural commodities.

To follow the complete circle of inter-connection between industrial and agricultural prices, we may start with an increase in wage rates in the steel industry. A similar sequence would follow whether the initial advance was in steel or transportation or some other industry and whether it began with wage increases, or independent advances in prices.

The increase in steel workers' wages quickly leads to an advance in the price of steel products. This involves an increase in costs of materials over the wide range of industries using steel—notably transportation, construction, hardware, farm machinery, and automotive vehicles. These advances in costs shortly find reflection in the prices charged by these industries for their goods and services; and in turn (through the operation of the parity system) in the prices of farm produce. In due course, the rising cost of food impels demands for compensating increases in wages everywhere. Where the escalator principle is incorporated in wage contracts, an automatic upward adjustment of wages to match the rising cost of living is guaranteed.

The impact of industrial price advances is soon felt throughout all sectors of the economy. A rise in the price of manufactured goods directly affects the costs of construction and supplies required by financial and service agencies, hospitals and educational institutions, and in the manifold activities of governments—federal, state, and local. Moreover, as the cost of living increases, compensating increases in salaries, wages, fees, etc. become necessary in every field of activity. Finally, the rising costs of government operations necessitate increased taxes which in some cases become a part of the industrial cost structure. The upward adjustment occurs unevenly, and belatedly, but nonetheless inevitably.

II. THE DOMINANT IMPORTANCE OF LABOR COSTS

Wage and salary payments to employees, together with supplementary benefits, constitute the major single element in production costs. In the economy as a whole in 1956 "compensation of employees" of corporate enterprises aggregated 241 billion dollars. Moreover, wages and salaries constituted a large part of the payments made by unincorporated enterprises, aggregating nearly 40 billions. In contrast, the aggregate net interest outlays, including those made by governments, amounted to only 7.3 billion dollars, while rentals of all kinds totaled only 10.3 billions.

It is difficult to give a precise figure for the labor element in the cost of a particular product because a part of the total labor cost is embedded in the raw materials, supplies, etc. which are purchased from other companies. But for manufacturing industry the U. S. Bureau of the Census periodically publishes data showing wages and salary costs as compared with the total "value added by the manufacturing process"—added, that is, to the cost of purchased "materials, supplies, fuel, electric energy, and construction work." In 1954 the labor item amounted to over 60 per cent of the total cost incurred at the manufacturing stage of the production process.

The table below shows the labor costs in the principal sub-divisions of industry in relation to the value added in the manufacturing process. In ten divisions wages and salaries account for more than two-thirds of the total costs entering into the *value added*. The range is from 32 per cent in tobacco to 78 per cent in fabricated metal products. The varying labor costs reflect chiefly the dif-

WAGES AND SALARIES AND VALUE ADDED BY MANUFACTURE, 1954
(In millions of dollars)

INDUSTRY GROUP	VALUE ADDED BY MANUFACTURE[a]	COMPENSATION OF EMPLOYEES[b]	PER CENT LABOR COSTS
ALL MANUFACTURING	$116,913	$70,960	60.7
Food and kindred products	13,400	6,170	46.0
Tobacco manufactures	988	314	31.8
Textile mill products	4,749	3,408	71.8
Apparel and related products	5,147	3,505	68.1
Lumber and wood products	3,188	2,219	69.6
Furniture and fixtures	1,966	1,317	67.0
Pulp, paper and products	4,581	2,441	53.3
Printing and publishing	6,265	3,818	60.9
Chemicals and products	9,444	4,137	43.8
Petroleum and coal products	3,583	1,729	66.9
Rubber products	1,904	1,172	61.6
Leather and leather products	1,637	1,141	69.7
Stone, clay, and glass products	3,822	2,276	59.5
Primary metal products	9,373	6,060	64.7
Fabricated metal products	7,596	5,749	75.7
Machinery (except electrical)	12,339	7,829	63.4
Electrical machinery	7,403	5,021	67.8
Transportation equipment	13,926	9,332	67.0
Instruments and related products	2,129	1,513	71.1
Miscellaneous manufactures	4,473	1,809	40.4

[a] U. S. Dept. of Commerce, Bureau of the Census, General Summary, *1954 Census of Manufactures,* Bull. MC-201, p. 4.

[b] U. S. Dept. of Commerce, *Survey of Current Business,* July, 1957, p. 16.

fering degrees of mechanization in the several industries.

The labor factor is equally important in mining, in contract construction, and in transportation. In railroad transportation, despite the great technological progress and resulting reduction in personnel that has occurred in recent years, labor costs in 1955 comprised as much as 65.3 per cent of the total operating expenses, having risen from 54.8 per cent since 1945.[2] The labor item also bulks large in two other very important sectors of the economy—*services,* and wholesale and retail *trade.*

III. WAGE COSTS AND PRICES

The paramount importance of labor costs may be indicated by comparing the movement of wage rates and the wholesale prices of finished manufactures. The fifteen year interval—1900-1914—was one of general growth and rising prices, punctuated by only two short recessions—in 1908 and 1913. During these years wage rates advanced considerably faster than prices. The over-all increase in wages was roughly 40 per cent as compared with a price rise of 19 per cent.[3]

In the 8-year peace-time expansion era from 1922 through 1929, we find a somewhat similar story. Wages in manufacturing rose gradually throughout the period; but after 1924 the wholesale prices of finished commodities declined somewhat.

The significance of the wage trend in recent decades is strikingly portrayed in the accompanying diagram, which shows the movement of hourly earnings in manufacturing and the prices of finished products. Since the revised Bureau of Labor Statistics indexes use the year 1926 as a base, the chart begins with that year.

Since 1933 the rise in wage rates has been almost continuous—through the recovery period of the thirties, in World War II, and throughout the postwar period. Except for minor dips in 1937-38, 1949, and 1953-54, the price rise has also been steadily upward. But, since

[2] *Annual Report of the Interstate Commerce Commission,* 1956, p. 180.

[3] Bureau of Labor Statistics.

WAGE COSTS AND PRICES OF FINISHED MANUFACTURES, 1926–57[a]
1926 = 100

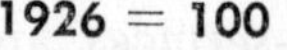

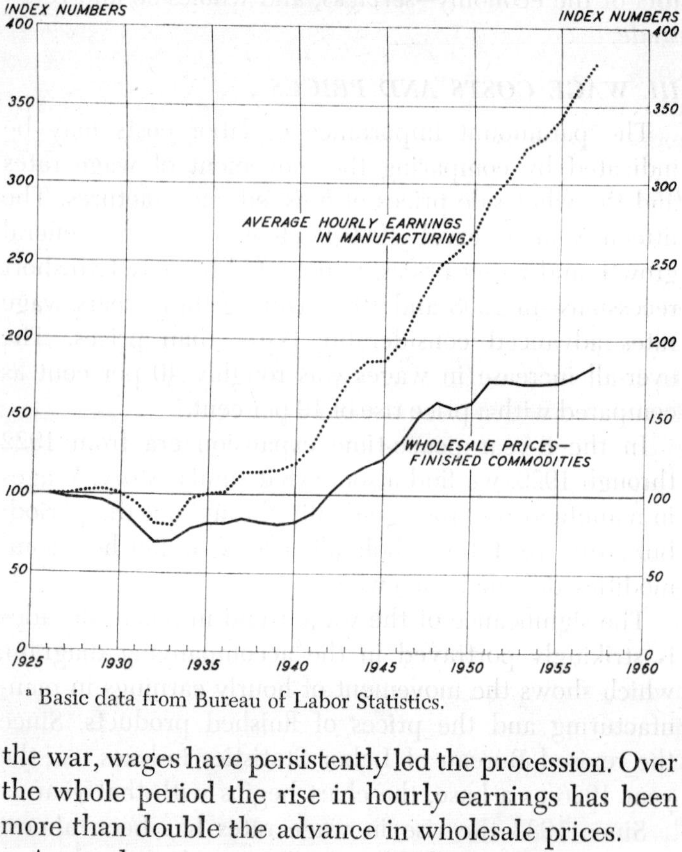

[a] Basic data from Bureau of Labor Statistics.

the war, wages have persistently led the procession. Over the whole period the rise in hourly earnings has been more than double the advance in wholesale prices.

As we have seen, wages and salaries make up over 60 per cent of the direct cost in the manufacturing process. In addition, wages constitute the most important single factor in the costs of materials and services which must be purchased by the manufacturing industry—which includes raw materials, transportation, contract construction, fuel, etc.

It is impossible, therefore, to escape the conclusion that the factor primarily responsible for the progressive advance in prices in recent decades has been the extraordinary rise in wage rates—the major element in costs of production. The fact that prices did not rise in proportion to the advance in wage costs is attributable chiefly to improvements in operating efficiency.

IV. THE SIGNIFICANCE OF PRODUCTIVITY

At this place it becomes necessary to bring into the picture a cost-reducing factor of basic importance. In modern times technological progress—based on science, engineering, and mechanization—has increased many fold the efficiency of the productive process. Productivity is commonly measured by dividing the aggregate production by the number of hours of labor involved. This is designated *man-hour* output.

In the industrial realm an increase in man-hour output is the result of a combination of factors—including improvements in industrial plant and equipment, larger scale output, better trained managers and workers, more satisfactory industrial relations, etc. In the agricultural realm it results from the substitution of machine for hand labor, larger scale farm operations, increased knowledge of soils and conservation practices, improved tillage, more effective fertilization based on soil tests, better control of animal and plant diseases, higher producing seeds and livestock, and greater attention to the elimination of waste and spoilage in the storage and processing of agricultural produce.

The rapid development of capitalistic enterprise throughout the nineteenth century brought a remarkable increase in productive efficiency in the realm of industry. But in agriculture technological progress was comparatively slow and confined chiefly to labor-saving machinery which had little effect on yields per acre. The so-called scientific age in agriculture which eventually brought phenomenal increases in yields per acre dates from roughly 1900.

Over the first half of the present century man-hour output in industry as a whole increased unevenly, but at an average rate of roughly 2 per cent a year. In agriculture the rate of increase was somewhat less rapid than in manufacturing prior to 1940.

Since World War II the United States has witnessed a remarkable advance in productive efficiency. In the industrial realm as a whole the annual rate of increase in man-hour output has averaged a good 3 per cent—though some signs of slackening have appeared since 1956. In agriculture, the increase in man-hour output has fully kept pace with that in industry and bids fair to continue without abatement.

It is this increase in man-hour output resulting from technological progress that has made possible our progressively higher plane of living. Moreover, it has been the remarkable increase in industrial productivity in recent years that has enabled profits in manufacturing industries to remain at a satisfactory level even though prices lagged far behind wages.[4]

V. SUPPORTING ANALYSES IN ECONOMIC TREATISES

In classical economic treatises formal discussion of the factors affecting the general level of prices was confined, as we have seen, to the section on *Exchange*.

[4] See chart, p. 162.

Money was assumed to enter the picture only after the productive process had been completed and the unpriced goods were in the market place awaiting sale. Thus the price level was said to be determined simply by the ratio of goods supply to money supply. Yet at other places in the same treatises there commonly are discussions of price-making factors of a different sort—operating within the productive and commercial system itself. Many of these, as we shall see, support the analysis presented in preceding pages.

1. Costs of production and prices. Notwithstanding the general price theory enunciated in the section on Exchange, standard treatises have recognized in other chapters that prices are governed by conditions affecting the efficiency of production. Indeed, *cost of production* is emphasized as of decisive importance. In the words of John Stuart Mill, the value of any commodity is determined "temporarily by demand and supply, permanently and on the average by its cost of production."[5]

Costs of production in relation to prices were commonly discussed both under conditions of increasing costs and decreasing costs. It was observed that the extractive industries—agriculture, mining, forestry, and fisheries—were subject to a law of *increasing costs* (diminishing returns)—as and when it became necessary to resort to less productive natural resources. Hence over the years it was held that the prices of such products must inevitably rise—and rise progressively. On the other hand, in the industrial realm, production was commonly conducted under conditions of steadily increasing efficiency—or decreasing costs per unit of out-

[5] *Principles of Political Economy* (N.Y. ed., 1864), Vol. 2, p. 24.

put. Hence the trend of prices of manufactured goods would be downward—until such time as the rising costs of raw materials might come to outweigh the economies in the manufacturing process.

This type of analysis was sometimes rooted in the conception of energy costs—the amount of product that might be yielded by a given expenditure of human energy. Thus it might be held that the *level* of money prices would still be governed by the over-all supply of money as compared with the supply of goods. But when the term *expenses* of production was expressly employed, money outlays in connection with productive operations were clearly in the author's mind.

2. *How the benefits of progress are disseminated.* In a competitive system, the way in which the benefits resulting from technological progress accrue to the masses of the people was set forth in standard treatises somewhat as follows: In a private enterprise economy, industrial managers strive always to increase the efficiency of production in order to make the maximum of profits. As efficiency increases, the lower cost producers gradually reduce selling prices in order to obtain a larger share of the market, at the expense of the less efficient producers. Thus, under the spur of competition, prices tend to move downward in line with the level of costs of the more efficient producers. In consequence of this process the buying power of consumers is progressively increased. The reduction in costs is assumed to be accomplished, not by a reduction in wage rates, but by technical improvements in the methods of production.

This analysis of the process by which progressively higher standards of living are achieved under a capitalistic system is based explicitly on factors operating within the productive system to reduce costs and selling prices. It is here recognized that the amount of money in circulation as compared with the amount of goods automatically declines as the level of money costs and prices falls.

3. *Administered prices.* Reference has been made in a previous chapter to the so-called *administering* of prices by large-scale business organizations. Because of the great importance of large-scale enterprise in modern times, it has been contended by numerous writers that the industrial price structure is determined chiefly by the practices of large corporations in fixing prices in the light of estimates of what the traffic will bear. We are not here concerned with the question whether competition is thus destroyed or merely placed upon a different plane. Our present interest is simply in noting that those who hold that the level of industrial prices is determined by large-scale quasi-monopolistic enterprises have (perhaps unwittingly) abandoned the conception that it is merely a result of monetary factors.

4. *The protective tariff and prices.* Discussions of the consequences of protective tariffs always start with the proposition that the levying of customs duties raises the prices of imported commodities—and more than proportionally. The levying of a 20 per cent tariff duty, it is held, would increase the price of imported goods 20 per cent, and then because of the prevailing system of percentage mark-ups through manufacturing, wholesale, and retail channels, the rise in prices would be cumulative all the way to the consumer. It would appear, therefore, that, if there were a universal, horizontal increase in the customs duties of all imported

commodities, the general level of prices would rise.

At this point the quantity theorist may object that, *unless* the quantity of money were meanwhile increasing, the prices of *domestically produced* products would have to decline in proportion to the price increase of the *imported* commodities. This simple arithmetic ignores the interactions of higher priced imports upon costs elsewhere. For example, the cost of producing minerals, or other raw materials, might well rise rather than fall because of the demands for increases in wage rates to compensate for the higher costs of imported products.

5. *Increases in direct taxes.* The literature pertaining to taxation emphasizes that taxes levied on business operations constitute increased costs of production. The excise and sales taxes are admittedly a net addition to the price of the commodity on which they are levied. All writers on taxation hold that a universal sales tax would become embedded in the cost structure and result in a general increase in the level of prices. Many forms of present-day taxes are regarded as business costs which must be covered by the selling price—notably those levied on physical assets used in the business. Such property taxes, are, as a matter of course, included as a part of the costs which regulated industries are entitled to recover from the rates charged consumers.

6. *Wage rates and prices.* Economic literature abounds with statements pertaining to the effect of wage rates on prices. Indeed, a standard argument against granting demands for wage increases has been that it will not do the laborers any good because when they come to spend the increased money they will find they can buy no more than before because prices will meanwhile have been raised. That is, the increased

wage costs will have been added to the price of the goods produced.

7. *Monetary requirements of business.* The literature of finance has long emphasized that a satisfactory monetary system is one that is responsive to the varying financial needs of business. The primary weakness of the old National Banking system was the *rigidity* imposed by the requirement that bank notes must be based on government bonds. A primary purpose of the Federal Reserve Act was to provide an elastic bank note and deposit currency system that would be responsive to the financial requirements of business—that would expand, or contract, in accordance with varying needs for more or less money.

The financial requirements of business, it was recognized, were governed by the volume of business and by the level of monetary costs. In periods of expansion, accompanied by rising wage and other costs, business operations required progressively more funds. It was clearly seen that monetary requirements, and the supply of money, were governed by what was commonly described as "the general state of industry and trade."

In the economic literature briefly summarized above, the authors were realistically discussing motivating forces in the price-making process. These forces were operating within the *productive* system to raise or to lower the general level of quoted prices. There is here no reference to the relative supply of money and goods in consumer markets and no suggestion that a changing supply of gold or money or credit is the motivating or propelling force—whether in price advances or price declines. In short, the reasoning is in no way restricted or circumscribed by the framework of thought found in the chapters dealing specifically with the relation of money to prices.

VI. GAUGING THE FUTURE OF PRICES

Is it possible in the light of the foregoing analysis to forecast the probable long-term trend of prices over the years ahead? Since the situation may be profoundly affected by new wars or other international complications, and also by political and social factors affecting the domestic situation, the answer has to be—not with any degree of precision. It is possible, however, to identify the primary factors which, given reasonably stable conditions, will govern the level of prices in the coming decades.

Two factors will be of decisive influence in determining the future trend of prices: (1) the rate of technological progress—which governs the output per man per hour; and (2) the wage and salary rates paid to employees. Increasing productive efficiency—a cost-reducing factor—exerts pressure toward lower prices. Increasing wages—a cost-raising factor—exerts pressure toward higher prices.

The outcome in the years ahead will reflect the relative weight of these factors—man-hour output and rates of pay. To state the alternative possibilities in simplest terms: (1) if rates of pay and man-hour output increase equally, prices will be virtually stable; (2) if rates of pay increase faster than productivity, prices will rise; (3) if productivity increases faster than wage rates, the price trend will be downward, assuming of course the existence of effective competition.

It is impossible to know whether the recent rate of technological progress can be maintained, or increased.

Since World War II we have witnessed an extraordinary burst of creative energy, resulting in a vast expansion of improved industrial plant, with installed equipment of ever-increasing efficiency. Another factor serving greatly to increase aggregate annual output in recent years has been a minimum of strikes and a sustained high level of operations. Thus, one may well question whether the recent rate of increase in man-hour output can be sustained indefinitely. It should be noted, however, that former fears that we shall soon be faced with decreasing productivity because of the exhaustion of virgin resources have been virtually eliminated.[6] Even in agriculture, as we have seen, modern science and technology are combining to produce much higher yields per acre than was formerly deemed possible. On the whole, the outlook for continued increases in man-hour output must be adjudged favorable.

On the cost side, it appears certain that continuing increases in wage rates will be a powerful force working for progressively higher prices of industrial products. The wage item (embedded in raw materials, transportation, fuel, and power, as well as directly in the manufacturing process) has, as we have seen, become of preponderant importance. And the economic and political power of modern labor organizations is such that continued pressure for higher rates of pay is to be expected. Escalator clauses in labor contracts, designed to lessen industrial strife, serve to accelerate the inflation process.

On the agricultural side the price trend might be ex-

[6] For extensive discussion of the adequacy of our national resources, see the author's *Controlling Factors in Economic Development*, Chap. VII.

pected to be downward in consequence of increasing yields per acre—except for two offsetting factors: First, the extraordinary increase in population since 1940 and the continuing high birth rate forecast a progressive increase in the demand for farm products for several decades. Second, the political power of farmers will doubtless continue to manifest itself in legislative programs in support of agriculture. If the price parity principle is continued, farm prices may be expected to move upward more or less in line with rising industrial prices. The alternative policy of restricting production would, if successful, have the same result.

In turn, rising prices of manufactured and farm products will exert pressure in every division of the economy and in every occupation for wage and salary increases to compensate for the "rising cost of living." Transportation and public utility rates, finance charges, professional fees, direct taxes, etc. will in due course be increased; and these ever-widening areas of advancing costs will become the basis for further increases in the prices of industrial products. Finally, salaries in government service, in educational institutions, and in philanthropic and welfare organizations will gradually be adjusted upward.

The advance in wage rates, one may well believe, will in the future, as in recent years, continue to outstrip improvements in productive efficiency. If so, we shall have a progressive increase in the general level of commodity prices over the coming decades. Only a depression of major proportions, resulting in a substantial reduction of wage rates, would reverse the trend. Even in such an event the upward movement would doubtless be resumed in the not distant future.

CHAPTER IX

The Problem of Control

In this final chapter we relate the findings of our analysis as a whole to the age-old problem of controlling inflation. Do we possess the means of preventing a progressively upward trend of prices over the years ahead? It will be necessary to consider separately the situation as it exists in war periods and under ordinary peacetime conditions.

It should be recalled that inflation has traditionally been ascribed to monetary causes. The several types of monetary factors involved include:

1. Debasing the standard money in which prices are expressed—by reducing the weight or content of the official dollar.
2. Increasing gold production, with a consequent fall in the value of the dollar unit.
3. Issuing irredeemable government Treasury notes.
4. Increasing the supply of credit currency by excessive bank loans.
5. Increasing the supply of money in circulation by means of Treasury deficits.
6. Financing long-term capital expansion by means of credit operations instead of solely out of savings.

All of these explanations of the great price rise of recent years are to be found in the quotations presented in Chapter I.

Implicit in most of these interpretations is an underlying assumption, namely, that the level of commodity prices is the direct result of an increase in the over-all supply of money as compared with the over-all supply of goods. An increase in the Treasury deficit is called inflationary; while a decrease is said to be deflationary. An expansion of bank credit is called inflationary; a contraction deflationary. An increase in the supply of bank reserve money is regarded as inflationary; a decrease is deflationary. Expressions such as these permeate current financial literature—both as it relates to the causes of, and the remedies for, inflation. A somewhat similar conception is involved when the increase in money supply is attributed to higher wages—though in this case the increase in buying power admittedly does not originate in monetary policies.

The analysis in foregoing chapters has shown that the traditional assumption that the supply of money and the supply of goods are independent of one another is invalid. Rather both originate in, grow out of, productive operations in a pecuniary economy. The money income generated in the process of production—and accruing to individuals in the form of wages, interest, rents, and profits—*is* the money supply available for expenditure by the people. The magnitude of this supply of spendable money is governed by rates of remuneration for services rendered and, as we have seen, these normally depend upon quite other factors than the supply of gold or bank reserves or fiscal and monetary policies. Treasury and Federal Reserve policies have always been ineffective precisely because they cannot directly reach the factors responsible for the flow of money income. They may indirectly affect the situation but only by positive restrictions of credit which impede productive operations.

I. UNDER WAR-TIME CONDITIONS

It *is* possible to maintain a comparatively stable price level in time of war. American experience in both World War I and World War II shows that the price control system, while belatedly established, ultimately became reasonably effective. Had the control machinery been instituted earlier—before the pressure of the cost-price spiral had become intense—the regulations would have been much easier to enforce. The facts show that the upward spiral begins almost immediately in the realm of raw materials and special types of finished products. Hence it is perhaps too much to hope that an initial price rise of this type could be prevented at the outbreak of war—for such a rise commonly begins well before the declaration of war or the outbreak of hostilities.[1]

War-time experience, both in the United States and in other countries, has conclusively shown that to be effective the price control authorities must have the power to control both the prices of labor and of agricultural produce and other raw materials. Not until costs of production were brought under control was it possible to control prices. Moreover, once costs were controlled, the price level was stabilized despite the continuance of deficit financing on a vast scale.

II. UNDER CONDITIONS OF PEACE

The problem of price control under normal peacetime conditions is much more difficult than in time of

[1] See discussion in Chapters VI and VII.

war. That is to say, the sharp advances that have been characteristic of war periods can be prevented, while the gradual advances in peace-time periods of prosperity cannot. The numerous types of preventive remedies outlined in Chapter I will here be briefly summarized and analyzed.

1. *Restoration of the gold standard.* Advocates of the gold standard, it will be recalled, hold that anchoring the money supply to a gold base would serve as an automatic brake on the actions of banks and government, thereby stabilizing both economic and financial conditions. While minor readjustments would from time to time be required, long-term price movements would be gradual in character, being governed by changes in the value of gold as a standard commodity.[2]

The factual record shows, however, (see chart, page 2) that long-term price movements were almost if not quite as marked before the departure from the gold standard as they have been since. The reason why the gold standard cannot prevent inflation is simply that the gold supply as such is in no way connected with the level of wages and other costs of production.

2. *Balance the budget and reduce the debt.* Our study has shown that there never has been any correlation between fiscal deficits or surpluses and the movements of commodity prices. Indeed, there has often been a sort of inverse correlation—for a simple reason: When business is expanding and prices rising, the demands upon government for relief are reduced appreciably; and at the same time tax collections are relatively high; thus there is likely to be a budget surplus. Conversely, when business is sluggish, the demands for federal ex-

[2] See statement, pp. 31-32.

penditure increase and tax collections decline; hence deficits expand while prices remain stable or even recede.

Treasury financial operations cannot control the level of prices because the Treasury has no control over the wage and other contracts which govern costs of production. An increase in income taxes in order to reduce consumer purchasing power will not prevent rising prices if wage and other costs are rising. Indeed, a series of annual budget surpluses, sufficient to bring about a very substantial reduction in the public debt, would not affect the level of monetary costs, and hence, the level of prices. To cite a single example, the cash surpluses of the fiscal years 1947 and 1948, aggregating 26.7 billion dollars, were accompanied by sharply rising prices.[3]

3. *Raise the rate of interest at the Federal Reserve.* This method of restraining inflation has long been extolled as an easily administered, almost automatic, control device. Primary reliance is placed on the deterrent effect of a higher cost of borrowed money—which would restrain borrowing, stabilize the money supply, and check the rise in prices. This method has been repeatedly tried and found wanting. In earlier crises it was contended that the remedy was applied belatedly; but such a charge cannot be made with respect to the crisis of the middle 1950's. Our analysis has shown that under modern conditions the rate of interest is an *inconsequential* element of cost—of virtually no moment in business calculations.[4]

4. *Restrict the over-all supply of credit.* This method, recognizing the ineffectiveness of interest rate control,

[3] For details see page 146.
[4] For discussion see Chapter III.

would rely upon an outright, positive restriction of credit.[5] In short the central bank authorities would allow credit to increase only in exact proportion to the increase in the volume of goods. The reasoning is that the maintenance of equilibrium between goods and money would automatically stabilize prices.

This suggestion fails to understand that the volume of funds required for the operation of business depends not only upon the volume of goods produced but also upon the money cost per unit of output—which is governed by the rates of pay for work performed. So long as more money is paid out for a given volume of output, the ratio of money in circulation to goods in circulation increases.

Both the fiscal and the monetary methods of control proceed upon the assumption that one or another (or both) of these agencies of government is in a position to restrict the money supply as compared with the supply of goods. Our analysis has shown that an increase in money supply as compared with goods originates in contracts calling for higher rates of pay for the same output. Since the monetary and fiscal authorities have no voice in wage contracts they cannot affect the ratio of either money costs or money income of prices.

5. *Maintain equality between money savings and capital investment.* One school of thought holds that the primary cause of postwar inflation has been the use of credit for capital expansion and that the remedy lies in bringing about an equilibrium between current money savings and current new investment. Such an equilibrium would require either increasing savings or limiting investments to the existing volume of savings.

[5] See statement, Chapter 1, p. 29.

This proposed remedy fails to appreciate that in the capital goods industries, as well as in the consumer goods industries, prices are based primarily on costs of production; and that wage rates here also are of decisive importance. In any case no means has been suggested whereby investment might be limited to available money savings without affecting the rate of capital expansion.

There is thus no simple control device by which a long-term rise in the general level of prices may be prevented. So long as the amount of money disbursed into the channels of circulation is governed by rates of remuneration for services rendered, the only effective point of control would be at the wage bargaining counter. Concretely, in the United States today a 10 per cent increase of wage rates would involve additional disbursements through wage envelopes of more than 20 billion dollars annually. Such an increase in disbursements would at one and the same time constitute higher costs of production and increased money incomes available for the purchase of goods at the higher prices which would prevail. Unless the ratio of wage rates to productive output is held stable, prices will inevitably rise.

We thus come to the question whether in a private enterprise system inflation can be prevented or circumscribed by the development of a spirit of reasonableness or by enlightened self-interest in connection with wage negotiations. The forces which we are here discussing are an inherent part of the private enterprise system. Involved are elementary *rights*, including the right to engage in business to make profits, to organize and bargain collectively, and to seek the aid of government in protecting or furthering group interests. Involved also are compelling *human interests*; such as the desire of labor groups to obtain higher wages for themselves—which, it is commonly assumed, affluent corporations can readily pay; and the desire of farmers to protect themselves through federal aid from the economic adversities from which they have long suffered. In the light of these rights and interests, it may well be doubted whether occasional preachments by government officials or professional economists urging upon businessmen, labor unions, and farm organizations a policy of voluntary restraint to safeguard general financial stability would have any appreciable effect. Moral suasion is not an effective instrument of control.

While one may thus hold out little hope for stable prices over the years ahead, the essential requirements for continued prosperity and price stability may be succinctly stated. As Brookings Institution studies of *Income and Economic Progress*[6] have shown, the gains accruing from technological advances should be divided three ways: (1) a portion should go to labor in the form of wage increases—as reward and as incentive; (2) a portion should go to business managers and stockholders—as reward and to provide funds for further expansion; and (3) a portion should, by means of lower prices, accrue to the general public—which includes farmers and those engaged in service and professional activities as well as the labor population as a whole.

[6] The analysis and conclusions were originally published in the 1930's in 4 volumes entitled: *America's Capacity to Produce; America's Capacity to Consume; The Formation of Capital;* and *Income and Economic Progress.*

Only as all groups in the body politic share in the gains of technological progress will maximum market possibilities be realized. The best long-term interests of labor will be served by demanding something less than the total gains from technological improvements. The best long-term interests of management will be furthered by passing along to the consuming public, whenever possible, some of the benefits of progress, through the medium of lower-priced products. Such a gradual but progressive reduction in industrial prices would not constitute a depressing factor. Rather, by sustaining and increasing mass purchasing power and relieving the pressure on agriculture, it would be a continuing stimulant to further expansion.

APPENDIXES

APPENDIX A

Appraisal of Traditional Theories

Traditional monetary theory as commonly conceived includes both the value of gold and the quantity of money explanations of price levels. While often regarded as amounting to pretty much the same thing, the conceptions involved are fundamentally different. In the value of gold approach the thought is rooted in a barter concept—goods being directly compared with gold as a standard. In the quantity of money approach, on the other hand, money is looked upon not as a standard of value but as a medium of exchange; and the price level is simply derived by dividing the national money supply by the national goods supply. In this appendix we shall discuss the origins of these theories and appraise their validity.

1. APPRAISAL OF THE VALUE OF GOLD THEORY

The value of gold theory, as noted in the text, grew out of the general principles of value as expounded by early philosophical writers. The central question seemed to be: What determines the value of the *standard* money in which the prices of commodities are expressed? The answer seemed evident: The value of gold, like the value of other commodities, is determined by supply and demand. The value of gold theory was thus simply an application of the general theory of demand and supply; and accordingly it was not deemed necessary to substantiate the theory by factual evidence.[1]

The factors governing the supply of, and the demand for, gold were, however, enumerated. The supply of gold was determined by: (1) the annual production of gold in the world at large; and (2) the accumulated stocks of this durable commodity. On the other side the demand for gold appeared to be of a three-fold character: (1) for use as money; (2) for industrial and artistic purposes; and (3) for hoarding or storing up wealth. Moreover, the intensity of the demand for gold as money was seen to be affected by the availability of supplementary forms of money and credit currency.

Under these circumstances it became impossible for anyone to gauge the changing value of the commodity, gold. Assuming it occurred to the average individual selling goods in the market place that he should compare his product with the commodity, gold, he would be confronted with such difficulties as the following: First, he would not know what source to consult for the facts as to gold production and even if he did he would find that the figures are published more than a year too late to be of current use. Second, he would not know how to merge annual figures with the accumulated gold stock. Third, he would not know whether it is world supply that is important or merely the supply of the nation in which he lives. Fourth, he would have no

[1] This position was expressly stated by Francis A. Walker as follows: "Prices being nothing more or less than values expressed in terms of money . . . it is not for those who hold this theory to prove their use. It rests upon the critics . . . to show some reason why a principle, admitted to be otherwise of universal application, should be suspected of failing at this point." *Quarterly Journal of Economics,* Vol. 9, pp. 372-79 (1895).

ready way of determining the magnitude of available substitutes for gold as a medium of exchange.

How do the adherents of the value of gold theory think such difficulties are surmounted? As a rule they have not been squarely faced. However, some writers have contended that the value of gold is determined by *marginal* buyers of gold—those who buy it for industrial uses or for hoarding purposes. Keynes, for example, explained the process as follows:

> A sufficient proportion of the gold supply has been able to find its way, without any flooding of the market, into the arts or into the hoards of Asia for its marginal value to be governed by a steady psychological estimation of the metal in relation to other things. This is what is meant by saying that gold has "intrinsic value."[2]

It will be seen that Keynes is here applying the marginal utility method of analysis to the determination of the relative values of gold and other commodities. Just as people make a psychological comparison of a unit of wheat with a unit of cloth, they also compare the marginal value of the standard, gold, with commodities in general.

But when a businessman wishes to use gold for industrial or artistic purposes, he does not need to make any comparison of the value of gold with commodities in general. He finds the price of gold to be so much an ounce, this price having been set by monetary legislation: In the United States the price was $20.67 from 1837 to 1935, when it was raised to $35.00. Thus the only comparison the businessman needs to make is between the fixed price of gold and the market prices of acceptable substitute materials. There is obviously no

[2] John Maynard Keynes, *Monetary Reform* (1924), p. 180.

reason why he should estimate the value of gold as compared with wheat or cotton.

Oriental hoarders have, to be sure, considered gold a good medium by which to save for the future. But the function of gold here is that of a *store* of value rather than a *standard* of value. The price which hoarders pay for gold is fixed by monetary legislation; and such comparisons as they may make would be only with other metals, or jewels, which might serve the same purpose.[3]

This conception—that the *non*-monetary demand for gold determines the exchange value of gold as money, and hence the general price level—differs fundamentally, it will be noted, from the gold demand and supply theory discussed in preceding paragraphs. Moreover, it is wholly at variance with the quantity theory

[3] Mention should here be made of the fact that there are markets where gold is bought and sold. The most important of these—the London gold market—is not a true market. That is, the basic price is set by monetary legislation and prices can fluctuate only between the gold export and gold import points. However, such a market operates only so long as some major country is on a full gold standard basis, standing ready at all times to buy or sell unlimited quantities of gold at the official price.

Since the early 1930's, however, the gold standard has been restricted in the scope of its operations. For example, while the United States has bought gold freely, this country has sold gold only to selected buyers, namely, central banks. Under these circumstances, individuals desiring gold must seek it elsewhere and pay whatever price prevails in unrestricted markets. There have been in fact a substantial number of free gold markets, notably in France, Switzerland, Portugal, Tangier, Beirut, and Macao, where gold may be bought and sold as a commodity at any price. In times of grave fear as to economic and financial stability, buyers have in fact been willing to pay far more than the official price of $35.00 an ounce. After World War II the price of gold bars in free markets rose at times above $50.00 an ounce; but with the return of greater international stability, it gradually fell to the level set by the official price of gold in the United States—to which, under International Monetary Fund agreements, the currencies of member countries are tied.

conception that the only gold that affects prices is that which, as money, is directly exchanged for commodities.

In sum, the idea that the price level is determined by individual comparisons of units of gold with units of commodities is wholly unrealistic in a complex economic system.

II. THE QUANTITY THEORY EXAMINED

The first writers to formulate the quantity theory approach in precise terms were apparently the Italians, Montanari and Davanzati. As Montanari put it: "All commodities in commerce between men, taken together, are worth as much as the gold, silver, and copper coined and in circulation."

The French philosopher, Montesquieu, more explicitly cast the matter in strict arithmetical terms:

> If one compares the mass of gold and silver in the whole world with the total of existing commodities, it is clear that each individual commodity may be compared with a certain portion of the entire mass of gold and silver. As the total of the one is to the total of the other, so part of the one will be to part of the other. . . . But since neither all property, nor all the metals or money tokens are being offered in exchange at any one time, *prices are fixed by the ratio between the total of things and of tokens actually brought to market.* However, since goods which are not on the market to-day may be there tomorrow, and the tokens which are not offered to-day may be tomorrow, prices ultimately depend on the proportion of the total of goods to the total of tokens. . . .
>
> If, since the discovery of the Indies, gold and silver in Europe have increased in the ratio of one to twenty, prices of commodities must have risen in the ratio of one to twenty. But if, on the other hand, the amount of commodities has increased in the ratio of one to two, it must be that prices have on the one side risen in the ratio of one to twenty, and

that, on the other, they have fallen in the ratio of one to two, so that they actually stand, in consequence, at the ratio of only one to ten.[4]

The English philosopher, John Locke, also endorsed the quantity theory approach, but with a somewhat divergent analysis. In his view the value of money arises solely out of its usefulness as a medium of exchange. Hence it is determined by the quantity of all the money in the world in proportion to all the trade. Accordingly, changes in the quantity of money would cause proportional changes in its value and hence in the prices of commodities. Locke held that since there is now ten times as much silver in the world as before the discovery of the West Indies, it will now exchange for "nine tenths less of any commodity."[5]

John Stuart Mill, whose great synthesis of economic thought was published in 1848, was long regarded as having rounded out the discussion of the theory of the general price level. Hence his views require summarization here.

At the beginning of his analysis of money, Mill says the problem is to determine what governs the exchange value of money itself. "Money is a commodity, and its value is determined like that of other commodities, temporarily by demand and supply, permanently and on the average by its cost of production."[6] Thus if the cost

[4] Baron de Montesquieu, *Esprit des Lois* (1873), pp. 58-60 (originally published in Geneva, Switzerland, 1748).

[5] John Locke, "Some Considerations of the Consequences of the Lowering of Interest and Raising the Value of Money (1691), from Arthur Eli Monroe, *Monetary Theory Before Adam Smith* (1923), p. 112.

[6] John Stuart Mill, *Principles of Political Economy* (1864), N. Y. ed., Vol. 2, p. 24.

of production of gold should fall and the supply be increased its value would decline and the prices of commodities would, other things equal, rise proportionally. He was here a pure *value of gold* theorist. But elsewhere he says, "We are comparing goods of all sorts on one side, with money on the other side, as things to be exchanged against each other."[7] He adds that only such portion of the money as is actually exchanged against goods in the market affects prices. "Money hoarded does not act on prices. Money kept in reserve by individuals to meet contingencies which do not occur, does not act on prices. The money in the coffers of the bank . . . does not act on prices until drawn out, nor even then unless drawn out to be expended in commodities."[8] Here he appears to be a *quantity of money* theorist, the emphasis being on money as a medium of exchange, rather than as a standard, or measure, of value.

Credit, or deposit, currency was also seen as a factor affecting the price level. At the time Mill was writing, credit had come to play an important role in business operations; and Mill was one of the first to take account of this phenomenon. In his view credit constituted an increase in purchasing power and it was thus "exactly on a par" with money in the effect upon prices.[9]

Mathematical Formulas

The next important step in the evolution of the quantity theory of money was contributed by professional mathematicians a century later than most of the writings to which reference has been made above. We

[7] *The same,* p. 28.
[8] *The same,* p. 34.
[9] *The same,* p. 84.

refer to the analysis by Simon Newcomb in 1885 and by Irving Fisher 25 years later. In common with numerous other mathematicians and natural scientists, before and after their time, Newcomb and Fisher were challenged by the phenomena of economic life and believed that by the application of rigorous scientific method it would be possible to arrive at an irrefutable body of principles or laws. In Newcomb's words: "Much of the confusion and difficulty which surround the subject arise from want of insight into the true significance and use of scientific propositions."

SIMON NEWCOMB'S FORMULATION

The publication of *The Principles of Political Economy* by Simon Newcomb, a distinguished American mathematician and astronomer, was regarded as a milestone in the development of the theory of money and prices. His analysis of the factors governing the level of prices may be summarized as follows:

1. There is a certain definite mass of money, notes, and credit in circulation, which we call the volume of currency—represented by the symbol V.
2. Each dollar of V circulates with greater or less rapidity —represented by the symbol R, which is the average number of times each dollar changes hands in the course of a year.
3. The aggregate physical volume of goods and services exchanged in a year is represented by the symbol K.
4. The trend of prices is represented by the symbol P. Accordingly, $K \times P$ equals total money value of all exchange transactions.
5. From the foregoing we derive the equation V (quantity of money) $\times$ R (rapidity of circulation) $=$ K (volume of business) $\times$ P(prices). $V \times R = K \times P$.[10]

[10] Book 4, pp. 338-47.

The quantities are, of course, recognized as being subject to change. The volume of currency may be affected by such factors as exports and imports of specie and changes in the volume of credit operations. The rapidity of circulation may be affected by the psychology of individuals and businessmen. K may change because of increased output.

Fluctuations in prices are regarded merely as a reflection of variations in the ratios of the other elements in the exchange equation. Assuming no change in K, or R, an increase in V would bring a proportional increase in P. That is, if the volume of money increased 50 per cent the price level would increase 50 per cent. With added money in hand everybody would proceed to purchase additional necessaries of life from the dealers; and the result of this increase in demand would be a rise in prices.

IRVING FISHER'S EQUATION OF EXCHANGE

Trained as a mathematician, Fisher early turned to the field of economics. In 1913 he published his treatise entitled *The Purchasing Power of Money*, which was inscribed to the memory of Simon Newcomb. This volume, which elaborated on Newcomb's simple equation of exchange, was widely regarded at the time as a definitive analysis of the factors controlling the general level of prices. The equation reads:

$$\frac{\text{M(money)} \times \text{V(velocity)} + \text{M}'\text{(credit)} \times \text{V}'\text{(velocity)}}{\text{T (volume of trade)}} = \text{P(prices)}$$

Fisher reasoned that "because this equation must be fulfilled . . . prices must, as a whole, vary proportionally with the quantity of money and with its velocity of circulation, and inversely with the quantities of goods exchanged."[11] Thus if the quantity of money should double, the price level, like the quantity of money, would have to double. Fisher explains that "this doubling may be accomplished by an even or uneven rise in prices. . . . If the prices rise unevenly, the doubling must evidently be brought about by compensation; if some prices rise by less than double, others must rise by enough more than double to exactly compensate."[12] In a reverse way, "a doubling in the quantities of goods exchanged . . . would halve the height of the price level, *provided* the quantity of money and its velocity of circulation remain the same."[13]

Credit currency serves equally with money to affect the equation of exchange. If the supply of credit is increased as a result of an expansion of bank loans, prices will rise proportionally—assuming, of course, the other factors in the equation remain unchanged. Similarly, changes in the velocity of circulation, of either money or credit, would bring proportional changes in prices. Velocity is defined as "the quotient obtained by dividing the total money payments for goods in the course of a year by the average amount of money in circulation by which those payments are effected."[14]

The gold supply remains, however, the factor of primary significance in the equation of exchange. In the first place, gold is (was at the time Fisher wrote) the base of the monetary system—other forms of money

[11] Irving Fisher, *The Purchasing Power of Money* (1913), p. 18.
[12] *The same*, p. 19.
[13] *The same*, p. 20.
[14] *The same*, p. 17.

being convertible into gold. The expansibility of subsidiary money is limited by the necessity of maintaining a safe relation to the underlying gold currency; the amount of credit currency is governed by bank reserve requirements; and velocity, rooted in habits, changes but slowly.[15]

Fisher illustrates the equation of exchange by means of scale pans—"a mechanical balance in equilibrium, the two sides of which symbolize respectively the money side and the goods side of the equation of exchange." At the left is placed a purse representing money in circulation. The distance from the fulcrum at which the purse is hung represents the efficiency of this money or its velocity of circulation. On the right side are three weights symbolizing a loaf of bread, a coal scuttle, and a roll of cloth.

> The distance of each from the fulcrum represents its price. . . . We all know that . . . an increase in the weights or arms on one side requires, in order to preserve equilibrium, a proportional increase in the weights or arms on the other side. . . . In general, a change in one of the four sets or magnitudes must be accompanied by such a change or changes in one or more of the other three as shall maintain equilibrium.[16]

When mathematicians like Simon Newcomb and Irving Fisher invaded the field of economics they built simply upon the framework of thought as they found it in the economic textbooks then current. They took for

[15] While Fisher's primary analysis relates to long-run, "normal," conditions, he recognized that there are occasional short-term variations growing out of business booms and depressions; but in his view these are merely *transitional* movements which do not affect the long-term basic relationship between money and prices. (*The same*, p. 17.)

[16] *The same*, pp. 22-23.

granted the validity of the underlying assumptions that the volume of goods and the volume of money are quite independent of one another. They had little knowledge of business organization or of the complex processes by which money is distributed to those who participate in the productive process. Their analysis began with an assumed volume of currency already in circulation and with an assumed volume of goods ready to be exchanged. The respective quantities of goods on the one side and money on the other were regarded as independent variables.

The use of a mathematical equation, and a mechanical balance in equilibrium, served to cement or crystallize the conception of independent variables. A packet of goods on the one side of the balance and a purse on the other: if more units are placed on the goods side of the scales, prices will fall; if more coins are put into the purse, prices will rise. There was thus erected, in effect, a stonewall barrier between the production of goods and the use of money. This is illustrated in Fisher's summarization of long-term trends:

> The history of prices has in substance been the history of a race between the increase in media of exchange . . . and the increase in trade. . . . Sometimes the circulating media shot ahead of trade and then prices rose. . . . Sometimes, on the other hand, circulating media lagged behind trade and then prices fell.[17]

1. *The Logic of Fisher's Analysis*

In the concluding section of Irving Fisher's analysis, he makes the following sweeping statement: "At the close of our study, as at the beginning, stands forth the

[17] *The same,* pp. 246-47.

equation of exchange as the great *determinant* of the purchasing power of money."[18] He asserts that "the price level is normally the one absolutely passive element in the equation of exchange"—that "prices are the effect and not the cause of the currency."[19] By implication, money is the cause of price changes. Indeed, at places he states explicitly that price changes are *caused* by the increase in money supply. For example, he says the sharp rise in prices from 1896 to 1909 has been "*in spite of* a doubling in the volume of trade and *because of* (1) a doubling of money, (2) a tripling of deposits, and (3) and (4) slight increases in the *velocities*."[20]

But at another place he qualifies as follows:

> While the equation of exchange, of itself, asserts no causal relations between quantity of money and price level . . . yet when we take into account conditions known quite apart from that equation, viz., that a change in M produces a proportional change in M′, and no changes in V, V′ [or the quantity of goods], there is no possible escape from the conclusion that a change in quantity of money (M) must normally cause a proportional change in the price level.[21]

The tell-tale phrase in this statement is "when we take into account conditions known *quite apart* (italics mine) from that equation." These conditions are that the volume of credit bears a virtually fixed ratio to the volume of money, that the velocities of money and credit are practically stable, and that the volume of goods is in no way related to changes in the money supply. In reality these so-called conditions are only

[18] *The same,* p. 150. (Italics are mine.)
[19] *The same,* pp. 172-74.
[20] *The same,* p. 307. (Italics mine.)
[21] *The same,* pp. 156-57.

assumptions; and they are the very assumptions on which the validity of the whole analysis depends. Since the conclusion as to causal relationship rests on the validity of assumptions which are unrelated to the equation of exchange, it follows that the equation of itself *determines* nothing. In fact the equation merely reflects the truism, that the quantity of goods times the prices at which they are sold equals the total number of dollars employed in exchanging them.

In replying to critics who had called Newcomb's equation a mere truism, Fisher insisted that:

> The greatest generalizations of physical science, such as that forces are proportional to mass and acceleration, are truisms, but, when duly supplemented by specific data, these truisms are the most fruitful sources of useful mechanical knowledge. To throw away contemptuously the equation of exchange because it is so obviously true is to neglect the chance to formulate for economic science some of the most important and exact laws of which it is capable.[22]

Again it is to be noted that the generalized truism was not derived entirely from deductive reasoning. It also depended on *supplemental* specific data—drawn presumably from observed phenomena. One may, therefore, again point out that the significance of the truism depends upon the validity of the supplemental data; and that the use of an equation is only one way of stating a fact or principle.

That Fisher's preoccupation with the *equation* served to becloud his reasoning is evidenced by the following: "To those who have faith in the *a priori* proof of the

[22] *The same,* p. 157.

equation of exchange the real significance of the remarkable agreement in our statistical results should be understood as a confirmation, not of the equation by the figures, but of the figures by the equation."[23] Here he forgets that the supplemental data essential to the proof are not derived from the equation or deduced by *a priori* methods.

The purely mechanical character of Fisher's thinking may be illustrated by his differentiation between an average of *individual* prices and a *general level* of prices. In his view an expansion of the over-all supply of money is a sort of swelling tide which automatically bears aloft the prices of commodities in general. This *price level,* he says, must be studied independently of individual prices. While the prices of individual commodities in the market places may be determined by supply and demand, the general level of prices is determined otherwise. "We cannot explain the level of the sea by the height of its individual waves; rather we must explain in part the position of these waves by the general level of the sea."[24]

As thus conceived the price level varies independently of changes in the average height of individual prices. Changes in individual prices, says Fisher, cannot raise or lower the level.

> The increased money expended for this commodity will be taken from other purchases. In other words the waves in the sea of prices have troughs. This can be seen from the equation of exchange. . . . Any increase in one of its many terms, due to an increase of any individual price, must occur at the expense of the remaining terms. . . . The reac-

[23] *The same.*
[24] *The same,* p. 177.

tionary effect of the price of one commodity on the prices of other commodities must never be lost sight of. . . .[25]

By *reactionary effects* Fisher does not have in mind a *structure* of prices subject to interacting influences. He simply means that if some prices rise, others must of necessity fall: every *plus* must be offset by a *minus.*

Notwithstanding his conception that the price level is something very distinct from an average of individual prices, Fisher used individual price quotations, as confirmation of his theory.

In short, Fisher is concerned with the truth of arithmetic in a static mold rather than with the price-changing process in a dynamic business world. He comes back always to the maintenance of the equation: Since M′ and the Vs are assumed to be virtually inflexible, a rise in the prices of certain goods must perforce be offset by proportional declines in other prices—unless the supply of gold is increasing.

2. *Broadened Concepts of Trade and Prices*

In the mathematical formulations which we have been considering, only final consumer goods appear in the picture—a loaf of bread, a roll of cloth, and a scuttle of coal. There are no factories, nor farms, nor machinery, nor raw materials, nor semi-finished products. It is worthy of note, also, that the money supply is symbolized by a purse of the kind a housewife carries to market. All of this was strictly in accordance with the assumption of the classical textbooks that money enters into economic activity only in facilitating the exchange of final consumer goods.

[25] *The same,* pp. 178-79.

Many writers eventually came to regard the original concept of *trade,* as relating only to commodities, and consumer goods at that, as too restricted. That is, it was eventually recognized that money is also used in many other ways. Indeed, to get all monetary operations into the equation, the concept of trade had to be broadened to mean financial *transactions.* This led to the inclusion of operations in real estate and securities, payments for services in the form of salaries, wages, and professional fees, and also remittances for rents, interest, and dividends.[26]

Thus extended the T of the equation is no longer units of goods merely; it is also services rendered by labor, capital, land, and management. Hence to determine the aggregate number of units in T it would be necessary to add to commodities such disparate items as laborers, managers, professional people, plant and equipment, apartment buildings, and farm acreage. [It will be apparent that one cannot achieve the essential commensurability by adding, for example, wages (rather than laborers) to commodities because wages are on the other side of the equation—a part of P.]

The equation of exchange in its original form was concerned, as we have noted, only with the prices of consumer goods. Logically, then, the supply of consumer goods should have been compared only with that portion of the total money supply which is spent for consumer goods; but in fact the money side of the equation included the entire supply of gold and other forms of money. When, in due course, the goods concept was

[26] At one place Fisher made reference to such operations as involving the use of money.

broadened to cover all transactions involving the use of money, there was achieved—in principle—a balance sheet which included everything. But, as a practical matter, since commodities, land, plant and equipment, labor, securities, government services, etc. cannot be added together, their inclusion in the equation along with commodities leads to an intellectual *cul de sac.*

In this broadened conception the P of the equation (the price level) covers not only the prices of commodities but also the rates of remuneration accruing to the various factors engaged in production. It is reasoned that wages, interest, and rents are in effect prices—paid, respectively, for the services of labor, land, and capital. In the words of Professor Ellis, "Incomes are also prices, and all prices appear simultaneously from solving the equation."[27] According to this line of reasoning, what one obtains from "solving the equation" is a combined price index consisting of commodity prices, wages, rents, interest and profits. The thought evidently is that the over-all supply of money *determines* not only the level of commodity prices but also the levels of money incomes.

This conception is a striking illustration of the way in which concentration on a mathematical formula has circumscribed thought and obscured the operation of the price system. If all prices, including wages, interest, etc., were determined *simultaneously*—at the moment "the equation is solved" by dividing total money supply by total transactions—there could be no divergence between the movements of wages, interest, and rental rates, and no interaction between commodity prices and

[27] Howard Ellis, *German Monetary Theory, 1905-33* (1934), p. 184.

wage rates, or, for that matter, between the rate of interest and the volume of borrowing operations. Everywhere else in economic analysis it is recognized that the magnitude of each distributive share is determined by independent factors pertaining to supply and demand or to relative bargaining power. While the remuneration accruing to the factors engaged in production finds reflection in the over-all monetary transactions of the nation, the respective shares of each producing group are determined by other than monetary factors.[28]

3. *The Concept of Velocity*

A central feature of the quantity theory is the concept of velocity of circulation, represented by V and V′ in the equation of exchange. An increase in velocity, like an increase in the quantity of money, will, it is contended, raise prices proportionally; and *vice versa*. We shall show in the succeeding pages that the conception is without validity—that velocity has no bearing on the level of prices. But first it is necessary to explain precisely what is meant by the term.

Professor Fisher employed the term in two different, and contradictory, ways. First, he defined the rate of turnover of money, as had Newcomb, in terms of its efficiency in use. "It is the quotient obtained by dividing the total money payments for goods in the course of a year by the average amount of money in circulation."[29]

In Fisher's second conception, velocity is said to be

[28] This conception that the level of wage rates as well as of commodity prices are automatically affected by changes in the quantity of money is also embedded in the theory of international specie movements and the mechanism of price and trade readjustments. See p. 281.

[29] For statements of Newcomb and Fisher, see pp. 192 and 193.

determined by the amount of money that is more or less continuously withheld from expenditure. He noted that it is necessary for individuals to maintain some pocket cash for purposes of convenience and to meet emergencies; for traders and dealers of all kinds to keep substantial sums in the till—to make change and to meet "petty cash" needs; and for producing corporations to keep reserves of cash in order to meet contingencies and fluctuating business requirements. It was observed that a spendthrift, always short of funds, has a high velocity, while a thrifty person, always in cash, has a slow velocity. The habit of charging at the stores tends to increase velocity because the man who has things charged does not keep as much money on hand as would otherwise be necessary. Similarly, the greater the regularity of income receipts, the smaller the sums which must be kept on hand to bridge the gap. Since in Fisher's view these factors are deeply rooted in habits, customs, and practical necessities, the velocity of circulation seldom changes appreciably.

In reality such permanent withholdings of cash merely constitute a reduction in the quantity of money currently being offered in exchange for goods. In effect such cash is *out* of circulation; it is not in the sum totals which make up the money side of the equation of exchange. Consequently, it is not related to the rate of turnover of the money that *is* in active circulation, and hence affords no support for Fisher's concept of velocity as a *constant*. As Mill pointed out: "Only such portion of the money as is actually exchanged against goods in the market affects prices."[30] Reserves of ready cash, held

[30] See p. 191 above.

for convenience and as a precaution against emergency, do not affect the number of times that the money which *is* spent changes hands in a year.

Is Rate of Money Turnover a Price Factor?

The first conception of velocity, defined as the rate of turnover of the active circulation, may now be considered on its merits. First, it is to be noted that in its origin the rate of turnover idea was in no way related to the level of prices. It first appeared in economic literature in connection with discussions of the mercantilist philosophy that national policy should be directed to the accumulation of ever-increasing quantities of the precious metals. Sir William Petty and John Locke—the first writers to use the velocity concept—were not interested in the price level but were considering the question "How much money does a country need?" Petty noted that the amount required in the course of a year depended in no small degree upon the "frequency of payments." In Locke's words, the amount of money needed is not merely a matter of its quantity but also of the "quickness of its circulation." The more rapid the turnover of money, or the greater its efficiency, the less would obviously be the total required to meet a nation's annual monetary requirements. Later writers, following this pattern of measuring turnover in terms of a year's time, jumped to the conclusion that the use of the money supply over and over, say ten times in a year, has the same effect upon prices as would a ten-fold increase in the money supply.

However, the theory requires that the money be exchanged many times for the *same* goods. It is true that the existing money supply *is* used several times in the course of a year; but it is exchanged several times, not for the same goods, but for successive installments of new goods. Those who espoused the velocity conception failed to note this crucial fact. John Stuart Mill recognized the point and was troubled by it; for he wrote that the difficulty with the velocity conception—which he held to be confusing rather than enlightening—arises from the use of the time interval.[31] Mill did not, however, carry his thought to its logical conclusion.

Newcomb appeared at one place to recognize that velocity, defined as the number of times money changes hands in the course of a year, has no effect on prices. He said, "If we divide the year by R—Rate of Money Turnover—we shall have the average length of time that a dollar remains in one man's hands. If we take this period instead of one year as our unit of time we shall have $R = 1$."[32] Unfortunately, Newcomb apparently did not see the implications of his statement.

Adherence to the *annual* time interval conception appears the more surprising in view of the classical analysis of the way in which market prices are determined. The supply and demand schedules employed to illustrate the point at which, under varying assumptions as to supply and demand, the price will be set, are always cast in momentary terms. As a result of the higgling process, it is held that the price settles at a point which clears the market of goods.

Since, in fact, the production and the marketing of

[31] John Stuart Mill, *Principles of Political Economy*, Vol. 2 (1864), pp. 31-33.

[32] Simon Newcomb, *The Principles of Political Economy* (1885), pp. 346-47.

goods is a continuous process, comparisons between money supply and goods supply—if they are to be made—should be in the shortest practical unit of time. Considered on a daily basis, the flow of money to the markets would meet the flow of goods some 300 times in a year, resulting in 300 separate sets of prices. Money would be spent each successive time for a new supply of goods; and in each new time interval there would be a new price determination. In short, the velocity concept disappears when the money side of the equation and the goods side are considered in the time interval in which the price is actually set.

We may now return to the question whether in any given time period the money supply available to consumers is in fact spent for the *same goods* more than once. Common observation indicates that nearly all *consumer goods* pass out of the markets forever after being purchased once. That is, final consumers *consume* them; the merest fraction is ever resold. The one important exception is automobiles; and here there is usually a time lag of several years. *Capital* goods immediately become embedded in brick and mortar or permanently installed as operating equipment; and resales are seldom involved.

There are, to be sure, a few instances in which it may be said that the same identical commodity is bought many times within the course of a year. Such is the case, for example, in occasional real estate booms, when the ownership of a given plot, lot, or section may be rapidly transferred from speculator to speculator. Similarly, in a booming stock market, ownership certificates may change hands almost from day to day. Speculation also occurs in organized commodity markets. But these were not the kind of transactions with which the exponents of the velocity conception were concerned.

In summary, since few commodities re-enter the markets after they are purchased by consumers, the money supply as a whole cannot be used several times over in purchasing the same goods. The money laid out by final consumers endures, to be sure, and is shortly again disbursed as wages, interest, etc. and thus again becomes available for purchase of a continuing flow of consumer goods. But the money is spent each successive time for a new supply of goods, and in each new time interval there is a new price determination. Thus the number of times money is turned over in a year cannot be an independent factor affecting prices in retail markets.

The situation is, of course, somewhat different when goods are still in the channels of production and distribution. When goods are sold by a manufacturer to a dealer they are not yet out of the market. They may possibly exchange hands several times before they pass into the hands of final consumers. But even here the number of times money changes hands and the number of times goods change hands are not independent of each other.

It may be noted here that the velocity concept is ignored in current discussions of "disposable national income." The aggregate income available for expenditure by the public is simply the sum total of wages, interest, rents, and dividends, minus withholdings. Business enterprisers gauge their sales possibilities from month to month and over the year as a whole by the expected levels of purchasing power; and in such calculations it is not assumed that anyone can spend his current income more than once. Insofar as a velocity concept enters the national income picture, it pertains to the possibility of a slackening or acceleration of business activity and hence in the prospective aggregate flow of disposable income.

Money Velocity and Goods Velocity

Still another method may be employed to show the basic fallacy in the velocity conception. In Fisher's arithmetical calculus, it will be recalled, velocity is regarded as an independent variable unrelated to the goods side of the equation. Implicit in this assumption is the notion that the money supply revolves all by itself, so to speak, without being articulated in any way with business operations.

The validity of this independent variable idea has been attacked by various foreign writers,[33] by the present writer in class lectures at the University of Chicago prior to 1921, and by Herbert J. Davenport, the well-known American economic theorist. Davenport states the case as follows:

> To assume that one sort of velocity or turnover [money] can change without an equal change in the other [goods] is to misconceive the facts. . . . These two sorts of changes are parallel, equal, and offsetting. . . . The media can arrive at more turnovers per period only if the goods take on a similarly accelerated velocity in exchange against the media.[34]

That is, changes in money velocity are offset or negated by corresponding changes in goods velocity. In Daven-

[33] For extensive citations from foreign writers holding this point of view, see Arthur W. Marget's *Journal of Political Economy* (June, 1932), Vol. 40. See also, Howard S. Ellis, *German Monetary Theory, 1905-33* (1934), Chaps. 8-11.

[34] "Velocities, Turnovers and Prices," *American Economic Review* (1930), Vol. 20, pp. 9-13.

port's view, the two rates of velocity, that is of money and goods, always change equally and in the same direction.

Arthur W. Marget, defender of "received doctrine," has undertaken to refute Davenport's argument.[35] Marget recognizes the necessity of equal changes on both sides of the equation, saying "Of course it is true, that, with every spending of money there is a 'spending' of goods, and vice versa. . . ." But he adds, "This does not make it necessary that the rates at which the stocks of money and goods, respectively, are being spent, should be mathematically equal."[36] This implies merely that Davenport is not 100 per cent correct.

However, Marget undertakes to prove that velocity remains an independent factor affecting prices. He argues that the "transactions" side may be kept identical with the money side by a *combination* of increasing goods turnover and an increasing quantity of goods—*newly produced.* Thus, the increased velocity of circulation need not be fully matched by an increased velocity of goods turnover. Hence the more rapid spending of money for the already existing supply of goods would still serve to bid up prices.

This is an interesting logical exercise; but it should be noted that if Marget had carried it to its ultimate possibilities he would have discovered that all of the goods to be exchanged might equally well (as a matter of logic) be assumed to be *newly produced*—in which case the money side would be completely matched by new goods. With no opportunity for velocity to operate

[35] *Journal of Political Economy* (June, 1932), Vol. 40, pp. 289-313.

[36] *The same,* p. 300.

against already existing goods, it would automatically disappear as a price-making factor. The dilemma into which Marget gets himself may be stated as follows: If he admits that *all* of the money is exchanged against already existing goods, he is all the way with Davenport; money velocity as a price-making factor disappears. On the other hand, if he goes the route in the other direction and assumes that the money is exchanged wholly for new goods, velocity again disappears as a price factor.

In any case this line of reasoning does not squarely meet the basic issue. The velocity concept which Marget defends has always been based on the assumption that money is spent many times for an existing volume of goods—that there is no direct connection between spending money more frequently and more frequent sales of goods: The underlying assumption is that the goods side and the money side are independent variables. In contrast, the other analysis regards money turnover and goods turnover as *inter*dependent—that an increase in the velocity of money is inextricably associated with an increasing rate of turnover of goods.

Marget in a long and tortuous analysis finally faces this issue and attempts to meet it. He argues that in a period when the velocity of money is increasing, the transfers are made against goods in every case, but they are being made against *smaller units* of those goods. That is to say, a dollar instead of buying one bushel of wheat eventually buys only three pecks. This conclusion is, of course, based on the assumption that the increase in money velocity has in fact raised prices—which is the point to be proved. As Davenport observes, "The thesis to be established turns out to be assumed to start with, and to constitute the entire movement of thought by which it is arrived at."[37]

To this charge Marget replies that "There is no reason for assuming that changes in the velocity of circulation of money will necessarily be counteracted by a *precisely equivalent* change in the velocity of circulation of goods. . . . Why is our assumption more arbitrary than that of Davenport who assumes the contrary?"[38] In this statement Marget merely returns to the position already noted, namely, that the increased rate of spending *may* possibly go in part for existing goods and in part for newly produced goods. To this the former rebuttal still stands.

In short, those who developed the velocity idea noted that the money supply has a rate of turnover, but commonly failed to note that the goods supply also has a rate of turnover. However, later writers, preoccupied with short-term "cyclical" fluctuations, have at times clearly recognized that trade fluctuations and money flows are associated phenomena. When business conditions are favorable, trade is said to be active and the velocity of circulation is said to be high; while in periods of dull business, the rate of spending and the rate of business activity both decline. Yet, velocity of money circulation is still commonly referred to as a factor operating independently to affect the level of prices.

III. VARIANTS OF THE QUANTITY THEORY

Two principal variants of the Newcomb-Fisher analysis require mention at this place. Since neither is now

[37] *The same,* p. 305.

[38] *The same,* pp. 305-06. (Italics mine.)

regarded as significant, only a brief statement is necessary with respect to each.

1. The Cambridge Equation of Exchange

This equation was developed in the 1920's by economists of Cambridge University. Derived from Alfred Marshall's reasoning, it has been expounded in somewhat varying forms by several writers, notably Pigou and Robertson. In brief, these writers simply reverse the order of reasoning followed in the Fisher equation. Instead of focusing on changes in the prices of commodities as expressed in terms of money, they focus on changes in the price of money as expressed in terms of commodities. The Cambridge formula is thus in essence merely the reciprocal of the Fisher formula.

The conclusion reached is the same as under the Fisher equation, namely, that prices vary directly with the quantity of money. The only apparent difference lies in the fact that the analysis includes a concept of real income (in terms of goods) which is used instead of total transactions. While a new term is employed, this *real* income does not differ from the goods of the Fisher equation.

In the view of its advocates, the new formula and the attending analysis is more realistic. But since the practical problem in which people are interested is why commodity prices rise or fall rather than the abstract question why the value of money, in terms of commodities, rises or falls, the Cambridge equation would doubtless appear to the average person as both less realistic and more difficult to grasp.

2. The Cash Balance Approach

This approach, developed in the 1920's by R. G. Hawtrey of Great Britain, has had considerable vogue. It is difficult to explain because of the terminology employed and also a lack of clarity with respect to some of the concepts involved. Keynes at one juncture found the approach engaging but eventually abandoned it as confusing.[39]

Hawtrey posed as a primary question: How do members of the community settle what margin of purchasing power they shall keep, either in the form of cash or in the form of credit? Attention is called to the well-known reasons for maintaining reserves of purchasing power. First, since an individual's income and expenditures seldom keep pace exactly, it is necessary for some money to be kept in the pocket or in the strong box to bridge the gap. Second, the prudent man keeps a supply of money on hand to meet unforseen emergencies. Third, it is inconvenient to invest savings in driblets; therefore one accumulates a considerable sum before making an investment. Similarly, business organizations must keep on hand money or available bank deposits for a variety of purposes: They must have till money; they must have funds with which to meet emergencies or to take advantage of special opportunities; and they must have substantial bank balances as a basis for credit. The difference between the current income of individuals and business enterprises and their current outlays is designated the community's "unspent margin."

The analysis, thus far, is virtually identical with that of earlier writers who discussed the factors affecting

[39] See *Treatise on Money* (1930), Vol. 1, pp. 229-33.

velocity of circulation. However, in their view such reserves were regarded as significant only as they affect the rate of turnover of the whole money supply—or its efficiency in use. Such habitual reserves were regarded as relatively stable in amount.

But Hawtrey goes on to contend that these reserves of cash—the *unspent margin*—are in reality equal to the total national money supply. As he puts it:

> Changes in the consumers' income and the consumers' outlay are inseparably bound up with another factor, that is, the total stock of the means of payment in the hands of the community. This I call the "unspent margin." It is the total of money and bank credit in the hands of everyone who receives and pays money, whether individuals, businesses, public bodies or any others; it is so much of their money receipts as they have at any time retained unspent. But it is also the aggregate of the money and bank deposits in the community, and is found by adding together the deposits shown in the bankers' books and the money issued into circulation and not withdrawn.[40]

In the light of this language it is not surprising that students should not agree as to the precise meaning or implications of the cash balance approach. The author certainly does not make it clear just how the cash balances, that is the *unspent* margin, come to equal the *total* money supply. He apparently reaches this position by simply shifting his focus—from the normal cash balances which individuals and business enterprises find it necessary to keep on hand to the total cash balances—in banks and elsewhere—at a given moment of time. It is true, of course, that if one were to examine the financial statements of the entire bank-

[40] R. G. Hawtrey, *The Gold Standard in Theory and Practice* (1933), pp. 11-12.

ing system, say on a Monday morning, he would find reflected there the aggregate deposits of the entire population; and if to these be added the cash held in pockets, strong boxes, business tills, etc., we have the entire money supply of the nation. Moreover, it might be said that as of the instant all of this money supply is *unspent*. But this is a static fact only and as such throws no light on the operation of the economic system. The unspent margin, or withdrawn or hoarded portion of the money supply, cannot be the same thing as the total money supply.

The relation of the "unspent margin" to commodity prices is explained as follows:

> Let the unit of value be settled, and the numerical measure of the unspent margin is determined. Conversely, if the number of units of value in the unspent margin is settled, the unit of value is thereby determined, and the determination of the unit of value determines all the other quantities, such as the prices of commodities and services, which are measured by it. Thus we see that, given all the economic conditions, the prices of commodities are directly proportional to the number of units of value contained in the unspent margin of purchasing power.[41]

It is difficult to be sure just what this statement means. My interpretation is that what the author is trying to say is that the value of the monetary unit determines the price level. If so, he comes out at the same place as does traditional analysis.

In any event, the cash balance conception cannot be regarded as a separate and distinct theory of prices. The exponents of this point of view were in fact value of gold or quantity theorists so far as long-term prices

[41] R. G. Hawtrey, *Currency and Credit* (1923), p. 34.

are concerned. Their interest in cash balances grew out of their preoccupation with short-term or business cycle fluctuations.

Later writers have stressed the highly volatile character of cash balances. Their thinking was evidently profoundly affected by the stagnant economy of the 1930's. Confronted with the phenomenon of idle money, as well as idle machines and idle men, the emphasis of these writers was placed not on normal cash balances held as a matter of practical convenience but upon volitional withholdings for the purpose of storing up values. At times both spending and investing are deferred because general conditions are not deemed propitious; indeed, a strong cash position may be regarded as indispensable to personal security.

Fluctuations in the desire for cash (liquidity preference in Keynes' terminology) are held to be of primary importance in price fluctuations. The process has been described as follows:

> Under normal circumstances, merchants have certain expectations of the amounts of goods that they will be able to sell at current prices and stock their inventories accordingly. But suppose that, for whatever reason, a considerable group of the public decides to hold more income in cash and spend less for goods. The demand for goods then would fall off and merchants would be left with unsold merchandise on their shelves. In order to move inventories, they would then have to cut prices. At the same time they would naturally curtail orders to suppliers unless the latter reduced prices (which they might do if they had substantial inventories which they wished to move in anticipation of a reduced market).
>
> It may be that the initial reduction in prices will not have the desired effect. The public, noting the price decreases,

may, in fact, actually increase their holding of money in the hope that prices will be reduced still further. Merchants and manufacturers may make further reductions to move existing inventories, but, since this move means the incurrence of losses, they will not go below a certain point. Sooner or later, consumers who have been holding a larger than usual proportion of money will decide that prices have dropped as far as they are going to, whereupon they will buy goods at the lower level of prices then existing.[42]

This analysis, it will be observed, relates only to short-term fluctuations in business and prices. It is an explanation of business depressions and does not pretend to explain the long-term, or secular, trend of prices. In fact, it does not conflict in any way with the analysis of Irving Fisher. The latter was primarily interested in the long-term secular movements of prices rather than in short-term fluctuations, though he gave some consideration to the latter in his analysis of so-called transitional periods.

In concluding this appraisal we would emphasize that the quantity theory of money, whether expressed in the form of mathematical symbols or in words, throws no light on the process by which prices move from lower to higher levels; or *vice versa.* It cannot indicate whether the increase in currency is a *causal* or merely a *permissive* factor. It merely registers a result.

IV. A DOUBLE APPROACH

More or less coincident with the evolution of the approaches to the problem of price changes outlined

[42] Frederick A. Bradford, "The Purchasing Power of Money," Robinson, Adams, Dillin, *An Introduction to Modern Economics* (1952), pp. 257-58.

above, there was developing what may be called a double approach. In brief, it was contended that price changes may result either from forces affecting the value of the standard, gold, or from forces operating independently in the production process. As we shall see, this means something very different from mere changes in the volume of trade as compared with the quantity of the medium of exchange.

Professor J. Laurence Laughlin, writing in the early years of the present century, was the leading exponent of this double approach. Laughlin was so vigorous a critic of the quantity of money theory, that few of his contemporaries realized that he was at the same time a vigorous advocate of the value of gold approach. To him it seemed a truism that if the supply of gold should increase relatively to the demand therefor, its value would fall and commodity prices would automatically rise proportionally; and *vice versa.*

But Laughlin differentiated sharply between the function of gold as a standard and its function as a medium of exchange. He held that it is in the former capacity only that money is related to prices—that the number of monetary units used in effecting exchanges is not a price-making factor. In his view prices are made *prior* to the exchange process. This conception is in line with the classical view that all trade is essentially barter—that in reality goods are exchanged for other goods at *pre-established* values, and that the money *medium,* as the term implies, merely facilitates the exchange process. As Laughlin put it:

> The offer of "money" for goods is only a resultant of price-making forces previously at work, and does not measure the demand for goods. That is, the quantity of the actual media

of exchange thus brought into use is a result and not a cause of the price-making process. The supposed offer of money has no money as its basis, but is only the offer of a purchasing power, previously existing, based on saleable goods, which at the moment of payment appears expressed in the terms of the standard. . . . In reality (as in foreign trade) goods are exchanged against goods.[43]

This line of reasoning is deeply embedded in the classical theory of bank credit in relation to prices. The traditional commercial banking theory held that bank credit currency arises out of commercial loans—the credit being backed by specific commodities moving through the channels of distribution. When the goods which support the credit are sold, the credit currency will automatically be extinguished by the payment of the loan. Since the credit transaction grew out of, and was based upon, goods in transit, between seller and buyer, the checks drawn against the credit could not, it seemed obvious, be a price determinant; rather, the amount of the credit was governed by the already established price of the goods.[44]

While Laughlin adhered to the value of gold conception, and believed that gold had once been of major significance, he held that it had come to be a factor of minor importance. He argued that because of the durability of gold and the massive world supply, changes in annual output could have relatively little

[43] *Causes of the Changes in Prices Since 1896,* Bulletin of the American Economic Association, 4th Series, No. 2, Papers and Discussions of the Twenty-Third Annual Meeting, December, 1910, pp. 27-36.

[44] Laughlin recognized that in periods of great business prosperity, credit might be used to finance speculative activities and thus affect prices. But he dismissed this as being *abnormal credit*—having no significance in the longer run. This is somewhat analogous to Fisher's dismissal of cyclical variation in the relation of gold to credit and velocity as *transitional* phenomena.

effect upon the value of a unit of gold. Accordingly, he concluded that the explanation of the price changes in the latter years of the nineteenth and the early years of the twentieth century, are to be found mainly in factors operating in the productive process. Among the factors on the goods side which might operate independently to raise or to lower prices, Laughlin listed: Lowered expenses of production; increased expenses of production; increased demand for the product; diminished demand for the product; and monopoly.[45]

Laughlin did not claim to be the originator of the conception that changes in the level of prices may be affected by factors having nothing to do with the existing money supply. For example, he pointed out that although Ricardo was an advocate of the value of gold approach, he also held that prices of commodities may be affected by non-monetary factors when he wrote, "The prices of commodities which are subject to competition, and whose quantity may be increased in any moderate degree, will ultimately depend, not on the state of demand and supply, but on the increased or diminished cost of their production."[46] He also noted that Henry Thornton, one of the authors of the famous British *Bullion Report* of 1810, who usually adhered to the quantity theory approach, contended:

> The price at which the exchange takes place depends on two facts: on the proportion between the supply of the particular commodity and the demand for it, which is one question; and on the proportion, also, between the state of the general supply of the circulating medium and that of the demand for it, which is another.[47]

[45] *The Principles of Money* (1903), p. 336.
[46] David Ricardo, *Works*, McCulloch's Ed. (London 1888), p. 234.
[47] Horner, Thornton, and Huskisson, *The Bullion Report*, p. 194.

Finally, Laughlin observed that Thomas Tooke in his monumental work on the history of prices had come to believe, from his observations as a merchant and his extensive studies of commodity markets, "that the great alterations of prices originated, and mainly proceeded, from alterations in circumstances distinctly affecting the commodities, and not in the quantity of money, in relation to its function. . . ."[48]

It is of interest to note, also, that the American economic and business analyst, David A. Wells, in his *Recent Economic Changes,* covering the period from the Civil War to the late eighties, also held that changes in the general level of prices may be the result of *non-monetary* causes. He stated that the extraordinary downward movement of prices must, in the main, be due to one of two causes: "First, a great multiplication and cheapening of commodities through new conditions of production and distribution . . .; and, second, that . . . gold, has, through relative scarcity, owing to diminished production and increased demand, greatly appreciated in value."[49] His own studies led him to place primary emphasis, not on changes in the value of gold, but on factors directly affecting the production and marketing of goods.

The conception that price movements may be due to a combination of monetary and non-monetary factors also finds reflection in a report of the British Committee on Finance and Industry in 1931—commonly referred to as the *Macmillan Report.* In Great Britain the persistent depression in many trades and the exten-

[48] Thomas Tooke, *History of Prices* (1838), Vol. 2, p. 350.
[49] David A. Wells, *Recent Economic Changes* (1898), p. 123.

sive unemployment throughout the late twenties was being currently ascribed to a variety of factors: a rise in the value of gold resulting from the re-establishment of the gold standard; an inadequate expansion of credit; and adverse changes in the general economic position of Great Britain. In late 1929 the British government appointed an official body to investigate the causes of this unhappy situation. The membership consisted of government officials, professional economists, and bankers and industrialists.

The *Macmillan Report* called attention to both monetary and non-monetary sources of price disturbance. On the one hand, great importance was attached to the operation of the world's monetary and banking systems as affecting the general level of prices. But, on the other hand, the economic difficulties of the time were held to be "primarily due, not to any wanton misbehaviour on the part of the monetary factors themselves, but to unusually large and rapid changes on the part of what are rightly described as non-monetary phenomena, these non-monetary factors again themselves producing monetary changes." Among the non-monetary factors reference was made to capital losses consequent on the war, changes in established relationships between debtor and creditor countries, the rapidity of technical changes in manufacture and agriculture, the rigidity of wage rates, the growth of tariffs, etc. It was concluded "that the price level is the outgrowth of interaction between monetary and non-monetary factors."[50]

Throughout the discussion there was sharp cleavage

[50] The *Macmillan Report,* p. 93.

between the "theoretical" and the "practical" members of the Committee. The theoreticians, led by John Maynard Keynes, held that the quantity of money was exclusively—or at the least primarily—responsible for price fluctuations, while the practical men held that non-monetary factors were of primary, if not exclusive, importance. The final statement represented a compromise between these extremes, giving a place (weight unspecified) to both monetary and non-monetary influences.

Attention should also be called at this place to the fact that it is generally conceded that wide fluctuations in prices associated with booms and depressions are not altogether due to monetary factors. Indeed, many writers on business cycles accord little place to monetary influences—though it has usually been assumed that the situation might be controlled by the wise use of monetary policy.

It is apparent from the statements presented that there are several types of double approach. On the money side the authors are in some cases *value of gold* theorists, and in others *quantity* theorists. As for the goods side, emphasis is sometimes placed on the costs of production, sometimes on the demand and supply situation with respect to commodities, and again on general factors in the national and international economic situation. They are alike in the conception that factors may be operating in the economy at any given period to raise or lower the general level of prices which are unrelated to the existing money supply. This is abundantly borne out by the analysis of this study.

V. THE DEVELOPMENT OF THE INCOME APPROACH

The focal point of attention with this approach is the money income available for expenditure by individuals. At first glance it may seem that this approach differs little from that of the quantity theory; for is it not implicit in the latter that the money supply constitutes the demand for goods? Numerous writers indeed, among them Cantillon, Smith, and Mill, expressly used the term *demand* in discussing the money supply in relation to goods. Yet, as we shall see, the difference between these approaches is fundamental.

The writer primarily responsible for the emphasis upon money income as the determinant of prices was Thomas Tooke to whom reference was made in the preceding section. In the thirteenth of his conclusions Tooke laid down the following basic proposition, or thesis, as he called it:

> It is the quantity of money, constituting the revenues of the different orders of the state, under the head of rents, profits, salaries and wages that alone forms the limiting principle of the aggregate money prices. . . . As the cost of production is the limiting principle of supply, so the aggregate of money incomes devoted to expenditure for consumption is the determining and limiting principle of demand.[51]

It may be observed in passing that Tooke, like the quantity theorists, was concerned primarily, if not exclusively, with demand for *consumer* goods.

Tooke's influence was exerted primarily through Continental writers. Lacking academic status and being deeply involved in controversial issues pertaining to

[51] See T. E. Gregory's reissue of Tooke and Newmarch's *History of Prices*, Vol. 3 (1928), p. 276.

banking legislation it was perhaps not surprising that the thirteenth thesis, which appeared only in the final volume of a series of studies, should have been largely overlooked or ignored by contemporary British economists. Tooke came, however, to be greatly admired by such Continental writers as Adolf Wagner of Germany and Knut Wicksell of Sweden. It appears that Wagner did not appreciate the implications of the thesis that money income was the *determining* and *limiting* principle of demand. But he was much engaged by the emphasis upon the stream of money income and its expenditure; and he himself pointed out that there were two main segments—consumers' money on the one hand and producers' or business money on the other hand. Wicksell was primarily influenced by Tooke's conception of money income as setting the *limit* to demand, and like Tooke, was principally interested in expenditures for objects of immediate consumption, the prices of which constituted the truest gauge of the general price level.

It is of interest to note that there was a fifty-year interval between the writings of Tooke and of Wicksell and Wagner—the former's *Interest and Prices* appearing in 1898 and the latter's *Socialeconomic Theory of Money* in 1909. In the same year the Austrian economist, Professor F. von Wieser, published an article which emphasized the significance of money income in relation to prices. Joseph Schumpeter, a student of Wieser, followed this approach in an early book (1917). However, in his final volume, published posthumously in 1954, he virtually abandoned it. (See below, pp. 228-29.)

Albert F. Aftalion of France, also a student of Wieser, deserves a high place in the evolution of the income approach. He explicitly adopted the term *income theory* and used an algebraic formulation to disclose the relation between income and prices.[52] "If we call R the national income in money, Q the total production, and P the average price of articles in which it is figured, one can write $R = PQ$." In Aftalion's view, variations in R were commonly the effects of variations in PQ, especially Q.[53] That is, fluctuations in money income are dependent upon fluctuations in business activity and prices. It is significant that the old velocity concept (V) does not appear in this equation.

In Aftalion's view, the income theory is essentially different from, and superior to, the quantity theory. In the quantity theory it is variation in the over-all quantity of gold and other money that is important; in the income theory the emphasis is on changes in the flow of money income, as governed by wages, interest, dividends, and profits, and the resulting effect on consumer spending. No direct proportionality is necessary between variations in total money supply and prices; nor is it the quantity of money which gives the motive force to movements of income and prices. In his view the great advantage of the income theory is that it explains how there can be variations in prices (due to fluctuations in income) without any alteration in the over-all supply of gold and other forms of money—which he calls a "mystery under the quantity theory."

The shift from money supply, as governed by gold

[52] Aftalion's views were adumbrated in an article appearing in 1917, entitled "Periodic Crises and Overproduction." It was elaborated in an article published in 1925, entitled "Recent Monetary Experiences and the Income Theory." His position was more systematically set forth in *Money, Price and Exchange,* published in 1933.

[53] *Money, Price and Exchange,* p. 156.

stock, subsidiary forms of money, credit currency, and their rates of turnover to the money income currently received by individuals for services rendered is a crucial change. Under the income conception the magnitude of the flow of money income may vary widely from the stock of gold and other forms of money, and may vary independently. The failure of many writers on money and prices to grasp this vital difference between the income theory and traditional monetary theories has been a persistent source of confusion.

Confusion With Respect To Income and Quantity Theories

Many writers on monetary theory, failing to perceive the vital difference between the income approach and traditional monetary theories, have sought to harmonize them. Evidence of this practice is found in some of the quotations from current treatises given on page 34 of the text. Two other citations are here given in order to reveal more clearly the prevailing confusion of mind that exists.

Joseph Schumpeter and the income approach. Reference was made above[54] to the fact that Joseph Schumpeter endorsed the income and expenditure approach in an early book published in 1917. He emphasized the *rate of movement* of the money stream—later designated the *income velocity* of money. But in his posthumous volume (1954) Schumpeter minimizes the significance of this approach, holding that it yields no result that cannot be obtained by the equation of exchange.

In his *History of Economic Analysis* (1954), Schumpeter summarizes his views on the income approach as follows:

[54] P. 226.

We have noticed that Tooke, in his "13th thesis," had suggested that the explanation of money prices should start from consumers' incomes. As we know, he offered this as an alternative to the explanation of price levels by the quantity of money which he rejected. Ever since, the Income Approach has appealed to analysts—though it was also adopted by others—who disliked the quantity theory or even the equation of exchange. But it is easy to see that, in itself, the former is nothing but another way of writing the latter. Moreover, the amendment might seem to be of doubtful value since incomes evidently "determine" prices in the same sense only in which prices "determine" incomes. Yet Wieser's and Hawtrey's preference for this approach is quite understandable, though it yields no result that cannot be obtained via the equation of exchange: like the cash balance approach, it points to individual behavior; more than the cash balance approach, it removes mere quantity of money from the position of a proximate "cause of the price level" and substitutes for it one that is still nearer to prices—income, or even consumers' expenditure; finally it relieves the theory of money prices from such questions as what is to be considered as money. The effect of an increase of money upon prices is indeterminate so long as we do not know who gets the additional money, what he does with it, and what the state of the economic organism is on which the new money impinges. The income formula does not in itself take account of all these questions but it directs our attention toward them and thus helps monetary analysis to step out of its separate compartment. This advantage is particularly obvious in analyzing an inflationary process. Though there is really not much more sense in quarreling over the question whether it is the increased quantity of money or the increased pay roll that "causes" inflation than there would be in quarreling over the question whether it is the bullet or the murderer's intention that "causes" the death of the victim, there is still something to be said for concentrating on the mechanisms by which the increased quantity of money becomes operative—not to speak of the additional advantage which counts for so much in economics, namely, that the income-expenditure formula does not meet with some of the prejudices that the equation of exchange encounters.[55]

It would almost seem from this statement that Schumpeter is both against and for the income approach—holding that it contains nothing essentially different and yet has distinct advantages over the quantity theory. He holds that the income theory is but another way of writing the quantity theory, and that its chief virtue is that it obviates prejudices which have come to surround the equation of exchange. But he clearly departs from this view when he says that the income approach removes mere quantity of money from the position of proximate "cause of the price level," and that we cannot gauge the effect of an increase in the money supply until we know what is happening to the income stream. The vital question is ignored—Does an increase in gold or other forms of money automatically become a part of the income stream, and, if so, by what process? See our discussion on page 44 of the text.

Howard Ellis' interpretation. In his book on German monetary theory, Ellis devotes no little space to the income theory, which had considerable vogue among German economists. He asks, "How does the income theory relate to the quantity theory?" and concludes "the answer is not easily found."[56]

The reason for Ellis' difficulty is that he has not grasped the vital distinction between a *stock* of money, consisting of the supply of gold and other forms of currency, and a *flow* of money income, governed by the level of wages, interest, rents, and profits (disposable income). He refers extensively to the somewhat am-

[55] Pp. 109-10.
[56] *German Monetary Theory, 1905-33* (1934), p. 176.

biguous Wieser, but nowhere cites the explicit thesis of Tooke, nor does he refer to the analysis of Aftalion.

The author's mind is still rooted in a static equation analysis which involves a comparison of quantities at a moment of time. He says that Wieser "was one of the first in Germany to recast the quantity theory in terms of rates," and he notes that the quantitative data are flows and not stocks. But he evidently does not appreciate that the volume of the flow of disposable income is not necessarily the same as the volume of the stock of specie and other money. In fact, the income flow may bear little relation to the money stock; for example, in the United States following World War I, the expanding gold supply (and credit potential) was not matched by any corresponding expansion in the flow of money income to the public (See discussion page 242 below). The accumulations at Fort Knox bear mute testimony to this fact.

The fundamental weakness of the income theory, as held by modern writers, is the implicit assumption that the price level is determined wholly by the level of demand, based on disposable money income. It gives no thought to money costs of production as a factor affecting the prices of commodities entering the markets. This assumption, as has been shown in foregoing chapters of this treatise, is sustained neither by factual data nor realistic economic analysis.

How Crystallization of Thought Retards Economic Analysis

At the conclusion of this appraisal, attention should be called to a generalization advanced in the introductory chapter to this volume. We refer to the tendency in all realms of thought for principles and doctrines once enunciated and incorporated in formal treatises to be regarded henceforth as eternal truths or axioms. This is especially the case where they are expressed in mathematical form. Such crystallization of thought tends to estop further analysis—precluding periodic examination of the validity of underlying assumptions in the light of changing conditions and new evidence.

The formulation of the quantity theory in mathematical terms was engaging to most economists because formulas have an appearance of exactitude and finality. The equation of exchange continued to dominate thought and to deter thorough-going reappraisal for decades. Its influence over men's minds was of a subtle character. New evidence based on statistical data or observation gradually led to qualification or refinement of the "established theory" but not to fundamental reconsideration.

Many economists came to take exception to the rigidity of Irving Fisher's analysis. Concretely, it was observed that Fisher tended to minimize the possible variations between money supply (M) and credit supply (M′); that his conception of trade should be broadened to include other things than final consumer products; that the velocity of circulation might at times be greatly affected by *volitional* withholdings of cash; and, also, that there might be interactions among the several items comprised within the equation.

By way of illustration, reference may be made to the evolving thought of an economist who early in his career had accepted the equation of exchange without appreciable qualification. Twenty-five years later in a textbook he expressed his reservations as follows:[57]

> The equation of exchange is merely a useful device for bringing together the factors which enter into the determination of price. We should not label any one set as "causes" or the others as "effects". . . . In the first place, as we well know, an increase in the circulation of money or bank deposits usually calls forth a greater supply of goods (T) instead of raising prices (P) by the amount of the increase in M or M′. Second, P is not a completely passive factor. The very position of the price level at a given time affects the quantity of the other factors M and M′ placed in circulation by buyers and the rapidity (V and V′) with which they circulate. Third, T, the quantity of goods offered for sale, may change for reasons entirely independent of the other factors, and not only will cause changes in the price level (P) but also will influence the quantity of money and deposit currency which will be placed in circulation as well as the activity with which they circulate.

In order to make the theory conform to the facts, a highly qualified re-statement is suggested—reading as follows:

> The level of prices will vary directly with changes in the quantity of money, provided (1) that its velocity of circulation is not influenced by the change; (2) that the quantity of credit and its velocity of circulation are likewise not disturbed by this increase in the quantity of money; and (3) that the volume of trade is not changed by it. As we have already observed, such a static condition probably never exists. Furthermore, we shall then have to add the caution that even the price level itself is not a passive factor, upon which changes in the amount of money do the acting, but that, on the contrary, the position of the price level at a given moment not only affects each of the other members of the equation but also helps to determine the course of the price level in the future.

Although these qualifications clearly challenge the

[57] George W. Dowrie, *Money and Banking* (1936), pp. 70-72.

very premises of the Fisher analysis, the author still regards the equation as significant. He concludes:

> The fact that the relationship of the various elements entering into the determination of the value of money is a complex one does not justify us in concluding that no such relationship exists. . . . It [the equation of exchange] will continue to serve as a most useful device for setting forth the factors which enter into the determination of the value of money, provided that it does not delude us into thinking that their interrelationship is a simple one.

The author had in the intervening years obviously been influenced by factual observations of business and financial trends; but he was nevertheless still bound by the framework of thought underlying the equation of exchange. As he saw it, the elements making up the two sides of the equation are highly complex and somewhat, somehow, interrelated; that is, there are repercussions from one to another—based chiefly on psychological influences growing out of fluctuating business conditions. But the adherence to the equation nevertheless served to perpetuate the mold of thought which implies that money enters the picture only after the productive process has been completed and that the supply of circulating media and the volume of goods are mainly, if not wholly, independent each of the other.

VI. THE FAILURE OF TRADITIONAL THEORIES IN PRICE FORECASTING

One method of appraising the validity of a theory is by gauging its reliability in forecasting future trends. Since World War I both the value of gold and the quantity of money theories have been invoked by their advocates as practical guides to price movements. A number of specific predictions may be cited.

1. *That Prices Would Not Fall After World War I*

In 1919 Irving Fisher announced that there would, indeed could, be no appreciable fall in the American price level. He held that there had been a price revolution similar to that which followed the discovery of precious metals in the New World four hundred years earlier—that the huge existing supply of money and credit in the channels of circulation would naturally remain in circulation and maintain prices at, or very near, the existing level. The most that might be expected was a slight decline in prices about a year later—in consequence of increasing production following demobilization.[58] Within a year after this prediction there occurred the most precipitous price collapse in American history.

2. *That the Price Adjustment Mechanism Would Ensure Reparation Payments*

The international price adjustment theory was invoked by Professor Taussig in 1919 to reveal the way in which the German reparation obligations would be met. First he outlined what the steps would be if the countries involved were operating on the gold standard.

> The order of events would be foreseen as follows. First, a rise of foreign exchange in Germany, due to the government's demand for bills wherewith to effect remittances to foreign countries. Pounds sterling, francs, dollars will be in demand. The specie export point will soon be reached and gold will flow out of Germany. Next, a period of lower

[58] Pamphlet issued by the Division of Public Works and Construction Development, U. S. Dept. of Labor (1919). For the author's concurrent analysis of the factors that would necessitate an extensive price adjustment in 1920, see Harold G. Moulton, "Banking Policy and the Price Situation," *American Economic Review,* Vol. 10, No. 1 (Papers and Proceedings of Annual Meeting, American Economic Association, December, 1919).

prices in Germany and of prices continuing steadily to become lower. Conversely, there will be rising prices in foreign countries. Third, exports from Germany will increase, being stimulated by lower prices; imports into Germany will decline, being checked by that same situation. The gap between merchandise imports and exports will steadily increase, until finally that stage is reached when the total spread between the two will be equal in money value to the sum total which the German Government needs annually to remit. . . . Merchandise exports from Germany will exceed merchandise imports by a billion a year (or whatever is the amount of the reparation remittances). . . .[59]

Since Germany was operating on a paper money basis, it was necessary to consider how this fact affected the situation. In Taussig's view the process would be essentially the same but would be accelerated under a paper money regime. This is because the depreciation of the mark in the foreign exchanges made Germany, as every tourist knows, a bargain counter for foreign buyers but a very poor market in which to sell. Taussig elaborates the results of this situation as follows:

For a long time there will be a divergence between the general price level and the rates of foreign exchange. The divergence means that exporters will be in a position to profit. They can buy cheap (comparatively cheap) in Germany, sell the German goods abroad, draw on the foreign purchasers and sell their exchange to advantage at home. Quite the reverse will be the situation of importers. They will not be able to sell to advantage in Germany and will have to pay high for the means of remittance to the foreign vendors. The whole situation obviously will tend to attract

[59] F. W. Taussig, "Germany's Reparation Payments," Address before the American Economic Association, December, 1919. See "Papers and Proceedings of the Thirty-Second Annual Meeting of the American Economic Association," *The American Economic Review,* Vol. 10, No. 1, Supplement, March, 1920, pp. 33-34.

labor and capital to the German exporting industries and to repel them from the importing industries. . . . The exporting industries provide goods which go to foreign countries. No imports arrive in return.[60]

Since the depreciation of the mark made Germany a good market in which to buy and a poor market in which to sell, an impetus was thus undoubtedly given to the trade readjustment process; and so long as the exports were from accumulated stocks of goods, this was helpful. But as soon as the exports had to come from new production, insurmountable difficulties were encountered. The great bulk of German exports had to be made from imported raw materials; and, at the same time, a substantial proportion of the food required by the working population had to be purchased abroad. With high-priced imported materials and high wages, made necessary by high-priced food imports, the cost of German manufactures became very high. High-priced imports required high-priced exports if profits were to be earned.

Taussig's reference to "importing industries" and "exporting industries" shows a lack of understanding of the structure of the German industrial system. The importing industries and the exporting industries were commonly one and the same—*companies* buying cotton, wool, or ores in foreign lands and converting them into finished products for sale, partly in Germany and partly abroad. The selling price had to cover the cost of the imported materials, labor, etc. Under these circumstances, imports of raw materials and of foodstuffs for the working population could not be reduced without curtailing export possibilities.

[60] *The same,* pp. 39-40.

The early collapse of the German monetary and financial system under the pressure of reparation payments proved that the fundamental production and trade difficulties could not be corrected by mere adjustments in relative price levels in consequence of the depreciation of the German currency.[61] Germany, in fact, did not develop any export surplus, the reparation payments being made possible by new foreign loans.

3. *That the Huge American Gold Supply in the Twenties Would Raise Prices*

In consequence of World War I and its aftermath of economic and financial readjustment, there occurred a vast redistribution of the world supply of monetary gold—that is, of the gold stocks held by central banks and governments as the basis of monetary systems. In the early stages of the European conflict, both groups of belligerents shipped gold to the United States in payment for war supplies. After the United States entered the war, gold was received only from allied powers; and in due course gold payments were superseded by credit arrangements. Beginning in 1921, imports were resumed on a huge scale, aggregating 1.450 billion dollars in the four years, 1921-24, inclusive.[62] These huge imports of gold, added to continuing large domestic production, served to expand enormously America's monetary stock of gold—from 1.526 billions

[61] For a detailed analysis of the economic aspects of the reparation problem, see Harold G. Moulton and Constantine E. McGuire, *Germany's Capacity to Pay* (1923).

[62] For the remainder of the decade the net change was negligible; and during the panic period, 1932-33, there was an outflow of some 620 millions.

in 1914 to as much as 4.306 billions in 1930. The credit expansion potentials were at least twelve times the increase in the gold reserves.

The continued rapid expansion of the American monetary gold supply during and after World War I, and the consequent building up of the huge lending power of the Federal Reserve banks, led traditional monetary theorists confidently to predict an early great rise in the American price level—a prediction which was periodically repeated for a decade. It was contended that this would make the United States a good market in which to sell but a poor market in which to buy; and the resulting trade readjustments would, in due course, bring about an outflow of gold and a correction of the existing maldistribution of the world's supply of monetary gold. However, as the chart on page 2 shows, no such price advance occurred; indeed, the wholesale price index in the United States showed a slight decline in the later years of the decade, notwithstanding the prosperity of the period.

The failure of prices to rise in the twenties led many theorists to conclude that the gold supply had somehow been *sterilized.* To those who regarded the theory as unquestionably true, it seemed that there *must* have been some arbitrary interference with normal operations. However, no restrictive policies had been adopted by the Federal Reserve Board. The Board's revised policy of 1923 (set forth on page 54) was essentially passive—designed merely to make sure that credit was available to meet the legitimate needs of business. The Board persistently refused to assume responsibility for control of the price level.

Writing in 1927, Taussig admitted that in the twenties, "It was not the expected that took place, but quite the unexpected. . . . Neither inflow nor outflow had the effects which the 'received' doctrines contemplate. . . ."[63] That he was, however, still reluctant to abandon the theory is evident from the following passage:

> When more time has elapsed and a nearer approach to a normal economic situation has been reached, the enigmas may prove less baffling than they appeared at the time, the eventual outcome more in accord with familiar doctrines. But it is clear that we must be cautious in applying the familiar doctrines of international trade to the interpretation of this quite extraordinary situation. . . . It will prove most interesting to watch the course of events during the next decade or so, say till 1935.[64]

According to the "received" doctrines, the adjustments were supposed to occur promptly, if not immediately, rather than over a long period of years. In any case, the history of succeeding years provided no support for Taussig's cautious hope.

4. That Devaluing the Dollar Would Raise Prices Proportionally

The validity of the value of gold theory received a direct test in the devaluation of the dollar experiment sponsored by Professors Warren and Pearson in 1933. The objective of the plan was to raise commodity prices by devaluing the dollar; that is, by reducing the amount of gold in the official dollar unit. The process involved an increase in the price paid for gold from $20.67 to $35.00 an ounce. It was contended that the effects of changes in the price of gold upon the prices of com-

[63] F. W. Taussig, *International Trade* (1927), pp. 330-31.
[64] *The same*, pp. 330-32.

modities would be mathematically precise. "If prices rose 0.1 per cent in a week, the weight of gold purchasable by a dollar would be increased 0.1 per cent until any rise was corrected." Conversely, "if prices fell 0.1 per cent, the weight of the gold purchasable by a dollar would be increased 0.1 per cent."[65] Thus, in consequence of the 60 per cent increase in the price of gold commodity prices would rise 60 per cent.

The evidence is conclusive that the devaluation of the dollar did not lead to an automatic revaluation of commodities in terms of the dollar. In fact, the devaluation directly affected prices only in the case of imported commodities. A reduction in the weight of the dollar unit, of course, reduced the value of the dollar relatively to pounds, francs, etc. in the foreign exchanges. Since United States' imports have to be paid for in foreign currencies, when the exchange value of the dollar depreciated Americans had to offer more dollars than before for the same amount of foreign currencies. Hence, to avoid losses, importers marked up the selling prices of the imported goods. The effect of devaluation upon the prices of American exports worked itself out somewhat differently. Since foreign currencies would now buy more American goods than before, the demand therefor naturally increased, leading to a rise in price. The rise in the early stages was expedited because speculators hastened to buy exportable goods in anticipation of the price rise.[66]

Despite the stimulus to the prices of internationally traded commodities, and the added stimulus afforded

[65] G. F. Warren and F. A. Pearson, *Prices* (1933), p. 164.

[66] For further discussion of the technical features of the plan, see Appendix B.

by general business recovery and widespread increases in wage rates under the National Recovery Administration codes, the general advance in prices was only one-third what had been so confidently predicted—20 per cent instead of the promised 60 per cent.

The experience of other countries during the same period affords even less support for the theory. In Great Britain and Sweden a depreciation of the currency of roughly 30 per cent, which is equivalent to a rise in the price of gold of more than 40 per cent, was followed by a slight decline in the level of commodity prices. In Japan the price of gold more than doubled, but the general level of prices showed a rise of only 19 per cent.[67]

It should be added here that the trends of the last quarter century afford no support either for the value of gold theory or the quantity theory anchored in gold production. The supply of gold dollars increased fantastically in the thirties—in consequence of continued domestic production, importations, and, especially, the devaluation—which served to increase the number of dollars in proportion to the reduction in the amount of ore required in the official dollar unit. The gold accumulations in government hoards and vast *potential* credit supply remained dormant—unwanted by business. Idle money characterized the decade as a whole.

Throughout the buoyant war and early postwar years the gold base could have supported a price level several times as high as that which prevailed. Indeed, the central bank reserves remained so great that it was deemed desirable to raise sharply the reserve require-

[67] For a detailed discussion of this experiment, see Leo Pasvolsky, *Current Monetary Issues* (The Brookings Institution, 1933), pp. 114-26.

ments of the member banks in order to lessen available lending power and tighten the credit situation so that the Federal Reserve authorities might regain some measure of influence over member bank activities.

It is not without significance that in current price discussions one seldom finds reference to the gold supply as a factor in the situation. The explanation of the price revolution since 1939 runs chiefly in terms of money in general, of the expansion of credit through the medium of fiscal policies—or, in the case of the income theorists, of constantly increasing purchasing power. In the standard textbooks, as we saw in Chapter I, the focus of attention has been shifted from the value of *gold* to the value of *money*. Only those who would restore the former system of convertibility of all forms of currency into gold now attach much importance to the gold standard in relation to prices.

APPENDIX B

Attempts at Statistical Verification

Traditional monetary theory, as we have seen, was developed mainly through the process of deductive reasoning. However, a number of attempts have been made to substantiate theory by citations of statistics pertaining to specie supply and price movements. Since it has been contended that such inductive inquiries confirm the results achieved by deductive reasoning, it is necessary to appraise the more pretentious of these analyses. Such studies pertain to domestic price movements within given countries; to world price trends; and to the international price adjustment mechanism. As we shall see, none of these studies substantiate the theoretical reasoning.

We shall review in this appendix the following studies:

Earl J. Hamilton's analysis purporting to show a close correlation between imports of precious metals from the New World and the price revolution in Spain in the sixteenth century.

Irving Fisher's data allegedly showing a remarkable correlation between gold *stocks* and price movements in Great Britain in the nineteenth century, and in the United States between 1906 and 1909.

Gustav Cassel's analysis of world gold *production* and world price *trends* over the sixty-year period from 1850 to 1910.

Warren and Pearson's evidence relating to world supply of and demand for gold, 1839-1933, which constituted the basis for their gold stabilization plan.

Viner's attempt to *verify* the international price adjustment mechanism by Canadian experience—1900-13.

The studies by Frank D. Graham and John H. Williams, pertaining to the international adjustment mechanism under depreciated paper money regimes.

I. NEW WORLD PRECIOUS METALS AND THE PRICE REVOLUTION IN SPAIN

The discovery and exploration of the New World by Spain was quickly followed by the exploitation of the rich mineral resources of Latin America. Shipments of specie to Spain began as early as 1503. During the first quarter of the century they consisted almost entirely of gold, but after 1530 the great bulk was silver. The amount shipped increased gradually until 1570, nearly doubled in the ensuing decade, and reached its peak in the 1590's. The flow began to taper after 1601 and by 1660 was of negligible proportions.

Attention was first called to the possible connection between these imports of the precious metals and the general rise in commodity prices by a sixteenth century French writer, Jean Bodin,[1] who had apparently been influenced in his thinking by the fact that prices had risen rapidly in Rome after Julius Caesar brought great stores of the precious metals to the city from conquered countries.

[1] Jean Bodin, "Reply to the Paradoxes of Malestroit Concerning the Dearness of All Things and the Remedy Therefor" (Paris, 1568), from Arthur Eli Monroe, *Early Economic Thought* (1924). See quotation on p. 4.

Over the succeeding centuries the Spanish price revolution of the sixteenth century has been cited as *prima facie* evidence of the causal influence of the precious metals on commodity prices. The conclusion has seemed equally clear both to those who adhere to the value of the standard conception of price determination and to those who emphasize the quantity of money units available for exchange against goods.

During the constructive reign of Ferdinand and Isabella, Spain had established, in 1497, a bimetallic coinage system which was steadfastly maintained until almost the very end of the sixteenth century. With currency debasements thus eliminated as a price-distorting factor, and with credit currency of minor importance, sixteenth century Spain offers an exceptional opportunity for testing the theory that changes in commodity prices are directly proportional to changes in the quantity of the money standard or in the volume of the media of exchange.

The Study by Earl J. Hamilton

Statistical materials with respect to imports of specie and Spanish prices were meager until Professor Earl J. Hamilton published in 1934 a comprehensive study entitled *American Treasure and the Price Revolution in Spain, 1501-1650.* Thanks to extraordinary enterprise, Hamilton was able to compile from official records in Spain and Latin America the annual import figures for silver and gold, respectively, for a period of 150 years—1500 to 1650—showing separately the amounts owned by the government and by private individuals. He also constructed rough indexes of commodity prices and wages in the principal Spanish provinces. On the basis of these two sets of data Hamilton, as we shall see, reached the conclusion that the rise of prices in Spain in the sixteenth century was strictly in accordance with the expectations of *a priori* reasoning as embodied in the quantity theory. He concludes:

> The extremely close correlation between the increase in the volume of treasure imports and the advance of commodity prices throughout the sixteenth century, particularly from 1535 on, demonstrates beyond question that the "abundant mines of America" were the principal cause of the Price Revolution in Spain.[2]

Before appraising the evidence presented, a few words of explanation are desirable with respect to the way in which the specie was handled. According to Hamilton, the New World colonists specialized in mining activities and the specie was exported to Spain in exchange for essential commodities. "The treasure fleets sailed from Spain laden with provisions, wares, and all sorts of merchandise"; but the return cargoes were usually about 95 per cent specie. The metal was weighed in the New World at government assay offices. The well-to-do miners usually carried their own metals to the assay offices, while others sold theirs to dealers or to capitalists who had advanced subsistence and equipment.

About three-quarters of the bullion was privately owned. The public, or Crown, bullion was derived chiefly from sales of papal indulgences, fines and confiscations, profit on token money, and tribute levied against Indian tribes—though on at least three occasions it was obtained through the seizure of private treasure.

[2] Hamilton, *the same*, p. 301.

Spanish law required that upon reaching Spain all of the private bullion should be coined at government mints. Once coined it was of course available to the owners for any and all purposes. In the early years most of the bullion owned by the Crown was also minted but later much of it was delivered directly to foreign creditors—especially to the Austrian bankers—the Fuggers—who had advanced vast sums to Emperor Charles V, King of Spain from 1516 to 1555.

Hamilton divided his analysis into two half-century periods. He compiled price indexes for each of the four regions, Andalusia, Old Castile-Leon, New Castile, and Valencia. He says that in the earlier period the price data for Old Castile-Leon were "infinitely superior" to the others. Included in this index were 41 varied commodities as against only 12 for New Castile. He found that prices roughly doubled in the first half-century and that they doubled again in the second half-century. In his view, "It is a remarkable coincidence that the advance of prices during the second half of the century so nearly duplicated that of the first half."[3] We shall review the data for each period separately.

APPRAISAL OF HAMILTON'S EVIDENCE

The conclusion that specie imports were responsible for doubling prices in the first half of the century is not warranted by the data presented.[4] A strong upward trend in prices was under way in Spain, as Hamilton shows, prior to 1500; and from 1501 to 1506 his combined index shows a rise of 41 per cent. Specie imports

[3] *The same,* p. 201.

[4] For price table, 1501-1550, see *the same,* p. 189.

did not begin until 1503 and the amounts were negligible until 1506. The rise of 100 per cent for the half-century is obtained by comparing the year 1501 with 1550 (composite index). If we use the "superior" data for Old Castile-Leon and measure the upward movement from 1506, the rise to 1550 appears to be only 34 per cent; and if 1506 be compared with 1547, the indicated rise is only 10 per cent.

The rise in prices was far from continuous. As Hamilton notes, in the first half-century the rise occurred chiefly in the first, third, and fifth decades. From 1511 to 1520 and again from 1530 to 1540 no upward trend is shown in the combined index number. In Old Castile-Leon prices rose from 73 in 1502 to 98 in 1506; but by 1512 the figure was back to 78. The index reached 101 in 1523; but three years later it was again down to 92. A new peak of 121 was reached in 1532; but in 1534 and 1535 the index was once more only 92. Not until 1548 was the 1532 level again reached. The fluctuations in New Castile were similar but more pronounced.

For the second half of the century the price data are said to be much better—the years 1571-1580 being used as a base in constructing new indexes. For this half-century the price series for New Castile are the most satisfactory.[5] The rise in the combined series from 1551 to the year 1600 was approximately 100 per cent. But if 1596 be compared with 1551 the rise was only 70 per cent. The very sharp rise after 1596 may well have been largely explained by such factors as the accession to power of the irresponsible Philip III, the threatened debasement of the monetary standard, the repeal of sumptuary laws, and the catastrophic plague of 1599-1600.

[5] *The same*, p. 198.

While the rise in the second half-century was somewhat more continuous, there were also interesting reversals in trend, especially in the later decades. In 1552 the index for New Castile was 71; by 1556 it was down to 62; in 1579 it stood at 113; but in 1588 it was only 104. The composite index for all provinces shows a moderate rate of increase in the 1550's and 1560's, comparatively stable prices through the 1570's, a moderate rise from 1580 to 1595, and a very sharp advance thereafter.

The occasional wide price fluctuations that occurred over the century as a whole are attributed by Hamilton to special factors: the peak of 1506-08 to bad harvests; the sharp rise in 1521 to wars; and that in 1522 to poor harvests. The marked decline of 1531-36 is said to be cyclical in nature; similarly, with the drops in 1554-56 and again in 1576-77, following the royal bankruptcy of 1575. The peak for New Castile in 1579 is attributed largely to an exceptionally poor fruit crop; and the downward movement of prices in Old Castile in the eighties is said to reflect bountiful harvests of fruit, nuts, and grains.

The fluctuations in prices shown in Hamilton's tables bear a general resemblance to those covering the nineteenth century in the United States. It is difficult to avoid the conclusion that the business cycle was manifest in Spain pretty much throughout the century. While Hamilton frequently ascribes downswings to cyclical factors, he makes no similar comment with respect to the upswings.

There is no real correlation between specie imports and price movements. In contrast with the wide fluctuations in prices, specie imports showed a virtually continuous increase—slowly until about 1530 and rapidly thereafter—until a high was reached in the 1590's. It is thus clear that there was no automatic adjustment of prices to the annual increments of specie, as the value of gold theory assumes. In any case, the theory requires, as Hamilton notes at one place, that the comparison should be not between *annual* imports of specie and the movement of prices, but between the *accumulating aggregate* stock of specie and prices. Data on specie stocks are not avaliable.

Moreover, one finds little correlation over longer intervals of time between private specie imports and price changes. (We use *private* specie here because most of the public specie is known to have been exported to meet regal debts.) For example, between 1503 and 1530, when specie imports were at much the lowest level of the century, prices rose 70 per cent. From 1531 to 1540, when specie imports increased approximately five-fold, there was no price rise. When specie imports were at their maximum between the middle eighties and the middle nineties, prices remained practically stable.

Nor do the half-century comparisons of specie increments and price movements give support to the theory. In the first half-century the private specie imports *aggregated* roughly 15 million pesos; while in the second half-century an additional 138 million pesos were received. With 10 per cent coming before 1550 and 90 per cent thereafter, the theoretical expectation would be a vastly greater price rise in the second half-century—cumulative in character because of the durability of specie. To be sure the effects might, theoretically, have been nullified by (a) a corresponding increase of specie exports, or (b) a vast increase in the quantity of production. But, in view of the embargo on private specie exports, it seems unlikely that the bulk of the specie left the country—though it is known that smuggling operations were common. Mention should also be made of the known fact that substantial amounts were used for ornamentation. But, as offsets, it appears that credit operations were gradually increasing. Since economic conditions were apparently deteriorating after the middle of the century,[6] the failure of prices to rise more rapidly then cannot well be attributed to an increase in the volume of trade. Thus, data which pertain only to specie imports and commodity price movements do not provide an adequate basis for the conclusion that the theory is substantiated by the available evidence submitted.

Hamilton presents a chart which he says "demonstrates beyond question that 'the abundant mines of America' were the principal cause of the price revolution in Spain." The chart, entitled "Total Quinquennial Treasure Imports and Composite Index Numbers of Commodity Prices,"[7] covers the entire period 1500-1650; but the close correlation claimed relates only to the sixteenth century. After that time the situation was complicated by the abandonment of the specie standard. The chart is reproduced at the top of 253.[8]

Unfortunately, the chart was not properly constructed. There are two flaws in the method of statistical presentation employed which together serve com-

[6] See discussion on p. 264.

[7] Presented on p. 301 of the book.

[8] The specie imports data and the composite index figures on which the chart is based are to be found in Hamilton's book referred to above, on pp. 34, 189, and 198.

SPECIE IMPORTS AND COMMODITY PRICES

I. HAMILTON'S CHART, 1501–1650

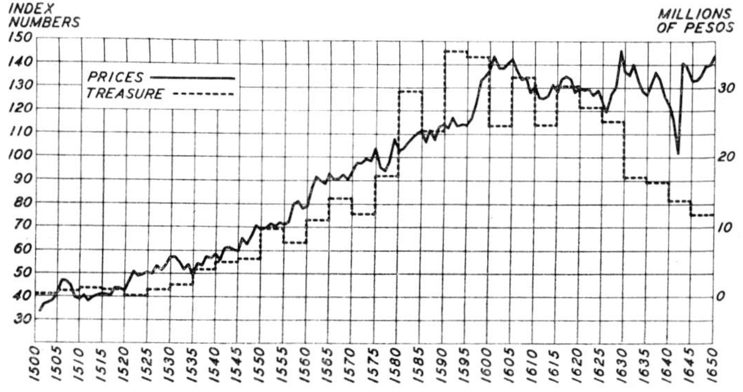

II. CORRECTLY DRAWN CHART, 1501–1600

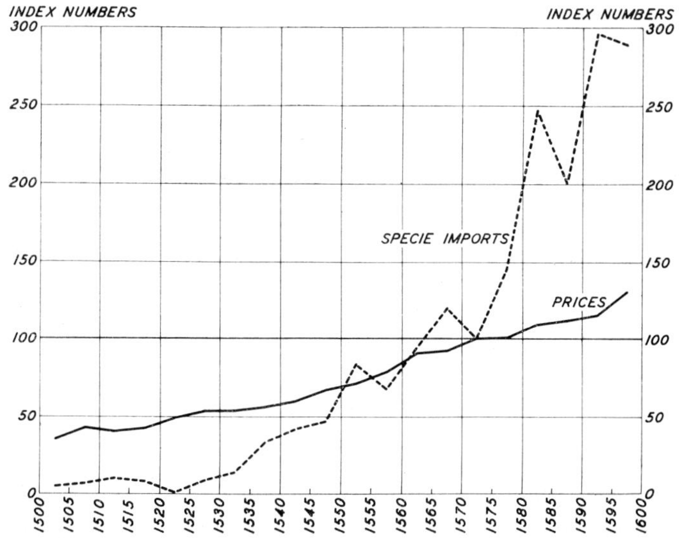

pletely to distort the picture. First, Hamilton uses index units for the scale of prices but actual quantities, as expressed in *pesos*, for the scale of specie movements. The result is to distort the relative trends and bring the lines into closer juxtaposition. Second, the author also forces the two graphs (specie imports and price indexes) into superposition by starting them at substantially different levels. The scale of prices starts with the zero at 20 index units *below* the base line; while the specie import scale on the opposite side has the zero considerably *above* the base line. The respective origins—the zero points—of the two curves differ on the chart by 4 scale units out of a total range for the variables over the entire period of somewhat less than 12 units. The author fails to adhere to the well-established statistical practice of placing the origins of two curves on a common base line. When the difference in the base, as in this case, is one third of the total range, the impression of similarity in trend is quite misleading.

A correctly drawn chart in which both curves are expressed in index numbers and start from the same base line will be found at the bottom half of page 253. Inspection of the data presented indicated that the years 1571-75 should be used as the base period. As will readily be seen, there is little similarity in the movement of the two lines over the period as a whole; and there is no resemblance between the trends of the first half-century and those of the second half.

It should be added here that Hamilton expresses reservations about the significance of his chart when he points out: that the velocity of circulation is not taken into account; that the growth of credit currency is unknown; and that there are no data pertaining to the volume of trade. Nevertheless, the only evidence for his conclusion that the price revolution was caused by the mines of the New World is the chart in question.

The Price-Changing Process in Early Spain

The statistical analysis which we have reviewed was focused on the question whether specie movements and price movements correlated. It was not directly concerned with the price-changing process—that is, with the forces operating to bring about a progressive upward movement of prices. It is suggested here, though available data are far from adequate, that the great price advance over the course of the sixteenth century is to be explained by a combination of factors affecting the Spanish economy during this period—among which the expanding specie supply was of permissive importance only.

Spain was emerging from a feudal agricultural economy and becoming a commercial nation operating on capitalistic principles. The area over which trading operations were conducted was broadening, industrial production was expanding, and business operations were being conducted increasingly on a *financial* basis. That is, barter was being replaced by monetary exchange, and labor was coming to be paid with money rather than with commodities. Banking and the use of credit was evolving, and even the business cycle was manifesting itself. Another feature of sixteenth century Spain was the development of a fiscal system. Increasingly, as the years passed, revenues for the support of both provincial and national governments were derived from taxation levied on trade and industry.

These developments naturally involved the growth of

a complex cost-price structure. The principal items of business costs were raw materials, wages, and tax levies. A progressive rise in raw material costs could readily be explained by the meagerness of Spanish resources to meet the requirements of an expanding economy. The cost of imported materials was high because of transportation charges, traders' commissions, etc.

Of much greater importance, however, was the character of the prevailing tax system. Since the Crown specie was mortgaged to foreign bankers and since the lands of the church and the estates of great nobles were exempt from taxation, revenues had to be collected chiefly from trade and industry. According to the Spanish economic historian, Martin Hume,[9] revenues were derived from import and export duties on merchandise, from tolls on goods in transit, and especially from sales taxes. In Castile, in the earlier years, the principal source of revenue was the *servicio,* a regular impost voted every three years. Later, "The main revenue of the Castilian kingdom was derived from the *alcabala,* a 10 per cent tax upon all sales. Thus every time a commodity changed hands its value was raised by 10 per cent."[10] Tolls were levied by every township on goods in transit; and this "hampered business to such an extent that in the course of time Spanish manufactures could only be used at or near the places of their production. . . ."[11] Ultimately, when these fiscal devices proved insufficient, an excise called the "millions," was levied on the principal articles of food.

The fiscal system, based chiefly on sales taxes, supplemented eventually by direct taxes on foodstuffs, ham-

[9] *The Cambridge Modern History* (1903), Vol. 3.
[10] *The same,* p. 481.
[11] *The same.*

pered the development of industry and produced a vicious cycle of rising costs and prices. At the same time, commercial policies restricting foreign trade prevented Spain from realizing the potentialities of mutually profitable international commerce. Hume sums up the effects of the fiscal and commercial policies as follows:

> The mistaken idea that industries handicapped by the *alcabala* and excise, with the addition of municipal tolls, could be protected by prohibiting the introduction of merchandise from abroad, and the export of bullion from Spain to pay for it, was persisted in for a century and a half. At the beginning of Philip II's reign when Spanish America with her abounding new wealth was clamouring for luxuries, and Spain herself, in a whirlwind of sumptuary splendour, was squandering all her substance on fine stuffs and bullion embroideries, the manufacture of such things was prohibited in Spain to avoid waste, and the importation of them rendered illegal. The natural result was universal smuggling, and ruinous loss to the national exchequer. But this was not all; the killing of the most productive industries, together with the drain of the best Spanish manhood for the armies and for America, reduced a naturally industrious people to habitual idleness and pretentious poverty.[12]

Another factor operating on the cost side was the continuous increase in wage rates. Hamilton's combined wage series for the four major provinces indicates that, throughout the century, wage rates advanced quite as fast as prices; indeed, the wage line is more often ahead than behind the price line.[13] After 1570, Hamilton says, wages forged ahead of prices, without any compensating gain in efficiency.[14]

[12] *The same,* pp. 481-82.

[13] Earl J. Hamilton, *American Treasure and the Price Revolution in Spain, 1501-1650* (1934), chart on p. 273. Only in Andalusia did the wage rates lag somewhat behind the advance in prices.

[14] Hamilton "Prices and Progress," *The Journal of Economic History,* Vol. 12 (1952), p. 337.

The more or less continuous rise in wage rates was built into the cost structure, becoming the basis for ever-increasing prices. Thus the process of price change involved a spiral of rising wages, rising prices, and again wages and prices. The process was greatly accentuated by the fact that the sales taxes were levied on a steadily rising price base. These several factors combined to push prices upward in pyramidal fashion.

Still another force operating to raise prices was the prevalence of speculative operations. In a period of general expansion and rising prices money is to be made in buying up supplies for sale at an advance, and also in gaining control over the supply of specific products. That such activities were widespread in Spain is evident from the fact that there was a long series of legislative acts designed to check *forestalling* and *engrossing* operations—which terms mean commodity speculation and monopoly.

It should be noted at this place that the present-day idea that a rise in prices is a direct result of competitive bidding by consumers in retail markets is not confirmed by the Spanish story. On the contrary, permissible retail mark-ups were directly governed by wholesale price trends, which were directly affected by the sales taxes and the advances in wage costs. In 1549 "the principle that the wholesale prices in the leading fairs should govern retail prices won recognition in municipal legislation. . . . To fix the maximum retail prices which should obtain until the next fair, the *regidor* and justices . . . added to . . . wholesale quotations just compensation for the expenses and labor of the retailer"—the mark-up being fixed at 10 per cent.[15] This system came to apply to cloth, fish, groceries, medicine, and miscellaneous commodities. Hamilton concludes "that the influence . . . transcended the Spanish frontiers and linked domestic prices with those of the leading commercial emporia of Europe in the second half of the sixteenth century is amply attested by the accounts of . . . the great bankers and merchant princes . . . and their correspondence from factors [agents] scattered throughout the Occident."[16]

This account of the process by which price advances occurred in Spain, and were gradually extended through the influence of the great fairs to other countries, is, it will be seen, vastly different from that envisaged by the quantity theory. According to the pure monetary explanation, specie flowed to Spain from the New World and caused an automatic rise in Spanish prices. Thus Spain became a good market in which to sell but a poor market in which to buy; and in consequence of the resulting adverse balance, specie overflowed from Spain to other countries, causing prices to rise throughout Europe. According to the cost-structure explanation, the rise was motivated primarily by commercial, fiscal, and wage policies—the increasing supplies of precious metals being permissive but in no sense causal.

Views as to the Consequences of Spanish Treasure

The decline of Spain as a nation has been commonly ascribed by both philosophical and historical writers to

[15] Earl J. Hamilton, *American Treasure and the Price Revolution in Spain, 1501-1650*, pp. 203-04.
[16] *The same*, p. 204.

the vast inflow of precious metals from the New World. On the political side, the inflow of silver and gold is charged with responsibility for the extravagant ambitions of Spanish rulers at this period and the shedding of Spanish blood in ill-fated campaigns throughout Europe. On the economic side, it is contended that the heavy export of commodities in payment for the specie depleted the nation's supply of consumer goods, thereby impoverishing the country. On the moral side, it is held that the abundance of precious metals was destructive to Spanish character, that the illusion of wealth fostered extravagance and vagrancy while, at the same time, the El Dorados overseas induced extensive emigration at the most productive age.

In his *Spirit of Laws,* Montesquieu described the effects of the Spanish treasure in the following language:

> The Spaniards, after the conquest of Mexico and Peru, abandoned their natural riches, in pursuit of a representative wealth which daily degraded itself. . . . Spain has behaved like the foolish king, who desired that every thing he touched might be converted into gold, and was obliged to beg of the gods to put an end to his misery. . . . But this great kingdom was every where baffled by its misfortunes. Philip II who succeeded Charles V was obliged to make the celebrated bankruptcy known to all the world. There never was a prince who suffered more from the murmurs, the insolence, and the revolt of troops constantly ill paid. From that time the monarchy of Spain has been incessantly declining. This has been owing to an interior and physical defect in the nature of these riches, which renders them vain; a defect which increases every day. . . . That must be a bad kind of riches which depends on accident, and not on the industry of a nation, on the number of its inhabitants, and on the cultivation of its lands.[17]

[17] Baron de Montesquieu, *Spirit of Laws,* Vol. 2 (1873), pp. 48-52.

The specie was not squandered by extravagant rulers. Charles V succeeded Ferdinand in 1516 and became emperor in 1519. He was succeeded in 1558 by his son, Philip II, who ruled until 1598. The policies of both Charles and Philip were dictated by two related considerations of dominating importance: the preservation of the inherited possessions which made up the scattered empire—Spain, Burgundy, Austria, Milan, etc.—and the cementing of the power of the Catholic church throughout Europe. To this end it appeared necessary to resist the encroachments of France, to police the Low Countries, and to fight the Turks not only in eastern Europe but throughout the Mediterranean area. The rising tide of Protestantism in Germany and the ascension of the Tudors to power in Great Britain were added complications.

The financial resources necessary to the accomplishment of these imperial objects did not, in Charles' reign, come chiefly from Spain. He depended largely upon the financial backing of the Austrian Fuggers and other international bankers. In the earlier years much more financial help was derived from the prosperous Low Countries than from Spain, where so many of the resources were held by the church and favored nobles. Charles was, in fact, always in financial difficulties:

> Money was raised in Castile by pledging the taxes in advance, by issuing bonds at fixed interest charged upon the national revenues, by mortgaging to financial houses every possible source of profit. In this way the great House of Fugger took over in 1524 the estates belonging to the masterships of the three military orders, and later the quicksilver mines of Almaden, and the silver mines of Guadalcanal.[18]

[18] Stanley Leathes, *The Cambridge Modern History*, Vol. 2 (1907), Chap. 2, p. 63.

Throughout Charles' reign the public debt constantly increased; but he maintained his credit position abroad by always meeting his interest obligations. Charles was a conscientious ruler, consecrated to a primary purpose. He bribed where necessary; but he was no spendthrift.

Philip (1558-98) was a religious zealot, whose *personal* life was one of austerity and who gave himself indefatigably to the personal direction and detailed administration of the vast affairs of state. His financial difficulties were even more serious than those of Charles. Despite onerous taxation, and occasional levies upon the church and the nobility, the fiscal situation grew steadily worse, resulting in national bankruptcy in 1575.

The precious metals received from the New World were, of course, distinctly helpful in establishing and maintaining international credit. Most of the Crown bullion was immediately transferred to foreign creditors. However, this treasure was apparently never sufficient to meet the government's requirements outside the borders of Spain.

Nor were the economic consequences altogether bad. The facts clearly indicate that, at least during the first half of the century, Spain enjoyed her greatest period of prosperity and growth; it was at this time that "Spanish galleons sailed the Seven Seas, and the sun never set on the Spanish flag." This was also the golden age of art and literature. As already indicated, the internal expansion of Spain began during the reign of Ferdinand and Isabella. Charles, also, endeavored to encourage trade and industry.

In 1529 he opened the export trade to a number of cities

of the East and the North, and broke down to some extent the monopoly of Seville. As a consequence many industries increased by leaps and bounds. The silk industry in Toledo and Seville, the cloth industry in Toledo, Cordova, Cuenca and Segovia reached considerable dimensions. The same stimulus reacted upon agriculture and the wool-growing industry. For a time the new discoveries seemed to have opened an industrial era in Spain.[19]

Hamilton writes: "The phenomenal growth of Segovia, Toledo, and other industrial centers suggests that the production of manufactured goods flourished . . . until near the end of the sixteenth century." He adds:

There can be little doubt that the population of every city of Andalusia and the two Castiles . . . was substantially greater in 1594 than in 1530; and, with the possible exception of Valladolid, the same holds for the territory within each city's sphere of economic influence. . . . There is strong reason to believe that the loss of population through emigration to the Indies was altogether negligible. Many Spanish soldiers were sacrificed . . . on foreign battlefields; but, inasmuch as no enemy [invaded the Peninsula] the civilian population was almost entirely spared. . . .[20]

Though population may have continued to increase, there is evidence of economic retrogression in the second half of the century. According to Martin Hume of the Royal Spanish Academy, even at the time of Philip's ascension in 1558 economic conditions throughout Spain were deplorable.

Untilled fields cried out for patient labour, while hordes of idlers crowded the Court and hung about the palaces of nobles in the towns. The roads, where they existed at all,

[19] *The same,* p. 100.

[20] Earl J. Hamilton, *American Treasure and the Price Revolution in Spain, 1501-1650* (1934), pp. 298-99.

had decayed into rough mule-tracks, unsafe always, and often impassable. The inns were wretched and poverty-stricken, as they are painted in *Lazarillo de Tormes* and *Guzman de Alfarache;* and the only professions which ensured subsistence were those of arms, the Church, and domestic service in the households of the privileged classes.[21]

All accounts agree that export trade languished after the middle of the century. An act of 1552 was designed to discourage exports in order to increase the supply of commodities in Spain.

Forbidding the export of manufactured articles, even to the American colonies, deprived Spanish industry of its market, and strangled the trade upon which the revenue mainly depended. . . . The well-meant, but financially unwise sumptuary laws, which followed each other from year to year, prohibiting, with increasing but ineffectual penalties, the expenditure of money upon superfluities, reduced still more the demand for labour. . . .[22]

The decline of trade and industry in the cities could scarcely fail to have serious repercussions upon agriculture. Most of the vagrancy, so much condemned by moralist writers, was doubtless only unemployment. Since economic *security* could be found only in the army, in church activities, and in household service, these occupations were overcrowded; and large numbers were also dependent upon alms. It should be remembered in this connection that the natural resources of Spain were meager as compared with those of France, the Low Countries, and England.

The Spanish claim to commercial monopoly of the whole of America, although jealously enforced so far as was possi-

[21] *The Cambridge Modern History,* Vol. 3 (1907), p. 482.
[22] *The same,* p. 512.

ble, had from the nature of the case become impracticable. The crushing of Spanish industry by an unwise fiscal policy had made it impossible for Spain itself to supply the growing needs of the settlers, whilst the galling restrictions imposed upon foreign sailors and vessels in Spanish ports had immensely hampered the importation into Seville, the centre of the whole transatlantic trade, of manufactures from abroad. The natural consequence was a widespread smuggling trade with America both from England and France.[23]

The great decline of Spain occurred in the seventeenth century—after the defeat of the Armada in 1588, the resort to currency debasement, disastrous plagues, and the accession to power of irresponsible rulers and corrupt and extravagant ministries.

II. SPECIE SUPPLY AND PRICE TRENDS IN MODERN TIMES

Official data pertaining to stocks of money, volume of trade, and price movements are *not* available until modern times. There are estimates of gold and silver *production* for the world as a whole running as far back as 1493. But prior to 1800 the figures are by twenty-year periods; and annual data are not available until 1840. There are no official estimates pertaining to *accumulated stocks* of specie before 1880. While there are unofficial estimates of stocks of specie as early as 1800, the estimates are rough and vary widely. In the United States it was not until 1933, when the gold supply was withdrawn from circulation, that precise estimates of monetary stocks became possible. For Great Britain figures of stocks of specie are reasonably satisfactory as far back as 1789.

[23] *The same,* p. 492.

There are no official data pertaining to the volume of production or trade until very recently. Such unofficial estimates as have been made for earlier times are of the crudest sort, based on the output of a few important commodities believed to be representative in character. Not until after World War I were serious efforts made, under the auspices of the League of Nations, to compile world production data on a systematic and comparable basis. There are selected commodity price series running back into the nineteenth century, but adequate wholesale and cost-of-living indexes were not compiled until after 1900. In consequence, anyone seeking to substantiate deductive monetary reasoning by inductive evidence is confronted with grave difficulties. Nevertheless, such meager evidence as is available has often been cited as strongly confirmatory.

1. British Experience, 1789–1909

Since British data with respect to stocks of specie were available for a somewhat longer period, Irving Fisher centered his primary attention on British experience. He concluded that available data reveal a "remarkable correlation" between money stocks and price movements. The comparisons between price movements and money stocks in the 120-year period, 1789-1909, he summarized as follows:[24]

Prices rose 1789-1809—stock increasing.
Prices fell 1809-1849—stock stationary.
Prices rose 1849-1873—stock increasing.
Prices fell 1873-1896—stock increasing slightly.
Prices rose 1896-present—stock increasing.

[24] The data which follow are from *The Purchasing Power of Money* (1913), pp. 239-45.

Of the first period, Fisher said, "prices practically doubled in twenty years. This was due to the increased stock of gold and silver which in turn was due to their large production during this period."

Of the second period, when prices fell while money stocks were stationary, he says the decline "was presumably due to the lull in the production of precious metals, which prevented the aggregate stock from keeping pace with the volume of business. Even the development of bank currency was insufficient to offset the continued increase in the volume of business."

Between 1849 and 1873 the substantial rise in gold prices, it is said, "was presumably in consequence of the gold inflation following the famous California gold discoveries in 1849 and Australian discoveries in 1851 and 1852."

Between 1873 and 1896 there was a major decline in prices, though money stocks were increasing slowly. Fisher explains this apparent lack of correlation as "presumably due to the slackening in the production of gold; to the adoption of the gold standard . . . ; to the arrest of the expansion of silver money . . . ; to the slackening in the growth of banking; and to the ever present growth of trade."

Of the period 1896 to 1909, marked by the Alaskan gold discoveries, he says: "Prices have been rising because of the extraordinary rise in gold production and the consequent increase in money media of all kinds."

It appears from these excerpts that Fisher is satisfied when both stocks of specie and prices moved in the same direction. But whenever the movements were divergent, he explains the discrepancy by referring to a *presumably* counteracting influence arising from the growth of trade, or from changes in the volume of other forms of money. No data were available on which to base the *presumption.*

Fisher makes two casual references to the development of bank credit currency in Great Britain during this era—noting that it was increasing from 1816 to 1849 and that the "rate of growth" was slackening after 1873. But he makes no effort to show statistically the magnitude of this increasingly important portion of the money supply.

Since no data are available for vitally important items, the alleged correlation is obviously not statistically established. All the analysis does is to assert that, since the equation is true, prices *must* have increased when the stock of money was increasing, unless offset by an increasing volume of trade.

2. *American Experience in the Nineteenth Century*

American price trends over the course of the nineteenth century were similar to those in Great Britain. The generally downward movement from the end of the Napoleonic wars to 1849, the advance in the fifties, and again the decline from 1870 to the middle nineties, have commonly been attributed by many writers to fluctuations in the productivity of the gold mines. However, until late in the century, data pertaining to bank credit and to the volume of trade were so meager that statistical verification was impossible.

It should be noted here that traditional monetary theory implied that changes in money supply occur more or less automatically—with a slight time lag, at the most. If this be true, one would expect to find in periods of increasing gold supply a steady, persistent, upward trend of prices, and in periods of declining gold stocks, a constant downward trend. But as the chart on p. 2 indicates, there were many counter movements within the so-called long-term price trends. The slight downward trend over the period as a whole is explained by the depressions of 1819 and 1837.

In the long down period, 1816-48, there were 170 months of falling prices, 129 months of rising prices, and 109 months of virtually stable prices. Nor were the advances minor in character or of brief duration. For example, the trend was sharply upward in the 1830's; and if in 1839 one had drawn a curve showing the trend of prices since 1820, he would doubtless have concluded that the trend was upward. Similarly, the downward trend after the Civil War was interrupted by periods of advancing prices. For example, gold prices rose sharply from 1868 to 1872, and from 1879 to 1882; and they rose slightly from 1886 through 1888. The over-all downward movement from the sixties to 1895 is accounted for by the two drastic declines—1873-79 and 1890-95—both periods of protracted depression.

From 1896 to 1913 there was a substantial rise in gold production and a substantial rise in commodity prices. It is of note that this period was marked by long continued prosperity, while the business recessions were minor in character and of short duration.

Irving Fisher presented data for the years 1896-1909 which purported to show that in the United States "the quantity theory is statistically verified to a high degree of correlation." Here he uses not only data pertaining to stocks of money and price movements, but also estimates of the velocity of circulation of money and the volume of trade. The velocity estimates range from 19 to 22 times a year—a variation of 15 per cent. "The figures representing trade are based on data for only 44 articles of internal commerce, 23 articles of import and 25 of export, sales of stocks, railroad freight carried, and letters through the post office."[25] These items make up but a mere fraction of the aggregate monetary transactions of the country. They do not include such operations as transfers of real estate, the purchase and sale of securities, or tax collections—or wages, rents, interest and dividends—all of which involve the use of money. With such transactions excluded from the computation, the very basis of the correlation is faulty.

Moreover, Fisher takes no account of the fact that the ratio of credit to specie was rapidly expanding during these years. Perhaps the most striking economic phenomenon of the two decades preceding World War I was the enormous expansion of bank credit currency. Specie was being progressively concentrated in banks, and, as the banking system evolved, it became possible for a given volume of gold reserves to support an ever-expanding superstructure of credit. In 1896 the ratio of deposits to specie holdings in our national and state banking institutions[26] was 4.46 to 1; in 1909 it was 7.03 to 1; and by 1914 it had risen to 8.01 to 1. Had the 1896 ratio persisted, deposits in 1909 would have been only 10.6 billions, as compared with the actual figure of 16.7 billions. The figures for 1914 would have been 11.8 billions, as against an actual figure of 21.3. Thus the omis-

[25] *The same,* p. 291.

[26] These figures include both demand and time deposits.

sion of this 9.5 billion dollars of credit expansion completely invalidates the conclusion reached by Fisher.

3. *World Gold Production and World Price Trends*

It will be recalled that writers holding to the value of gold theory were concerned with gold and silver as commodities subject to world-wide influences of supply and demand and with world price levels. According to this point of view, changes in specie would more or less automatically be reflected in universal price changes; in all countries prices would move up or down together and in like degree. Two pretentious efforts to prove that the movement of world prices over a long period of years has been directly governed by the changing value of the metallic standard require consideration here. As we shall see, the methods employed are very different in character.

CASSEL'S ATTEMPTED PROOF

The Swedish economist, Professor Gustav Cassel, centered his analysis on the sixty-year period from 1850 to 1910.[27] Cassel held that "analysis of the factors which cause changes in the general level of prices" must take account of "the whole quantity of gold in the world," whether used as money or otherwise. The best available data indicated an accumulated supply in 1850 of roughly 10 billion marks, or about 2.5 billion dollars. Between 1850 and 1910 the supply increased by 42 billion marks, or at the rate of about 2.8 per cent annually. This average he designated the *normal* rate of growth of gold supply.

[27] *The Theory of Social Economy* (1923), English Ed., pp. 441-61.

Finding no usable trade data for comparison with this increase in gold supply, Cassel conceived a method of analysis by which he believed this difficulty could be surmounted. In brief, he reasoned that since, in fact, the general level of wholesale prices was approximately the same in 1910 as in 1850, it is evident that the increasing gold supply over this period as a whole had not affected prices—being offset by a corresponding increase in production and trade. In his words, "The increase in the gold supply from 1850 to 1910 was necessary and sufficient, in view of the economic development, to keep prices on the same level in 1910 as they had been in 1850." In short, the increase in gold supply and volume of trade had just kept pace with one another.

But Cassel pointed out that the 2.8 per cent annual increase was an average for the whole period and that at times there had been substantial deviations from the normal rate of growth. He says, "We must logically conceive every deviation of the effective gold supply from the normal as *pro tanto* the cause of a change in the general level of prices. . . . From 1850 to 1887 the effective supply is above the normal; from 1887 to 1910 it is below." In the first period, he says, prices rose; while in the latter they fell. He concludes that "the main cause of the secular variations of the general price level" is to be found in deviations in gold supply—above or below the normal trend. It will be observed that Cassel finds only two secular trends over this sixty-year period, instead of the three observed by the writers mentioned in the preceding section.

Cassel called attention to the many annual changes in

prices over this period; and contended that "these have no connection with the price level." In these conjunctures [cycles] "a group of non-monetary factors have a decisive influence." Yet in making his analysis he begins with a very depressed year, price-wise, namely, 1850. Had he used 1840 instead, the trend line of prices would have been downward to the middle 1880's instead of upward; and, similarly, had he used the year 1854 as the base.

A more fundamental criticism, however, pertains to the methodology employed—outlined above. Lacking data on trade, Cassel employed a logical strategem to prove that changes in gold production *caused* the secular variations in prices. The key to his thought is found in the phrase quoted above, beginning—"We must logically conceive." The assumptions underlying the logic are precisely those on which the value of gold theory is based. In short, he invokes the theory to prove the theory. It should be noted, also, that he could not know whether during the secular periods the volume of trade was uniform, or whether the demand for gold was remaining constant.

In concluding this section, attention is again called to the fact that the theory that there is a world price level governed by a world value of gold obviously implies identical, or at least closely parallel, price movements in all countries where gold is the standard of value. Accordingly, if a significant divergence should be found in the price movements of individual countries, doubt would obviously be cast upon the validity of this particular theory. In fact, the secular trends of prices in both the United States and Great Britain, as shown in preceding sections, do not coincide with the world price trends shown by Cassel.

THE WARREN-PEARSON STATISTICAL EVIDENCE

In 1933 Professors George F. Warren and Frank A. Pearson of Cornell University, building on the value of gold theory, devised a gold purchase plan for stabilizing the level of commodity prices. In common with other observers they had been deeply concerned over the great fluctuations in prices that had occurred since 1913 both in the United States and other countries.[28] These price movements were attributed by them primarily to violent changes in the value of gold as a commodity. They held that the great rise in prices in the early years of the century was directly due to a fall in the value of the commodity, gold. On the other hand, since the early twenties, they believed the value of gold had been steadily rising because of a rising demand in relation to supply.

Warren and Pearson expressed themselves as being in no sense opposed to Fisher's compensated dollar plan, the multiple standard idea, or other kindred plans for stabilizing the price level. However, they proposed a somewhat different method believed to be more feasible in its application. Concretely, they would achieve the desired result by raising or lowering the price the government would pay for gold bullion. Since 1834 the official gold dollar has contained 23.22 grains of pure gold, at which rate one ounce of gold would coin into 20 and 67/100 dollars; hence the official price of gold

[28] See chart, p. 2.

was $20.67 an ounce. Any person in possession of gold could always sell it to the government at this price, and anyone wishing to obtain gold could always buy it at this price.

According to the Warren-Pearson theory:

> If a country raises the buying price of gold at about the same rate as the gold value of basic commodities falls, it will maintain approximately stable prices. . . . If a country raises the buying price of gold at a time when the gold value of basic commodities is stable, prices will rise in proportion to the advance in the price of gold.[29]

The assumed relationship between changes in the price of gold and changes in the commodity price level may be illustrated as follows: If an ounce of gold when its price is $20 would exchange for 10 units of commodities, the average price of each commodity unit would be $2. Then if the price of gold is advanced to $30 an ounce, the average price of the commodities in question would automatically become $3.

Warren and Pearson pointed out that gold was an international commodity subject to world-wide factors affecting supply and demand. Although the *world* value of gold had thus to be reckoned with, this, it was believed, could readily be taken into account in determining the extent to which the United States price of gold in terms of paper should be increased—or decreased, as the case might be. It was recognized, also, that the operation of the gold purchase plan inevitably involved fluctuations in the value of the dollar as compared with foreign currencies as reflected in international exchange quotations. It was believed the raising

[29] G. F. Warren and F. A. Pearson, *Prices* (1933), pp. 120-21.

of the price of gold by offering more dollars per ounce would automatically depreciate the dollar in foreign exchange quotations. But as a safeguard the plan provided that in case there should be a lag, the government should *buy or sell* gold in foreign markets, thereby directly influencing foreign exchange quotations.

This plan was sponsored by the President and was approved by Congress in the Gold Reserve Act of January 30, 1934. The Act provided, among other things, that the President may set the amount of gold in the dollar at not less than 50 per cent and not more than 60 per cent of its former weight. It was set at $35.00 an ounce, or 59 per cent of its former weight; hence the expression "a 59-cent dollar."

It was announced by the President that this mechanism is designed "to establish and maintain continuous control. This is a policy and not an expedient [representing a step] toward a managed currency." In the future the effects upon prices of changes in the value of gold would be counteracted by arbitrary changes in the price paid for gold at the mints. To achieve stability it would merely be necessary to alter the price of gold, up or down, to the extent required.

The President's power was granted for two years, and was several times extended; but it was finally allowed to expire on June 30, 1943. Since that date the weight of the dollar has remained unchanged.

The authors of the stabilization plan assembled a vast collection of data in support of the theory that the level of prices over a long period of years has been directly governed by changes in the value of gold.[30] Their

[30] *Prices* (1933); and *Gold and Prices* (1935).

analysis relates first to the seventy-five year era from 1839 to 1914; and, second, to the much shorter period from 1914 to 1933. So far as the long-term trends were concerned, they claimed a satisfactory confirmation of the theory. They contended that the many short-term fluctuations could be ignored on the ground that they were due to cyclical and other factors having no bearing on secular trends.

The method employed by Warren and Pearson for the period from 1839 to 1914 was, in brief, as follows: They compared estimates of the growth of world monetary gold stocks and world physical volume of production, and the ratio between them is compared with wholesale price movements of commodities for the same period. The secular variations in prices during this long era are attributed to fluctuating trends in gold mining and hence in the supply of gold.

There are numerous shortcomings in this analysis. First, unlike Cassel and other adherents of the gold commodity theory, they included only *monetary* gold supplies. Second, although both gold and silver were standard money over much of this period, silver is omitted from the money stock. Third, for the greater part of this period estimates of monetary stocks are but rough approximations. For the United States there are no official figures of monetary stocks prior to 1873; and it was not until after World War I that reasonably satisfactory world data became available. Fourth, the estimates of world physical volume of production are wholly undependable. During this era no comprehensive production data were assembled in any country. The figures used are but rough estimates for varying periods of time, based on a relatively few commodities for which statistics were available; and these have been pieced together in the construction of a crude index number believed to give some idea of the rate of economic growth. Finally, although the value of gold is assumed to be determined by demand and supply, no data are presented with respect to possible changes in the demand for gold. For example, no consideration is given to any increase in demand for gold as a result of the abandonment of bimetallism and the establishment of the single gold standard; and there is no analysis of the bearing of the vast evolution of credit currency on the demand for gold as money. Changes in the supply of gold appear to be regarded as the sole factor affecting its value.

In the second period, 1914-33, Warren and Pearson shift their primary emphasis from the supply of gold to the demand for gold. The great rise in prices during World War I is attributed to a decreased world demand for gold, resulting from the abandonment of the gold standard by many countries. The sharpest price decline in our history (1920-21) is ignored. The collapse of prices following 1929 is ascribed to an increased world demand for gold as a result of the restoration of the gold standard. In their words; "The low value of gold and resulting high prices from 1916 to 1928 were due to low demand for gold for monetary uses. The gold panic of 1929 and the collapse in the price structure were due to a sudden world-wide return of the demand for gold."[31]

In fact, the restoration of the gold standard began in 1924 and was completed by 1928—which years are included within the authors' period of low gold demand.

[31] *Gold and Prices,* p. 107.

If the theory were true, the great price decline should have occurred long before 1930. Moreover, between 1929 and 1933 the volume of world physical production of commodities declined sharply while the world stock of gold continued to increase steadily. According to the theory both factors should have worked together to produce markedly higher prices, whereas, in fact, there was a catastrophic decline.

The shift for the later period from supply to demand as the primary factor affecting the value of gold, and thus the price level, was apparently forced upon the authors because gold supply figures—deemed of decisive importance in the earlier period—no longer afforded support for the theory. For the period 1914 to 1928 the authors' figures show that the world physical volume of production increased 38 per cent and that the world monetary gold stock also increased 38 per cent. "From this relationship prewar prices would have been expected, but prices in gold throughout the world were 40 to 50 per cent above prewar. There was no reason for assuming that the world could return to the gold standard and maintain such a price level."[32] Therefore, the collapse must, it seemed, have been due to an intense demand for gold.[33]

Warren and Pearson's statistical analysis pertaining to the value of gold is thus unconvincing. Moreover, no

[32] *The same,* p. 106.

[33] The view that the collapse of prices after 1929 was *somehow* related to gold had numerous adherents at the time. As a rule, however, the difficulty was attributed to a shortage of gold supply rather than to an intense demand. The facts with respect to the gold situation lend support to neither point of view. See Charles O. Hardy, *Is There Enough Gold?* (The Brookings Institution, 1932). Within a few years there was much concern over the superabundance of gold in the United States.

effort is made to show how or why an intense demand for gold would affect the level of prices. They merely adhered to the traditional assumption that changes in the value of standard commodity, gold, automatically find reflection in proportional changes in the level of prices. For a discussion of the relation between the devaluation and the subsequent level of prices, see Appendix A, pages 240-42.

In concluding this section of the analysis, reference should be made to numerous attempts that have been made to substantiate the quantity theory by comparing changes in the level of prices with changes in the quantity of currency in circulation. Such statistical undertakings have always been beset with difficulties because of the diversity of the transactions which make up the T of the equation and because of the difficulty of measuring the money supply that is effective in any given time period. Moreover, those who hold velocity to be significant have to deal with a factor of unknown weight. The velocity conception was, however, useful to quantity theorists in explaining away statistical discrepancies in data pertaining to volume of currency in relation to price movements. Such differences have commonly been attributed to presumed, though admittedly unmeasurable, changes of velocity.

III. THE ALLEGED PROOF OF THE INTERNATIONAL PRICE ADJUSTING MECHANISM

While the value of gold theory assumes a universal price level directly related to the value of gold as an international commodity, the quantity theory allowed for temporary price variations between countries. If, for example, there should be an inflow of gold from Great Britain to the United States, it is argued that prices would simultaneously rise in the United States and fall in Great Britain. However, these price changes would shortly bring about trade readjustments between the two countries sufficient to restore equilibrium. Thus, there is still an international price level—held in rough equilibrium by the flow of gold and the resulting counter price movements.

This theory of automatic international price adjustments was arrived at not by a study of facts but by deductive reasoning. The deductions proceeded from the quantity theory itself—the truth of which was regarded as established. In the words of Professor F. W. Taussig of Harvard:

> Everything . . . rests on the assumption that the flow of specie affects the prices and money incomes of the trading countries. An inflow of specie causes the prices and money wages to rise; an outflow causes them to fall. The whole train of reasoning rests, in this way, on the assumption of the quantity theory of money. . . .[34]

Although gold admittedly constituted but a minor item in the total circulating medium, it was the base on which monetary systems were erected; and Taussig held that the "specie constituent has a peculiar and determinative effect on the range of prices."[35]

Eventually an effort was made, under Taussig's direction, to "verify" the deductive reasoning by inductive study. Canadian experience in the years preceding World War I afforded an unusual opportunity. In Taussig's words, "The Canadian episode unfolds itself

[34] *International Trade* (1927), p. 198.
[35] *The same,* p. 199.

as if planned for the economist's purposes. It comes as near to experiment as we can ever expect."

To provide a background, the economic position of Canada during the period under review, as revealed in the study, may be briefly summarized as follows: During the last decade of the nineteenth century, Canada's international economic position had been comparatively stable. Accumulated interest obligations on earlier foreign loans exceeded such new loans as continued to be made; but the difference was readily met with the proceeds of an export surplus of goods. Then, in 1900, there began a new era of internal development, precipitated by the very favorable outlook in the world at large and the opening of the virgin western Canadian provinces to settlement and exploitation. This called for vast new foreign loans, running into hundreds of millions of dollars annually—aggregating approximately 2.5 billions in the fourteen-year interval ending with World War I.

This Canadian case is, in fact, complicated by the dominant importance of the loans. Instead of a simple situation in which the volume of trade is independent of loan operations, with the flow of gold promptly redressing changes in the commodity balance, we have here a situation in which gold movements are of minor importance in maintaining short-term equilibrium. Still, there was over the period a substantial, though somewhat intermittent, flow of gold to Canada—aggregating $123,000,000 in the fourteen-year period. The conclusion was reached that the Canadian experience confirmed in essential respects the results derived from deductive reasoning.

This study was undertaken as a doctoral dissertation

by Jacob Viner, then a graduate student at Harvard, and it was eventually published (1924) under the title *Canada's Balance of International Indebtedness, 1900-1913*. Since the theoretical significance of this investigation is more directly and succinctly stated in Taussig's subsequent volume[36] than in Viner's book, we shall first present Taussig's interpretation of the findings.

1. *Taussig's Interpretation*

In this Canadian experience Taussig finds "a striking verification of the essentials of the theory" derived by deductive reasoning. As already noted, he emphasizes that the *specie constituent* of the money supply is of dominant importance; and that the order of events is (1) imports of gold; (2) expansion of currency; and (3) rising prices. However, the facts show that in the Canadian case prices rose long before the gold was received. Taussig was little daunted by the fact that the price rise constantly preceded, rather than followed, the inflow of gold, remarking that:

> The looseness of the connection between bank reserves and bank deposits leads not infrequently to a chronological order different from that assumed . . . [by the theory]. An inflow of specie may follow, not precede, an enlargement of the circulating medium and a rise in prices. So it may be, at least for a short time, even for a period of many months. Indeed, if there be further forces at work than those merely monetary, it may remain so for years. . . . An upward movement of prices, even though initiated merely through deposit expansion, cannot persist unless supported by this same force—a sustained inflow of specie. . . . During the years of the upswing period, the import of specie into the borrowing country may seem to be due at each several date to the higher prices . . . [and to follow rather than precede].

[36] *International Trade* (1927).

But these higher prices could not be maintained, much less could move still higher, unless the flow of specie came to the rescue, so to speak.[37]

The Canadian story as a whole is summed up by Taussig in the following words:

> Expansion in Canada, rising loans and deposits, reserves becoming again and again too scant, a rate of foreign exchange favorable to Canada, the replenishment of the reserves again and again through the inflow of specie by way of New York—all this could persist only because of the continuing loans. Had it not been for the loans, the expansion of credit by the banks must have come to a halt. As it was, notwithstanding occasional interruptions, the round was repeated year after year. Specie did flow into Canada; the entire circulating medium did enlarge; in essentials what happened did conform with the previsions of the theory.[38]

However, the order was the reverse of that assumed. Instead of gold imports *preceding* the price rise in Canada, they *follow*. Instead of appearing as a *causal* factor, a gradual increase in the gold base is seen to be *permissive* only—an essential to the continuance of the boom. Moreover, it is admitted in the first quotation that other than monetary forces might produce a long continued price rise.

The theory, as stated above, holds that both commodity prices and wage rates automatically rise in consequence of the inflow of specie but with something of a lag in the adjustment of wage rates. It is interesting to note that the rise in wage rates in Canada constantly preceded the inflow of specie; and also that the increase in wage rates was very much greater than the increase in prices.[39]

[37] *The same*, pp. 207-09.
[38] *The same*, pp. 226-27.
[39] See table p. 292 below.

2. *Viner's Analysis*

As noted above, Canada was a borrowing country during the period under study—1900-13. Since Viner accepted John Stuart Mill's explanation of the mechanism of international adjustment between a lending and a borrowing country, Mill's statement may be taken as the point of departure. As summarized by Viner, five successive stages are involved in the process of adjustment—following the consummation of a loan:

(1) A rise in the price of bills on the borrowing country;
(2) A flow of gold from the lending to the borrowing country, accompanied by exchange at the gold export point of the lending country (and at the gold import point of the borrowing country);
(3) Relative changes in price levels in the two countries, prices rising in the borrowing country, falling in the lending country;
(4) Changes in imports and exports, the borrowing country acquiring an unfavorable balance of trade and the lending country acquiring a favorable balance;
(5) After the unfavorable trade balance of the borrowing country had become exactly equal to the rate of borrowing, the return of the exchanges to parity, the cessation of gold movements, and the stabilization of relative prices in the two countries at their new levels.[40]

Viner's confidence in theory based on deduction is evident from the fact that he states in the preface that the purpose of the study is to *verify* (rather than *test*) the accepted theory. This may help to explain why he evades the crucial point in certain instances and fails to accept his own data in others.

With reference to the first point, Viner states that "detailed inductive verification is not feasible, because

[40] Jacob Viner, *Canada's Balance of International Indebtedness, 1900-1903* (1924), p. 146.

the effect of the borrowings is inextricably bound up with the effect of . . . disturbances, due to minor and temporary causes."[41] However, he finds that, in general, the trend of New York exchange in Canada was in conformity with theoretical expectations. It is pointed out that, because of a peculiar relationship between American and Canadian financial markets, "it is highly improbable that variations in the New York exchanges . . . had an appreciable influence on the relative volume of Canadian imports and exports."[42]

Second, there was a modest and more or less steady inflow of gold to Canada, aggregating 123 millions over the fourteen-year period. Viner was troubled, however, by the smallness of the gold import movement over the period as a whole and by the fact that it came into Canada in driblets. He notes, for example, that in the five-year period, August 1901-August 1906, in only one month did the net change in the Canadian stock of gold exceed 3 million dollars. In the following passage he virtually admits that the facts with respect to specie movements afford little support for the theory.

> If variations in exchange rates and in gold movements, operating, through their influence on relative prices, on the profitability of import and export, comprise the entire mechanism of adjustment of trade balances, should not the tremendous and irregular inflow of capital to Canada have been accompanied by gold movements much more substantial and marked by much greater fluctuations than are indicated? . . . The general upward trend of Canadian monetary stocks of gold . . . can reasonably be supposed to reflect nothing more than the fairly steady growth in the Canadian need for currency and banking reserves during a period of

[41] *The same,* p. 154.
[42] *The same,* p. 155.

expanding population, industry, and commerce, and of world-wide buoyancy in prices.[43]

Notwithstanding this realistic passage, Viner concludes that if allowance is made for Canadian reserves on deposit in New York banks "gold movements operated in the manner indicated by Thornton, Mill, and their followers."

Though the crucial point in the general theory is that gold imports precede and cause rising prices, Viner made no attempt to correlate Canadian gold imports, plus the balances in New York, with price movements. And the fact that the rise in prices throughout the period *preceded* rather than *followed* specie imports is not squarely faced.

Viner shifts from gold imports to *loans* as the direct cause of the Canadian price rise. He states that the substantial relative rise in Canadian prices "must be explained as due to the import of capital and therefore must be accepted as confirmatory of the classical theory."[44] By "capital" Viner here has in mind not capital goods but capital funds derived from the loan operations. The transfer of such funds raises the price of Canadian exchange, and if it rises to the gold import point, an inflow of gold will result. While the loans thus made possible an inflow of gold, it is still the gold flow that the theory deems responsible for the Canadian rise in prices. As Taussig puts it: "Specie will flow. . . . Then will follow the chain of consequences. . . ."[45] Thus the loans relate only to the first steps—the disturbance of the exchange rate. To substantiate the deductive reasoning it is still

[43] *The same,* p. 162.
[44] *The same,* p. 218.
[45] *Quarterly Journal of Economics,* Vol. 31, p. 394.

necessary to demonstrate that Canadian prices rose in response to gold imports, that the gold came first and that the price rise followed.

The third point, that prices rose more in Canada than in Great Britain or the United States, is supported by price indexes of the three countries. The theory, as we have seen, attributes the relatively greater rise in Canada to the inflow of gold; but since the gold followed rather than preceded the rise, it cannot be regarded as the *motivating* force. The greater rise of prices in Canada might readily be explained by the more intense character of the Canadian boom.

The fourth point, that the borrowing country acquires an unfavorable balance of trade, is naturally confirmed. The loans, of course, made it possible for Canada to procure from abroad more than she was able to pay for from her own resources. The bulk of the excess was commodities; a small portion only was gold.

TESTING THE REFINED VERSION OF THE THEORY

The theory expounded by Mill and others was eventually amplified by Taussig to include, as a part of the mechanism of adjustment, variations in the price *structure* of the borrowing countries. Instead of a horizontal general price increase in the borrowing country in response to gold imports, as the classical theory had assumed, the newer version holds that there are marked divergencies in the price trends of domestically produced and consumed commodities, of imported articles, and of exported products. It is argued that the prices of domestically produced and consumed goods rise sharply because of the inflow of gold and the consequent expansion of deposits and purchasing power. The prices of export commodities are restrained because the purchasing power of foreign buyers has not been increased; but they, nevertheless, gradually rise because of increasing costs of production. The prices of imported commodities rise even less because they are largely influenced by conditions in the countries from which they come. It is these price differentials that bring about the readjustments of trade—encouraging imports and discouraging exports.

Viner finds that the Canadian experience was in strict conformity with this theoretical reasoning. Domestic prices rose most, export prices somewhat less, and import prices least. However, the author's analysis of the export trade gives little support to the theoretical explanation of the relatively low prices of exports. The index used was based on exports in the year 1900. Because of Canadian developments in the ensuing years, there occurred a phenomenal shift in the character of Canadian exports, as much as 98 per cent of the increase in export trade being in commodities which were of minor importance in 1900. Despite this fact, Viner makes no change in the weighting of commodities in the export index number which he constructed.

Moreover, his data show that the prices of the older classes of exports increased in line with the index of domestic prices. But the failure of export prices, as a whole, to keep pace with domestic prices was due solely to the fact that in those exports where the great expansion was occurring—chiefly wheat, nonferrous metals, and pulp and paper products—prices rose but slowly. The author admits that the prices of such commodities were determined, not in Canada, but in world markets. Thus the automatic adjustment mechanism was evidently not responsible. He goes on to explain that even though world prices in such commodities were relatively low, their production was, nevertheless, profitable to Canada because of relatively low costs of production there.

Viner expressed the view that "the trend of wages . . . offers perhaps the best single index of the trend of domestic prices in general."[46] The wage data—said to be good—show an advance of 49 per cent in Canada as compared with 27 per cent in the United States and only 3 per cent in Great Britain—which could, of course, be explained by the exceptional expansion in Canada. Since wage changes are supposed to be a part of the mechanism of adjustment, it would have been informative to compare wages in domestic industries, import industries, and export industries with a view to determining whether wage variations were similar to the price variations. This was not done; perhaps the requisite data were not available.

The theory assumes that the flow of gold causes a rise not only in commodity prices but in wages—conceived as the *price* of labor. One would therefore expect to find a more or less proportional rise in wages and prices—with allowance perhaps for what Viner refers to as the "well-known tendency of changes in wages to lag behind changes in prices." But the table of prices and wages presented shows (see page 292) that the wage index rose from 100 to 148.9, whereas the price index rose to only 124.8.[47] Viner missed, or in any case ignored, this arresting fact.

[46] Viner, *the same*, p. 247.
[47] *The same*, p. 243.

Notwithstanding the reservations expressed in the quotation on page 286 above, and despite the fact that the Canadian price rise preceded rather than followed gold movements, Viner concludes that his analysis "verifies the classical theory in essential respects."

3. *An Alternative Interpretation*

The process by which prices rose progressively in Canada following 1900 may be stated as follows: At the turn of the century Canada entered upon a period of extraordinary expansion, based in large part on the exploitation of virgin resources. The ensuing boom period was characterized by shortages of capital goods, shortages of labor, and shortages of loanable funds. The deficiency of capital goods was met largely by imports, financed by loans. The shortage of labor was met by increased immigration attracted by high wages—more than one million persons coming from Great Britain during the fourteen-year period. The shortage of funds was met by an inflow of specie and the expansion of credit which this made possible.

Data contained in Viner's study suggest that the primary motivating force in the price advance was the persistent shortage of labor and the consequent rapid rise in wage rates. The movements of wage rates and prices over the fourteen-year period are shown in the table at the top of the next page.

The wage advance over the period as a whole was practically double the price advance. Moreover, in every year the advance in the wage index was greater than the advance in prices. Even when in the depressed year 1908 the commodity price index fell five points, the wage index advanced 2.2 points.

INDEXES OF WHOLESALE PRICES AND WAGE RATES[a]

YEAR	ALL COMMODITIES[b]	WEEKLY WAGES[c]
1900	100.0	100.0
1901	98.8	101.6
1902	100.7	103.8
1903	102.1	106.5
1904	102.0	109.3
1905	105.1	113.1
1906	110.9	116.5
1907	116.6	122.6
1908	111.6	124.8
1909	112.0	129.0
1910	114.7	134.0
1911	116.8	137.9
1912	124.2	145.0
1913	124.8	148.9

[a] This official Dept. of Labor index is based on 272 commodities, unweighted.

[b] *The same,* p. 243.

[c] "As there was a steady downward trend during this period in the length of the working day, this index of weekly earnings minimizes the extent of the increase in rates of wages per hour. It is an index not of actual earnings but of weekly rates of wages. It is based 'on a series of over 1000 continuous and reliable records back to 1900. . . .'" Viner, *the same,* p. 243, note 5.

This steady increase in wage rates continuously increased costs of production, especially in such fields as manufacture, transportation, and trade. The failure of prices to be marked up in proportion to the increase in wage costs is no doubt attributable to the fact that other costs did not increase proportionally.

Thus the persistent shortage of labor, and the steadily rising wage rate appear to have been of dominant importance in pushing prices upward from the cost side. This interpretation squares with the known facts and the sequence of events: economic expansion, immigration, rising wage rates, and finally rising prices. The gold inflow—made necessary by antecedent business expansion and tightening credit conditions, induced by rising interest rates, and made possible by loans—came as the last step in the associated chain of events.

4. Experience Under Paper Money Systems

A brief analysis should be made at this place of two companion studies which were concerned with the operation of the international price adjustment mechanism under depreciated paper currency. Here the mechanism involved is somewhat different than it is when the gold standard is operating—because of the premium on gold and the resulting readjustment of exchange quotations. Frank D. Graham's "International Trade Under Depreciated Paper, the United States, 1862-79," was published in *Quarterly Journal of Economics* (February 1922). John H. Williams' study, *Argentine International Trade Under Inconvertible Paper Money, 1880-1900,* was published in book form in 1920.

Though handicapped by a dearth of reliable statistical material covering this early period, Graham nevertheless concluded that prices and wages moved in accordance with the expectations of theory. He introduced three time-periods in which the effects may work out—immediately, transitionally, and eventually. Sometimes the first is held to be dominant; sometimes the second is preponderant; and occasionally the long-term effects are most significant. If, for example, an upward price movement is called for by the theory but does not occur, it is explained that this is due to a countervailing long-term effect which is already strong enough to engulf the shorter-term influence in the opposite direction.

The author also introduces a convenient system of time lags, to explain tardy price movements not in accord with the expectations of the theory. He completely ignores cyclical movements of business and prices. The failure of prices to rise after 1873, when loans were no longer in the picture, vitiates the conclusion for the last six years of this depreciated paper era.

Williams was guarded in his conclusion with respect to the significance of the Argentine case. Although he finds "a pretty general correspondence with theoretical reasoning,"[48] he points out that while the movements of import prices in the Argentine are in accord with theoretical expectations, those of exports are not. The latter is attributed to the fact that the exports of an agricultural country are mainly sold at world market gold prices. In addition, since only a few agricultural products are exported, both the volume and the price may, at times, be markedly affected by the vagaries of nature.

How Was International Equilibrium Maintained?

It has long been assumed by monetary theorists that prior to World War I the international gold system unquestionably operated to maintain international price and commercial equilibrium. This inference was not, however, based on inductive evidence. Rather it was derived, as Taussig notes, from the assumed validity of the quantity theory of money. The only attempts to test the international price adjustment theory are those which have been discussed in preceding pages.

The question may be raised at this place—How, if

[48] *The same,* p. 255.

not by gold movements and accompanying shifts in the price levels of different countries, was international economic equilibrium maintained?—For it was, in fact, somehow maintained. To answer this question one need not invoke shifts in price levels. In the main, equilibrium was maintained by balanced trade and service relations, supplemented by both long- and short-term credit operations. If imports of goods and services to a given country are exceeding exports, that country has several alternatives: (1) export gold to meet the balance due; (2) reduce purchases abroad; or (3) borrow the amounts required to meet the exchange deficiency. All of these means have been employed, often more or less simultaneously.

It should be noted here that shipments of specie are also affected by changes in interest rates. Tight money conditions in country A will attract fluid funds from abroad to take advantage of interest rate differentials. It is thus unnecessary to wait upon readjustments in commodity prices and consequent shifts in the relative volume of exports and imports.

The theory originated at a time when credit operations were of minor importance. But, during the last 100 years, borrowing operations have been so extensive and so continuous that the very conception of an annual trade balance requiring a specie shipment is almost meaningless. Since World War I, credit operations have dominated the international economic situation.

Can Causation Be Deduced From Correlation?

In concluding this appendix, reference should be made to numerous attempts that have been made to substantiate the quantity theory by comparing changes in the level of prices with changes in the quantity of currency in circulation. Such statistical undertakings have always been unsatisfactory because of the diversity of the transactions which make up the T of the equation and because of the difficulty of measuring the money supply that is *effective* at any given time period. Moreover, those who hold the velocity conception have to deal with an *unknown* factor.

But assuming that one were able to show by reliable comprehensive data that over a period of years there was perfect correlation—that the movement of prices was in exact correspondence with the increase in the volume of monetary circulation (account being taken of changes in the volume of transactions)—what would have been proved? The answer is, only what we already know—namely, that a rising price level requires proportionally more money to effect a given volume of exchanges. However, the mere fact that more money is required when prices are higher throws no light on the cause of the rise in prices. The question remains open whether the increase in the money supply was *causal* or merely a necessary concomitant. The factors involved in the price-changing process would in no way have been revealed.

INDEX

Index